This Boy

www.**transworldbooks**.co.uk

This Boy

Alan Johnson

BANTAM PRESS

LONDON · TORONTO · SYDNEY · AUCKLAND · JOHANNESBURG

TRANSWORLD PUBLISHERS
61–63 Uxbridge Road, London W5 5SA
A Random House Group Company
www.transworldbooks.co.uk

First published in Great Britain
in 2013 by Bantam Press
an imprint of Transworld Publishers

A CIP catalogue record for this book
is available from the British Library.

ISBNs 9780593069646 (hb)
9780593069653 (tpb)

Addresses for Random House Group Ltd companies outside the UK
can be found at: www.randomhouse.co.uk
The Random House Group Ltd Reg. No. 954009

The Random House Group Limited supports The Forest Stewardship
Council® (FSC®), the leading international forest-certification organisation.
Our books carrying the FSC label are printed on FSC®-certified paper.
FSC is the only forest-certification scheme supported by the leading
environmental organisations, including Greenpeace. Our
paper procurement policy can be found at
www.randomhouse.co.uk/environment

Typeset in 11.5/15pt Minion by
Falcon Oast Graphic Art Ltd.
Printed and bound in Great Britain by
Clays Ltd, Bungay, Suffolk

10

For Linda, who kept me safe.

This Boy

Prologue

I'M STUDYING A photograph. A small black and white image taken with a box camera. By a friend? One of my uncles? A passerby? Two figures set in a bleak but indistinct postwar landscape, standing arm in arm in front of railings outside Kensington Register Office with what appears to be barbed wire behind them. He is in his army uniform, the single ribbon denoting merely that he'd served. He'd been a lance corporal. I don't know with which regiment, or where, or whether he killed anybody (the question asked by practically all small boys of their fathers after the war). What I do know is that it could be said he helped to kill the woman beside him.

But on that day in January 1945, they must have been full of excitement and optimism about the life that lay ahead of them. Stephen Arthur Johnson and Lilian May Gibson (when she was born, in May 1921, her grandmother said she looked like a lily in May).

His smile is slight, betraying a determination not to show his teeth. Tie beautifully knotted, beret – angled slightly too high on one side – covering his red hair. She seems happy. A pretty, petite Liverpudlian with a Doris Day nose (what she called her 'titty nose', which she insisted I had inherited); smart in her cockade hat, placed at the same rakish angle as his beret. Her suit, though, is dark; were it not for the two white carnations pinned to her lapel, she could be at a funeral rather than her wedding. In the high heels she must have been wearing, though her shoes are out of shot, she looks only a little shorter than him. He was small, but she was smaller – not much more than five feet.

Were they happy on their wedding day? Surely they must have been but the hand through his arm is curled and tense, not flat and caressing; almost a clenched fist.

The faded inscription on the back reads: 'To Jean with love from Steve and Lil xxx.' Steve and Lil. Does the fact that his name comes before hers mean he wrote it? Could that be his handwriting? Did he take charge of distributing what I believe to be the only photograph of their wedding? No, more likely it was simply the convention of putting the husband's name first. It would be my mother, Lily, writing to her sister with this record that 'Steve and Lil xxx' had decided to face their postwar future together. Although, as things turned out, they spent it together yet apart – and then just apart.

PART I

STEVE AND LILY

Chapter 1

M Y SISTER LINDA and I were born either side of the creation of the National Health Service in 1948. I like to think our relative birth weights had something to do with Labour's greatest achievement.

In 1947, Linda weighed just 5lbs 4oz and was so tiny that she slept on a pillow in a drawer, which was convenient given that there was no room for a cot. By contrast, I put the 'boom' into baby boomer, weighing in at 10lbs on 17 May 1950. It was a complicated birth and it took its toll on Lily. She and I nearly died: she from the strain on what it would later emerge was already a weak heart and me because the umbilical cord was wrapped around my neck.

Lily was advised to have no more children and agreed to be sterilized. When I heard this mentioned as a child, I could only equate it with sterilized milk, bottles of which were ubiquitous on Britain's doorsteps. I had no conception of the pain and anguish that 'sterilization' must have caused an attractive woman still in her twenties.

I was to be named Robin until Alan Ladd, the Hollywood film star, made a brief but lasting intervention in my life. I've always rather liked the idea of being Robin Johnson. But the woman in the next bed to Lily's at Paddington General Hospital was a big fan of the diminutive Mr Ladd (as, for some inexplicable reason, were most young women at the time), and rocking Robin was quickly renamed Alan, with the awful addition of my father's middle name: Arthur. Nobody calls their children 'Alan' or 'Arthur' any more. Come to think of it, there are very few Lindas under fifty, either. I hated 'Arthur' so much that I never used it: at secondary school, I pretended that the second 'A' of my initials stood for Alvis.

We lived, courtesy of the Rowe Housing Trust, at 107 Southam Street, North Kensington, London W10 – a street whose buildings had been condemned in the 1930s. At least one family occupied each of the four floors and the dank basement. Before my arrival, Lily, Steve and Linda had lived in one room, but when I was born the trust gave us two rooms on a higher floor. One for sleeping in and one for eating in. Everyone used the same front door and the single decrepit toilet in the small concrete yard that backed on to the railway line in and out of Paddington Station. There was no electricity in the house – or outside, for that matter. The street was lit by gas lamps, which a man on a pushbike came to light every evening. Lily told us he was the Sandman, come to send us to sleep.

Notting Hill has become the generic term for a whole chunk of West London, but we didn't call our bit Notting Hill then. It was North Kensington, or, to be more accurate, Kensal Town – known to us simply as 'the Town'. Notting Hill was at the other end of Ladbroke Grove.

Southam Street was famously immortalized by the

renowned photojournalist Roger Mayne in a series of photographs taken between 1956 and 1961. He recorded both the squalor and the vibrancy of life there, the spirit of survivors inhabiting the uninhabitable. The houses first condemned two decades earlier were eventually declared unfit for human habitation while we were in residence and by the 1960s they had all been demolished. In the meantime we lived in two houses in the street, moving in 1956 from number 107 to number 149, where we had three rooms and a cooker on the landing.

The street straddled both sides of the Golborne Road. Those of us in the west end of the street referred to the eastern part as 'the rough end'. Doubtless they said the same about our side. There were no cars but plenty of kids. Indeed, as I recall, Southam Street was designated a 'play street': a blue sign outside the Earl of Warwick pub, at the junction with Golborne Road, informed drivers that they could enter for access only. Since nobody in Southam Street had a car that meant a vehicle-free street teeming with children. Given the overcrowding and the lack of sanitation, it's hardly surprising that the street was where people gathered, kids and grown-ups alike, irrespective of the weather.

I'm convinced that the blurred image of a child in the background of one of Mayne's photographs is Linda. It's quite likely: she was always out playing in the road. Linda's character was completely different from mine. She had learned to walk and talk at the earliest age possible, whereas I was two years old before I uttered a word and would happily have been crawling into puberty if extra effort hadn't been put into keeping me vertical. Linda was flamboyant, a gifted raconteur who found it difficult to stop talking and impossible to keep still. She was, and still is, a natural leader.

Steve worked – intermittently – as a painter and decorator. His employment was spasmodic not because there was a shortage of work but because he routinely failed to turn up and was continually being sacked. He hated his day job, focusing his energies instead on his alternative life as a musician. To Steve, evenings at the piano were always more important than mornings at work. A gifted pianist, he would play in pubs and clubs, at parties and at weddings. He was completely self-taught and played entirely by ear. He only had to hear a tune once to be able to recreate it. His understanding of keys and chords, of rhythm and tone, was purely instinctive.

Steve had already lost what proved to be his one chance to become a professional musician. He had been approached at an army concert by the famous bandleader Bert Ambrose, who invited him to join his band on condition that he learned to read music. Steve turned him down. According to Lily, Steve had always been averse to any kind of studying, and learning how to decipher those notes sounded to him too much like going back to school. But the missed opportunity must surely have been something he regretted.

Steve and Lily had first met at a NAAFI dance in 1944. She was waiting to be demobbed, having left Liverpool at eighteen to join the NAAFI (Navy, Army and Air Force Institutes) in London. During the war she had been engaged to be married to Willie Dance, a man ten years her senior – an alliance that gave rise to her friends' favourite joke: 'Willie Dance? No, but Lilian May.' Sadly, Willie contracted tuberculosis and died.

Lily was aware of Steve's reputation as a ladies' man, but it's not difficult to see how, recovering from a broken heart, she could have been swept off her feet by his charm, his gift for music and the dashing white pianist's gloves he wore for NAAFI concerts. By the early 1950s, effectively coping alone with two children in grinding poverty, she probably already realized the mistake she'd made.

With Steve constantly out of work and the money he earned from playing the piano squandered on his clothes, beer, fags and gambling on the horses, Lily was forced, despite her poor health, to work relentlessly. She was a charlady in the posh houses of Ladbroke Grove and South Kensington, helping with the catering when the families she cleaned for entertained in the evenings. Later she took on a succession of part-time jobs in various shops and cafés. But her paltry income was rarely enough to cover our rent and food. If she managed to get any money out of Steve it was a bonus. No wonder there were fierce confrontations when he came home drunk and well fed. Lily was capable of holding her own in any slanging match but when Steve was drunk he was violent, and then it was an uneven contest.

In winter, Lily would buy coal from the yard several streets away and push it home in an old pram she'd scavenged from a scrapheap for the purpose. She'd supplement the meagre supply by going out with a shopping bag in the wake of the horse-drawn carts or lorries delivering industrial quantities to the big houses in Holland Park, picking up any coal they had dropped. We would help her, carefully following her instructions to spit on every piece we found, 'for luck'.

On cold nights we'd go to bed wearing jumpers with a pile of old coats substituting for blankets. We lived in constant dread of not having a shilling for the meter. Time after time the gas mantles would go out and we'd light candles, or, to be more accurate, night lights – little round blobs of wax, like tiny cakes, that were cheap and portable, requiring no candlesticks.

Lily's regular 'search for a shilling' would be accompanied by constant pleas for God (in whom she had unquestioning faith) to help her. When she found one, she'd offer up her profound gratitude, eyes tightly shut, face raised to the heavens, or at any rate, to the ceiling, with its dark, damp patches and, in the summer, its covering of flies. We were so used to swarms of flies we didn't register them. Like the trains clanking past at all hours on the line in and out of Paddington, we'd only have noticed them if they'd disappeared.

With no fridge and the buckets of urine in the bedroom (to avoid having to go out to the yard in the middle of the night), our house was a more attractive venue for the discerning fly than it was for us. There were also cockroaches, beetles and all manner of bugs. During an infestation of earwigs Linda and I took to stuffing our ears with paper at night – we'd heard that these particular pests liked to crawl into people's ears, intent on eating the brain.

It is ironic that after leaving home at eighteen, Lily spent almost her entire adult life on the council waiting list, hoping for the kind of house she had left behind. In a quarter of a century she regressed from a Liverpool home with all mod cons to Southam Street with none whatsoever. From electricity to gas, from a bath to a sink, from a garden to a grotty shared yard.

Lily was the second of ten children born to John and Maria Gibson of Anfield. John was a Scotsman, Maria an Irishwoman. Maria must still have been reasonably strong for the birth of her 'Lily in May' but by the age of thirty-eight she'd had eight more children and seen two of them die in infancy from measles leading to pneumonia – a common outcome in the days before immunization. Four years later she was dead, of cervical cancer. Her own mother, Lily's grandmother, had also died at forty-two and Lily worried all her life that she, too, was destined to go to her grave at that age.

When Lily was five the Gibsons had moved into a newly built estate in Anfield. The semi-detached house in Warham Road had three bedrooms and gardens front and back, a bath, inside toilet and electricity. This was unusually lavish accommodation for a working-class family in 1926. My Auntie Peggy, the youngest of John and Maria's children, still lives there.

While Lily would be spared the constant childbearing endured by her mother, her life was no less hard. As the eldest daughter of a large family, much was expected of her. It was Lily who had to run the household during her mother's periods of incapacity after giving birth; Lily whose own early years were spent as the child-rearing apprentice; and Lily who, as an obviously clever girl, was at the same time required by a despotic father to study for a scholarship. It's true that he recognized Lily's potential and wanted her to fulfil it, and equally true that he was in this one respect ahead of his time, since in those days it was rare in working-class families for education to be considered a priority for girls, but there was no question of her being given any respite from her other duties to aim for academic success. He drove her so hard and asked so much of her that her health suffered badly. When she contracted rheumatic fever, she went for a while to live with friends of the family called Mr and Mrs Ireland. This at least gave her temporary relief from the increasingly overcrowded conditions at home, but there is little doubt it was this childhood disease that left her with a damaged heart valve and laid the foundations of a lifetime of physical frailty and a premature death.

Lily then developed the related complication of Sydenham's chorea, colloquially known as St Vitus' Dance, a neurological condition characterized by rapid, unco-ordinated jerking movements. She was placed in a hospital ward with elderly patients and tied down with straps to a rusty bed that creaked when she twitched. The other patients would yell and curse at Lily, urging her to lie still and let them sleep. This frightened her so much that she forced herself to stay rigid and was thus declared 'cured'. As Sydenham's chorea usually clears up eventually by itself, to what extent Lily's recovery was a triumph of mind over matter is a moot point, but whatever the case it must have been a terrifying experience for a young girl.

Against all the odds, Lily won her scholarship but her achievement coincided with her mother's final illness. That terrible blow, exacerbated by the fact that her father, having pushed her relentlessly to qualify for a good school, refused to buy the uniform necessary to secure the place, meant that she was never able to take up the scholarship.

Though I must have first encountered Grandad Gibson as a small child, I have no memory of it. I recall meeting him only once, as a teenager, by which time he could be best described as merely cantankerous, playing on his war wound (he'd developed gangrene from a bullet in his ankle in the trenches as a second lieutenant in the First World War) and revelling in his reputation for awkwardness. I remember him peeking through the front curtains of the house in Warham Road at the neighbour opposite and telling us that 'the nosy cow is spying on me'.

Evidently he had mellowed into a comparatively benign character by then. Lily's sister Peggy describes her father as a 'mean, cruel man' who ruled his children with a rod of iron, never thinking twice about hitting, punching or kicking them, particularly the older ones, which he did regularly. He had a variety of jobs – he was a binman at one point and, during the Second World War, a firewatcher – but with his war wound, and as a widower with small children, he was mainly housebound.

Peggy tells an incredible story which illustrates his vicious character. After their mother's death, Lily's two youngest sisters, Rita and Peggy, went to live with relatives, Auntie Nin and Uncle Tom, in Bootle. When the Blitz began they returned to Warham Road. It was just as well they did: if they'd stayed in Bootle they would have been killed when Nin and Tom's house took a direct hit in May 1941. Their aunt and uncle died, along with their maternal grandfather, who had been staying with them at the time. All three were buried in a communal grave.

Nin and Tom had no children and no family apart from the Gibsons. They had managed to save a bit of money but had not left a will. So many people who perished in the Blitz were in this position that a national newspaper used to publish lists so that relatives could claim their inheritance. It was Lily, by then living in London, who spotted their names on one such list and she and the second eldest daughter, Jean, who did all the work necessary to secure the money for their two young sisters, Rita and Peggy. They each received £100 to be held in trust. It should, as Lily and Jean had intended, have given them a start in life; a nest-egg any loving parent would have cherished and protected.

Not John Gibson. He refused point-blank to provide anything for his two little girls on the grounds that they now had money of their own. Clothes, shoes, school uniforms, bus fares, school equipment – everything had to be paid for from the legacy. By the time they left school it was all gone. In spite of the lack of care he had shown them it was, needless to say, Rita and Peggy who looked after their father as age and infirmity made him increasingly dependent on others. No wonder Lily had wanted to escape this tyranny as soon as she could.

After leaving school, she had moved first to the Norris Green district of Liverpool, where she lived with friends and got a job at the Co-op. Then she had put Liverpool behind her altogether and headed for the NAAFI in London, a bright, pretty girl embarking on a journey she hoped would lead to a future significantly better than the life she had endured so far.

~

Like Lily's mother, Steve's father had died long before Linda and I were born. I knew about the tragically short life of Maria Gibson in Liverpool but nothing of my paternal grandfather – not even his name. Neither can I recall Nanny Johnson's Christian name. She died when I was four or five, but the regular visits we made with Steve (Lily never came) to see her every Sunday morning are among my earliest memories.

Steve held my hand on these journeys. That sticks in my mind because it is the only time I can remember any physical contact with him. I was tiny, just old enough to walk independently with proficiency, and he'd hold my hand all the way to Nanny Johnson's; me on the left, Linda on the right, until she cartwheeled away. We liked these visits because we considered Nanny Johnson's flat, at Peabody Buildings, Delgano Gardens, to be the height of luxury. It was always warm in winter and cool in summer. It had an indoor toilet and a bath (in the kitchen, where the wooden boards placed across it when it was not in use provided a handy extra work surface). There was carpet in something called a living room and a comfortable settee. There were no flies or bugs and it didn't smell of decay and dirt and damp.

Like all working men in those days, Steve wore his suit on a Sunday. He liked to look smart. Part of the morning ritual was watching him getting ready. Polishing his shoes, ironing his shirt, choosing his tie. It was probably the army that made him so meticulous. He always ironed his own shirt and put a crease into his trousers by placing a sheet of brown paper between the material and the flat iron, heated on the stove in the fireplace. The little Formica table served as an ironing board. After he applied the Brylcreem that ensured not a single ginger hair would be out of place, the final flourish of his toilette was the fixing in place of the elasticated silver armbands that held his shirt cuffs just so on his wrists. This was when we admired Steve the most. Linda would bring her little pair of red shoes to be polished as part of the routine, as I looked on in awe at the transformation.

Off we would go on our Sunday pilgrimage, Steve and Linda and I, turning left out of 107 Southam Street, past the crumbling façades of houses that had lost their grandeur some time in the nineteenth century. There was a lot of rubble on the road, as well as litter and dog mess. In the days before the Clean Air Act of 1956, London's 'pea-soupers', thick, noxious miasmas of fog, soot and smoke from coal fires mixed with industrial pollution, would blacken buildings and corrode lungs. None of this discouraged Lily and the other women in the street from keeping up their own standards: they would spend hours every week scrubbing and whitening their front steps.

But on Sunday mornings all was quiet as we walked towards the top of the street, past St Andrew's Catholic Primary School, whose pupils all appeared to have freckles and red hair to match their scarlet uniforms. None of them seemed to live near the school.

On the corner was 'the Debry'. The Luftwaffe could have made a contribution to urban planning by enacting the already overdue demolition order for Southam Street, but in fact they had managed to provide us with only one reasonably sized play area, known as the Debry. It was many years before I encountered the word 'debris', made the connection and realized that it wasn't just the name of one bomb site in Southam Street. The Debry was cleared for the local Coronation celebration in 1953, when Lily covered Linda in Cherry Blossom shoe polish (at Linda's request) to enter her in the fancy dress parade as a piccaninny. With her milk-bottle-top earrings and her mother's scarf wrapped around her head, she should have won something. But the Queen Doll prize went elsewhere and Linda was forced to spend hours standing in a basin while Lily tried to scrub the polish off. Had there been a prize for the most politically incorrect costume, she would certainly have walked away with it.

Along Southam Street, I'd look into the areas, or 'airies', as we called the sunken enclosures in front of the basement dwellings. These were dangerous places. Many of the metal railings had been removed for scrap and replaced by corrugated iron. The stairs down to the basements were steep and the poor souls who lived in them were continually bombarded with rubbish, footballs, and the occasional falling child. From Southam Street we'd walk into Southern Row, then up the Ha'penny Steps on to the top end of Ladbroke Grove and across into Barlby Road, where two huge gas towers loomed like sinister spaceships.

I can't remember anything about Nanny Johnson except that she was a formidable woman dressed in black – like the character in the old Giles cartoons. I don't know exactly how many children she had. The youngest, Uncle Jim, was a teenager still living with her at Peabody Buildings. Steve had at least two other brothers and a sister – Auntie Annie, who had married 'Tottsy' Barker. Judging by his nickname, Tottsy had presumably once been a rag-and-bone man, or 'totter', as they were called. Within a few years, these equestrian entrepreneurs would be popularized on television in the hit BBC sitcom *Steptoe and Son*, set just up the road in Shepherd's Bush. They were a common feature of my childhood. Their trusty horses pulled rickety old carts laden with all manner of unwanted tat and junk collected from local households while the totter usually stood to drive in order to get a better purchase on the reins.

At some point Tottsy must have given up totting for a more respectable occupation as by then he was the only man I knew who worked in an office and dressed in a suit on a weekday. He left for Paddington Station every morning wearing his horn-rimmed spectacles and carrying a briefcase. Lily encouraged

Linda and me to look out of the back window at around 8.30 to wave to Uncle Tottsy as he went by on the train. We often saw a man with horn-rimmed glasses in one of the packed carriages. It may or may not have been our respectable relative: nobody ever waved back.

Nanny Johnson's flat was provided by the Peabody Trust, established in 1862 by a London-based American banker, George Peabody. When he set up his donation fund, he wrote a letter to *The Times* stating that his aim was to 'relieve the poor and needy of this great metropolis and to promote their comfort and happiness'. And Nanny Johnson certainly seemed comfortable and happy as we took our leave.

Although visiting Nanny Johnson was the purpose of the outing, we never stayed very long. Afterwards we usually called at an adjoining block of flats called Sutton Dwellings, where Steve's friends Ted and Elsie lived. They had children of a similar age to Linda and me and we were allowed to go and play with them in the safe communal yard behind the flats.

After depositing us back at Southam Street Steve, like most of the men in Notting Hill, would go to the pub before his Sunday dinner (lunch was something you only heard about on *The Archers* and *Mrs Dale's Diary*, just like that other mysterious meal, supper – in the evenings, we had tea). Unlike most of them, he had a professional reason to be there: entertaining the customers as the resident pianist. When the pubs closed the men would return home noisily for their dinner, after which the afternoon would be passed in a listless stupor, with parents dozing off and children bored rigid. England was not yet godless enough to allow shops to open or entertainment to take place on a Sunday. Even card games were forbidden in working-class households, including ours.

Though nominally Church of England, neither Steve nor Lily ever went to church. While Lily believed fervently in God, she seemed to distrust organized religion, perhaps as a result of the sectarianism of her Liverpool childhood. Linda and I were briefly sent to Sunday School when we were small, probably as much to keep us occupied as anything else, but we hated it, and Lily soon gave in to our objections. The tedium of the long afternoon was relieved only by the arrival of a whelk and winkle man wheeling a hand barrow full of fresh shellfish. These vendors only appeared on Sundays and somehow managed to cover every street. Steve and Linda would scoff brown paper bags filled with shrimps and whelks doused in vinegar and carefully extract winkles from their shiny black shells with pins. Lily and I hated the stuff and would remain aloof during these seafood orgies.

~

The truth about Steve's Sunday morning visits to his mother was bound to emerge eventually. It's a shame that Linda had to be the one to spill the beans.

One summer Sunday, we walked round to see Nanny Johnson as usual and then dropped into Sutton Dwellings. Ted wasn't at home. He was, I think, a lorry driver and often absent. As we played outside in the sunshine, Linda was her usual boisterous self, hurtling round the play area with a gang of kids in tow. She may have been a restless spirit, but she was always fiercely protective of her little brother and would be keeping a careful eye on me – static as usual, sitting quietly in the shade.

The good thing about being static is that it's usually safe.

Linda, on the other hand, was for ever having accidents. As a baby at 107 Southam Street, she crawled through the window of our room on the ground floor and fell into the 'airie', landing on her head. Incredibly, a large bump was the only damage. On another occasion she fell over while fetching a bottle of vinegar from somebody called the Vinegar Man, who toured the streets with a huge barrel on a horse and cart, crying 'Vinegar!' at the top of his voice. The bottle broke and she cut her knee on the jagged glass.

On this warm Sunday the inevitable fall had happened on a patch of hard, gravelly shingle. She ran up to Ted and Elsie's maisonette, suppressing her tears, to show her blood-splattered leg to her father. The front door was open. Finding nobody in the living room, she dragged her bleeding leg upstairs and opened the bedroom door. She must have been very quiet because Elsie and Steve were caught by surprise – in bed together, and if not in flagrante delicto, certainly approaching the delicto stage.

As Linda was only five or six years old there would have been a reasonable expectation that she didn't understand what she had seen. At any rate, as Steve, Linda – her leg adorned with plasters – and I walked home together nothing was said. But Steve underestimated Linda's maturity and she was soon treating Lily to an honest appraisal of her discovery. The prospect of enjoying the Sunday dinner we'd been waiting for and a normal, boring Sunday afternoon evaporated when Linda announced to Lily: 'I saw Daddy kissing and cuddling in bed. He doesn't love you any more. He loves Auntie Elsie.'

A hush hung over 107 Southam Street. The calm before the storm. But Linda, it seems, though correct in the first part of her analysis, was wrong in the second.

Chapter 2

STEVE LEFT LILY for Elsie when the truth emerged about his Sunday visits. Unfortunately, he came back.

Linda's revelation had led to the kind of shouting and screaming that were a feature of Steve and Lily's life together. In those pre-television days (or rather, the days before TVs were affordable for people like us) it must have provided entertainment for the other families sharing our house. For Linda and me, though, these rows were gut-wrenching periods of fear and misery. We would lie in our beds trying to shut out the noise by pulling the covers over our heads.

Around the time Steve went off to live with Elsie, Linda and I both had measles and Lily was unable to go out to work until we'd recovered. Money from Steve was elusive enough when he was at home, and he made no attempt to send any after he'd left. Six months later, Steve returned and Elsie went home to Ted – pregnant with Steve's child.

I knew nothing of this for years: I didn't find out that I had a half-brother, David, until I was in my teens. We've never met. His existence helped to explain the mystery of the famous 'punch in the passage' incident. A man had knocked on our door one Saturday morning and insisted on seeing Steve. There was a commotion and the sound of a body falling to the floor. Apparently, little Linda then ran out into the passage to find Steve flat out with Ted standing over him. 'Leave my dad alone!' she yelled, but the damage had been done. Steve had been given a good thumping. I remember his grey face as he staggered back into our room, with Lily strangely unsympathetic to his plight.

Ted had agreed to bring David up as his own son, and Steve had agreed to make a financial contribution. When he failed to pay, Ted had come looking for him. The punch probably succeeded only in forcing Steve to prioritize payment to Ted and Elsie over his erratic support for Lily and us. When Linda asked Lily years later why she'd taken Steve back, Lily said that she loved him and, more importantly, that she wanted us to have two parents. Perhaps she also harboured a hope that he'd change his ways.

Early in 1954, after Steve returned from the six months he spent living with Elsie and fathering her child, there was a period of relative calm during which Steve and Lily tried to make a fresh start. It was during this rapprochement that we went on a holiday together to Liverpool. Lily missed her native city terribly. London in general and Notting Hill in particular were not welcoming to 'outsiders'. She was self-conscious about her Scouse accent and tried hard to lose it – not because she was ashamed of it, but out of a desire to conform. Linda and I never noticed her accent at all, apart from when she said words like 'look' and 'book' which became 'luke' and 'boowk', and the occasional 'Oh aye, yeah' to indicate consent. Otherwise it emerged only when she was excited or angry.

Lily didn't miss her domineering father but she pined for the company of her sisters and her favourite brother, John. Three other siblings had left Liverpool during the war. The eldest, Joe (always called Sonny), had joined the RAF and now lived in Coventry, and a younger sister, Dolly, had worked with Lily in the NAAFI. They fell out after Dolly lured one of Lily's boyfriends away from her – a dark, handsome soldier from Hull called Les Foster. The rift had become entrenched when Dolly and Les had married and moved to Hull, where they eventually raised nine children. It had taken several years for diplomatic relations to be re-established.

Jean had married another Londoner, George Heath, and moved to Walthamstow, where they lived in a semi-detached house owned by George's family. Auntie Jean was Lily's Liverpool lifeline in London but, with no phone, they couldn't talk to each other unless we trekked out to Walthamstow, which was something of an expedition back then. Jean and George never came to visit us: Lily would have been ashamed of the conditions we lived in and Steve generally wanted nothing to do with Lily's family, although he enjoyed flirting with her sisters. Lily, Linda and I managed to go and see Jean and George at least once a year, but Lily and Jean were very close and I'm sure it wasn't as often as Lily would have liked.

Uncle George was a tall man with a shock of black, wiry hair and a low, booming voice. He had a good white-collar job as a Post Office clerk and drove a motorbike with a sidecar, in which he ferried around our cousins, Pamela and Norman, who were roughly the same age as Linda and me. Their house in Walthamstow was immaculate. They were the first people we knew who had had a telly and a fridge. Seeing Auntie Jean's house with its neat little garden made Linda and me more aware of the kind of home Lily wanted so badly to provide for us.

Lily would have been pleased to see her sister doing so well and to have her at least within more manageable reach than her other brothers and sisters. I do remember making one visit to Coventry and Hull respectively when Linda and I were small. Uncle Joe and his wife, Auntie Peg, were settled in a lovely new council house on the outskirts of Coventry. I can still picture the hills, fields and trees, and recall having egg salad for tea.

Hull, by contrast, seemed to have even more bomb sites than London but Dolly and Les, living in the midst of them, were very happy together. We liked Les a lot. He was sweet-natured with a disarming smile. On one magical evening during our stay there he took us to Spurn Point in a wood-framed Morris Traveller (what Dame Edna Everage once described in a spoof TV travelogue about Shakespeare's heritage as a 'half-timbered' car).

Steve hadn't accompanied us on these trips but in the period of glasnost post-Elsie, he agreed to come with us to Liverpool. So it was that we lugged our suitcases to the number 52 bus stop, headed for Victoria Coach Station, on a hot Saturday in the summer of 1954. Linda was six and I was four. For Lily, this visit was hugely significant. We were to meet not just her family but Mr and Mrs Ireland, who had taken Lily in when she contracted rheumatic fever in the early 1930s. It was the first time she'd been back to Liverpool since the war and her first opportunity to show off her children.

The object was clear. We must like Liverpool and Liverpool must like us. The 'Provy' was milked for a loan to pay for new clothes for Linda and me: matching red blazers with shiny metal buttons, new shoes of black leather, neat little shorts for me and a flowery dress for Linda. These Provident loans worked like a credit card: you had to repay the money you had borrowed, plus interest, in weekly instalments. Lily grappled with debts like this throughout her adult life.

The coach station was bustling. Then, as now, coach journeys were much cheaper than taking the train, and with far fewer families possessing cars than is the case today it was a popular mode of long-distance travel. Linda and I were hugely excited to be going on this big adventure with Lily and Steve. We had to share a seat and for a while we were mesmerized by the landscape that unfolded through the large window beside us. As I was too young when we travelled to Coventry and Hull to recollect how we got there, this is my first memory of venturing beyond London's borders. In those pre-motorway days, in a non-air-conditioned coach without a toilet, the journey was long – eleven hours – hot and punctuated by frequent lavatory stops.

Aunties Rita and Peggy met us at the coach station in Liverpool and took us on the bus to Anfield and the estate where Lily had grown up. Lily gave us a little walking tour, excitedly pointing out the schools she'd attended and the streets she'd played in. It was incredible to us to be staying in the room that had been Lily's when she'd lived at Warham Road. I remember opening one of the drawers and finding a hairbrush that, she told me, she'd used as a little girl. Our grandfather must have been there, but I don't recall meeting him at that stage. It's possible that Lily deliberately kept us out of his way.

The people to whom she really wanted to show us off, apart

from our aunts and uncles, were the couple she considered her surrogate parents, Mr and Mrs Ireland. We spent a lot of time at their house where there was a pedal car that had belonged to their now grown-up son. I was thrilled to be allowed to play with it. It was a toy I craved throughout my childhood, but one to which I only had access that once at the Irelands'. I made the most of it, pedalling around happily for hours. The real high-light of our week, though, was our first trip to the seaside – we took the ferry, another treat in itself, across the Mersey estuary to New Brighton on the Wirral peninsular, where we paddled and ate ice-cream and built sandcastles.

There are photographs of our holiday in Liverpool. Me in the pedal car at Mr and Mrs Ireland's, Linda and me finding shells on the beach, stripped to our baggy underwear, and posing in our brand-new blazers. Steve doesn't appear in any of them and I'm quite sure he wasn't the photographer. In fact, I can't remember him being there at all – which, in the circum-stances, is perhaps not surprising.

If Lily thought this holiday might be a long-deferred honey-moon for her and Steve she had deluded herself. He didn't come anywhere with us, spending his time exploring the local boozers, having disgraced himself in the first few days by being over-familiar with his sisters-in-law. To Steve this would have seemed like mild flirtation, the kind of behaviour that made 'Ginger' Johnson, pianist par excellence, such a favourite with the ladies of Notting Hill. But this wasn't Notting Hill, and being suggestive to our aunties caused them great discomfort and gave grave offence to our uncles.

Lily's youngest sisters, Rita and Peggy, were and remained vivacious women with a great sense of humour; full of fun despite having to look after their miserable father. Like Jean and Dolly, they had good, dependable husbands in Harry Green and Bob Durham. In other circumstances, Rita and Peggy would probably have taken Steve's flirting in their stride. However, I think the family were all aware that Steve had temporarily left Lily for another woman (although I doubt if they knew about the child he fathered) and would therefore have considered his jack-the-lad behaviour to be in very poor taste. All I know for certain is that words were said, voices were raised and Steve kept out of their way for the remainder of our week in Liverpool.

Back in London, Steve soon returned to the lifestyle he enjoyed, doing the odd bit of painting and decorating and a good deal more piano-playing. He was out every night and would disappear at weekends to Brighton or Southend. Every year he would spend weeks as the resident pianist for the hop-pickers down in Kent. A lot of men from Southam Street took their families 'hopping' in the summer, but Steve always went alone. The coach would pick up the party from outside the Earl of Warwick and as it pulled away the men, in holiday spirits and fresh from a pre-journey session in the pub, would throw pennies out of the windows to the local kids. Hordes of children would scramble for the coins in the filthy gutter. I was too little (and timid) to compete seriously, but Linda was always in the thick of things.

She understood that every penny counted. Lily struggled to put food on the table and, in a good week, to stretch to a Saturday sixpence for Linda and me. Most of our clothes came second hand from Portobello market. Most of Lily's were given to her by the people she cleaned for. From the time we started school we qualified for free school meals and were under instructions from Lily to eat as much as we could in case there wasn't anything for us when we got home.

I was enrolled at Wornington Road Infants' School at the age of five and, after the initial shock of being separated from Lily, settled well into my place on the wooden bench seats in Miss Ockingbole's class. Thanks to Lily, who had registered Linda and me at the library in Ladbroke Grove almost as soon as we could walk, I could already read reasonably well by the time I began school.

∾

In 1956 we moved a few doors down from 107 to 149 Southam Street. The house itself was no more fit for habitation than the one we'd left, but the move brought us a badly needed extra room and, for the first time, electricity – supplied, like the gas, via a coin-operated meter. Linda and I shared a bedroom on a landing, with another family occupying the second room that led off it. Upstairs was our kitchen and a separate room for Lily and Steve.

The stove on the landing also provided an additional source of warmth in cold weather, at least when the oven was lit. At number 107, our one fireplace had served as both hob and oven. Since we had to boil the kettle, cook and heat the flat iron all year round, the fire had to be kept burning and the temperature in there could be unbearable in the summer months.

In the winter we'd all sit round this iron stove to keep warm. At Christmas Lily used to invite 'Pop' Walker, who lived on the top floor of number 107, to share our festive fare, eaten by the dull, yellow glow of the gas mantle: chicken, followed by tinned fruit from a Christmas club hamper to which she'd been contributing a few pennies each week. Pop was thought to be in his nineties; he was certainly too old to have been conscripted for either of the world wars that had killed so many over the previous forty years. He spent his last days smoking his pipe and listening to old records on a wind-up 'His Master's Voice' gramophone. One Christmas, I remember, Pop fell asleep smoking a cigar in front of the stove. Suddenly flames were leaping from Pop's armchair and Lily had to run for a saucepan of water to rescue us all.

With air-conditioning a rare feature of British homes, today's city-dwellers will be familiar with the discomfort of scorching urban summers, even if, mercifully, they no longer have to put up with a roaring fire as well. But it's hard to convey just how cold it could be during the freezing winters of the past in the days before central heating.

At 149 Southam Street warmth was limited to a radius of about three feet around the coal fire and the vicinity of the stove. The bedrooms were ice-boxes and we dreaded the moment when we had to get dressed or undressed. Lily would tell us to imagine we were entering a warm, cosy cave as we got into bed. She had an old earthenware hot water bottle which she filled from the kettle and transferred from bed to bed. I doubt if I've ever been motivated to move as quickly as I was by the prospect of my bare feet coming into contact with the icy linoleum in the sub-zero bedrooms of my childhood. We had no carpet, save for a tatty scrap that served as a mat in front of the coal fire. Everywhere else the floorboards were covered with 'lino', cold and cracked, cheap and nasty. Getting up to pee in the bucket in the middle of a frosty night was no fun, but it was infinitely preferable to having to go out into the back yard to use the toilet, which often seized up when the water in the cistern froze. Bowel movements were conditioned by the weather and the availability of newspapers to be cut into squares and used as toilet paper.

In the early 1950s, before the arrival of the plethora of labour-saving devices most of us take for granted nowadays, every housewife's life was dominated by drudgery to a certain extent. For Lily, hankering after a car, a phone or a television would have been to dream of unattainable luxuries. It was basic household equipment she really needed. Not having a washing machine or a vacuum cleaner made housework (more or less universally regarded as the exclusive responsibility of women) a perpetual battle. The slums of Southam Street gave it an added dimension. The houses were literally crumbling. Damp seeped through walls and ceilings, there were holes in the skirting boards and doors and windows were sagging and misaligned.

Not having a fridge didn't matter in the winter, when the whole house was like a giant deep-freeze anyway. In the summer it was a different story, though nobody was in the habit of storing perishable foods whatever the weather. Lily, like most women, habitually trudged to the shops every day to fetch the eggs, bread and butter that formed our staple diet. The food rationing imposed during the war continued for some years into peacetime – it was 1954 before it ended completely – and the concept of stocking up or buying more than what was required to meet immediate needs would have been considered outlandish. In our case, it was just as well, because living hand-to-mouth was the only system our budget would withstand.

Our milk was delivered fresh every morning, and on hot

days it would be kept in a bowl of cold water. Butter was placed in the coolest corner of the pantry – a small cupboard with an outside wall and at least one air-brick.

If Lily could have been granted a wish for just one appliance, my guess is that she'd have chosen a washing machine. The effort involved in washing by hand, wringing to get as much water out as possible, then putting the clothes through the ancient mangle in the yard, drying them and ironing them with the stove-heated flat iron, was hugely debilitating. Lily did acquire an electric iron when we moved and, when she could afford it, she'd send the washing to the 'bagwash', the predecessor of the launderette. Ours was on the corner of the eastern end of Southam Street, at the junction with Golborne Road, opposite the blue police box, from which local policemen could telephone the station in an emergency. Washing was stuffed into a sack, secured with a drawstring, handed over the counter and returned ready for ironing in the same bag a few days later in exchange for a shilling.

In that pre-supermarket era, high streets in London and towns all over Britain were teeming with small, family-run shops selling anything and everything and our area was no exception: indeed, we were better served than most given that the Portobello Road – 'the Lane' – was also nearby. In Golborne Road there was Humphreys' the butcher's, next to the Bridge Fish Shop, just over the railway bridge walking towards Ladbroke Grove; then Burgess's, the greengrocer's; and, on the corner of Wornington Road, a shop selling nothing but faggots, pease pudding and saveloys. Faggots, for the uninitiated, were rolls of chopped liver, baked or fried; pease pudding was made of split peas, boiled with carrots and onion and mashed to a pulp. Saveloys were pork sausages that had been seasoned, dried and smoked. Even though I spent my childhood in an almost permanent state of hunger, the smell of this shop, which I passed every day on my way to school, put me right off this nutritious 1950s 'fast food'.

For me, ambrosia was available a little further down Golborne Road at Renee's Pie and Mash Shop, where you could get a nourishing meal for sixpence. With its tiled walls and heavy marble tables, there was a solidity to Renee's that was as comforting as the food. To me, no Michelin-starred restaurant could have matched it. Linda and I went there so often during the first nine, ten years of my life that we deserved shares in the business. Of course, we ate pie and mash (and in Linda's case, eels – she ate everything, whereas I added eels to my fussy blacklist along with faggots, saveloys and shellfish). The prosaic description 'pie and mash' really doesn't do justice to a meat pie that had a crust unlike (and in my view vastly superior to) any other kind of pie. It was made, we were told, to a secret recipe jealously guarded by the many pie and mash shops across London. What transformed the dollop of mash and enhanced the pie was the 'liquor': a thickish, clear sauce freckled with parsley. Renee's was the place to which children gravitated at lunchtime during the school holidays, or on a Saturday. I don't remember ever going there with Lily, let alone Steve.

Our second favourite shop was Holmes's, the German baker's. Just inhaling the scent of bread and fresh doughnuts as we walked past on our way to or home from school was enough to fortify us. But the vendors who saw most of our custom were the proprietors of the two rival sweetshops that faced one another across Wornington Road. They were both small but the competition between them was every bit as intense as today's battles between Tesco and Sainsbury's. Their weapon of choice was fizzy pop.

On one side of the road was the Kabin, a smart, modern establishment run by a smart, modern guy named Reg. With his dark, swept-back hair and checked shirt, sleeves rolled up to the elbows, he looked a bit like Roy Rogers, the cowboy star of the Saturday morning pictures at the Royalty Cinema in Lancaster Road. The fizzy drinks Reg served were sophisticated – Tizer, R. White's lemonade and cream soda – and cost three-pence a glass. Opposite was what had apparently once been a neat little place called the Tuck Shop but which was now known to everybody as Bert's. While it still sold what would qualify as 'tuck', the original sign had faded and old Bert – a ringer for Mr Pastry, the famous children's entertainer of the time, with his pure white moustache and matching frizz of hair – had become increasingly eccentric. As he lurched around the shop in his long, brown shopkeeper's coat, or climbed up and down the ladder required to reach the ancient sweet jars on the top shelf, he would emit a constant stream of invective, aimed mainly at Reg across the road.

Bert undercut Reg's modern, popular fizzy drinks with unbranded alternatives he concocted himself – a kind of non-alcoholic home brew – and poured from a huge bell jar. He sold these for a penny, and they were absolutely delicious, tasting of a sort of amalgamation of different fruits. Goodness knows what this stuff was made of or what it did to our intestines but there was a high level of customer satisfaction among us Wornington Road pupils.

Both Reg and Bert would be puffing away on a cigarette as

they dispensed our drinks. The vast majority of grown-ups smoked, including Steve and Lily. Given how common the habit was in the 1950s, it would have been unusual if they hadn't. Lily didn't smoke heavily – probably around five cigarettes a day. You could buy cigarettes in packs of five back then, and she'd convert hers into packs of ten by cutting the cigarettes in half with an old razor blade to make them go further. She smoked Weights until brands like Kensitas and Guards began to offer coupons, which she collected meticulously. If you got through enough fags to trigger emphysema you could acquire a bedside lamp with the coupons.

Steve smoked roll-ups. His fingers were permanently stained a brownish yellow, as were his false teeth. He played the piano with a roll-up dangling from the side of his mouth. Lily wouldn't have dreamed of smoking roll-ups: it would have offended her sense of femininity. An essential element of the image of the film stars she admired, like Bette Davis and Grace Kelly, was the elegant way they held a cigarette, sloping upwards from between the first and second fingers. Lily loved 'the pictures'. When we were little she went at least once a week – without Steve, needless to say. Her daily working uniform of wraparound floral overall and turban would be discarded, her lovely, chestnut wavy hair brushed and styled with the help of a platoon of pins, grips and clips. Face powder would be dabbed on, creating little clouds of perfumed dust. Finally she'd apply glamorous bright red lipstick, using a broken hand mirror held at an angle directly under the naked light bulb. The results would be checked in the full-length mirror on the inside of the door of the dark wooden wardrobe.

I loved seeing Lily fully made up and glowing with

anticipation. Those cinema trips were one of the few bits of happiness in her life. When we all slept in the same room at 107 Southam Street, I remember Lily's scent as she bent over to kiss me goodnight before escaping for the evening to Hollywood or Pinewood. Linda would be left in charge of me, since Steve was always out. Sharing Lily's excitement, I tried, but usually failed, to stay awake so that when she returned she could tell me all about the films she had seen.

We were used to being left alone from an early age because poor Lily never stopped working. Cleaning and scrubbing for Mrs McLean and Miss MacDougal, a widow and spinster, who ran an upmarket residential boarding house off Church Lane in South Kensington; up on a chair, dusting lampshades for Mr and Mrs Dehn, of Lansdowne Crescent; polishing the furniture and disinfecting toilets in the spacious flat in Notting Hill Gate where she cleaned for three young brothers, a solicitor, a journalist and a stockbroker, whose mother had hired her to tidy up after them. And in the evenings she would often be pressed into service at those dinners in the big houses between Ladbroke Grove and Kensington Park Road.

The nightly rows with Steve were invariably about money and his failure to contribute very much, if anything, to the household budget. He had very quickly returned to his old ways and seemed to consider it Lily's responsibility to put a roof over our heads, clothes on our backs and food in our bellies. He even resented the few pennies she spent on going to the pictures. Her hourly rate for cleaning would have been a pittance and Steve probably gambled in a day as much as she earned in a week.

A myth seems to have taken root in our retrospective view of the 1950s that women didn't work outside the home and that the husband was always the breadwinner. That may have been the convention in middle-class households, but it certainly wasn't the case in the working-class families in our street. As for us, if we'd depended on Steve to win the bread, we'd have starved. Even if he backed the winner in the 3.30 at Kempton Park, it didn't translate into bread for us. Yet if any woman shouldn't have been working in 1950s London it was Lily, given her heart condition which, like her relationship with Steve, was becoming progressively worse.

There is no doubt Steve could be a charmer. Those who heard him play at the Earl of Warwick, the Mitre or the Lads of the Village must have thought we were lucky to have 'Ginger' Johnson as a father. And we were proud to see how respected he was when, as tots, we were taken to wedding receptions to sit on top of the piano, taking care not to knock over the line of pints of mild and bitter that grew longer as the evening wore on.

We were also proud of him at the Cobden Club children's Christmas party, which for some reason was always held in January, where he was the master of ceremonies. The Cobden Club, on Westbourne Grove, later became a trendy private club and music venue: my son Jamie played there with his band a few years ago. In the 1950s, however, it was a working men's club, and Steve, as its regular pianist, hosted its annual children's treat.

He was rather less charming when he lay in bed all morning after a night of entertaining, surfacing only when it was time to put his bet on. Every morning we would have to take him up a cup of tea, only to find the previous one untouched, cold and congealing by his bedside, next to his dentures, which smiled up at us from the glass of water they were kept in overnight. The bold and brave Linda took to putting salt in the tea as an expression of her increasing bitterness. It was a futile gesture since he never drank it anyway.

We hated having to go into that dark, dank room, heavy with the stench of alcohol, but it contained the only mirror we owned, on the inside of one of the wardrobe doors. Though Lily, to guard against any tendency to vanity, warned us that if we stared into a mirror for too long we'd see the devil, we did occasionally have to go in to check that we were suitably presentable while Steve lay comatose in the bed.

The rudest thing I'd ever seen was in that wardrobe. It was a hardback book, the size of a comic annual, which belonged to Steve. Every page contained a series of photographs of a naked woman. I doubt if it qualified as pornography, even in the more innocent 1950s. The women had waxed pudenda and posed artistically like blonde statuettes. I don't know where the book came from or whose work it contained, but I dare say that in the big houses at the Holland Park end of Portobello Road it would have been considered art and probably displayed on a coffee table. To us, though, it was truly shocking.

It was Linda, as usual, who initially made this discovery and urged me on to self-corruption. When Steve and Lily were out, I'd sneak in, open the wardrobe, with its rows of Steve's ties hanging on a wire across the inside of the other door, the one without the mirror, stand on the little wooden chair that served as a bedside table and stretch into the dark recess at the top. I would then ogle the pictures for as long as I dared.

Impressed as we were by Steve's talent for music, he made no effort to share it with us. There was always a battered old piano taking up precious space in our rooms – hardly any furniture, but always a piano – and yet not only did he never try to teach us how to play, he made sure we couldn't teach ourselves, either. He kept the keyboard locked and possessed the only key.

He did come home once with a cardboard box full of old 78rpm records that he'd bought in Portobello market. These huge, pre-vinyl discs, made of shellac, were extremely brittle. For a long while we had nothing to play them on. All we could do was treasure them and read the labels: 'In a Shady Nook by a Babbling Brook' by Donald Peers, on Columbia; 'With Her Head Tucked Underneath Her Arm', 'Tap Your Feet and Sing Bop Dee Bop Dee Doo' by a forgotten orchestra, and a spoken-word recording of 'The Giant's Beanstalk'.

In the meantime our only source of entertainment was the wireless, rented by Lily from Radio Rentals, which was cabled into a brown Bakelite switch fixed to a window frame. It had three BBC settings – the Home Service, Light Programme and Third Programme. I grew up listening to *The Archers, Mrs Dale's Diary, Letter from America, Down Your Way* and *Have A Go*, with Wilfred Pickles ('Put your feet on the mantel shelf, tune in your wireless and help yourself'). Over the years Lily must have paid out enough rental fees to buy a hundred radios, but renting was her only option.

We wanted to listen to our ancient records, too, but no money meant no gramophone.

Then Lily won the pools.

Chapter 3

LIKE A HUGE percentage of the population, Steve and Lily did the football pools every week (Steve with Vernons, Lily with Littlewoods). It's difficult to grasp now how important the pools were to families, regardless of wealth and background. When, many years later, I became a postman in leafy, prosperous Barnes, we had to do special deliveries to clear the mountain of stubby, thick brown envelopes sent from the big Merseyside duo of Vernons and Littlewoods, along with Zetters and Cope.

When the football results were broadcast on the wireless on *Sports Report* at 5pm on a Saturday afternoon, they were listened to with hushed reverence across the nation, and nowhere more so than in Southam Street. Those who criticize the poor for spending some of the little money they have on the pools, or nowadays more often on the National Lottery, can never have experienced the profound motivational force of the prospect of a win.

Lily relied on the 'tick' for groceries, the 'never-never' – or hire purchase, as it used to be called – for anything more substantial and the tallyman for loans she had no hope of fully repaying. The designation 'tallyman' covered anyone who offered credit and then came to collect the repayments. As well as the Provident, which had funded our holiday in Liverpool, Lily borrowed from the Prudential and it was their tallyman, the most persistent, with whom we were most familiar. When we heard four knocks on the front door, we knew the caller was for us (the custom was one knock for the ground floor, two for the first and so on – and the third floor was us). Invariably it would be a tallyman of one stripe or another.

We were well practised in ducking down away from the windows and remaining silent as soon as we heard four knocks, and lying low until the tallyman gave up. We also knew we had to walk straight past the house if we saw one of them on the doorstep. They were easy to spot with their uniform belted raincoats and the thick, black ledgers they all carried.

The Man from the Pru, however, wouldn't be content to knock four times. When that elicited no response he would persevere by knocking once, twice or three times to get some-one else to open the door, then stride up to our floor and rap on the two doors leading off the landing, where the stove was. If we were very quiet he'd go away, and to his credit, he never opened the doors to look inside. But he caught Lily often, particularly if she happened to be using the stove.

Small wonder Lily did the pools every week, and dreamed of the better life that over twenty-two points on the coupon could provide. The first thing she'd buy if she ever won, she used to say, was a house. She always longed to have her own front door. We once had an offer of a council house that would have taken us out of the slums and through a front door that was exclusively ours. The trouble was that the front door in question was in Crawley, in Sussex. The offer was probably made during a push to populate the new towns being built to ease the housing shortages after the war. Steve was adamant: he had no intention of moving out of Notting Hill, let alone going anywhere near a new town.

Since Lily had no roots in West London, and given her desperation to improve our circumstances, I'm pretty sure we'd have decamped to Crawley if it had been up to her. She consoled herself with the thought that at least our landlords were the respectable Rowe Housing Trust and not the notorious Peter Rachman, who was by then busy enriching himself by driving out sitting tenants in Notting Hill, who had statutory protection against high rents, in order to exploit the growing demand among new immigrants from the Caribbean for cheap housing. At that time new tenants did not have the same protection as sitting tenants, and people arriving from the West Indies after the war in response to the call for workers in Britain found it almost impossible to find a place to live. They had no alternative but to accept poor conditions and extortionate rents, and Rachman packed as many of them as he could into shared accommodation by subdividing houses into multiple small rooms.

Rachman's domain never extended to Southam Street, or at any rate, not to our end of it, largely because our houses were already so overcrowded and mainly under the control of housing trusts. His principal area of operation was the streets south of Westbourne Grove, including Powis Square, Colville Terrace and Talbot Grove.

So Crawley was rejected and we remained in Southam Street with the Rowe Housing Trust. I used to go with Lily from time to time to their offices in the Portobello Road to pay the rent. There was a funny wooden, concertina-style hinged door that led directly into the offices from the street. We'd push it open and walk up a couple of floors where we queued to talk to a woman behind a steel and glass grille. I can still vividly remember the cream woodwork, brown lino and the smell of disinfectant.

The pools were Lily's only flutter, although she did embrace bingo a few years later, once the Betting and Gaming Act of 1960 paved the way for the bingo halls that began to spring up in towns and cities across the country. For Steve, though, the pools were a mere Saturday diversion from the horses. I think he must have placed a bet every day there was a horse to bet on. Had he lived in today's world of easy access to gambling on anything and everything, he might well have taken it up as a full-time occupation.

Before the 1960 Act, off-course cash betting on the 'gee-gees' was illegal and there was no such thing as a licensed high-street betting shop. Linda and I would be press-ganged into running Steve's bets. He would collar whichever one of us he found first and send us off with a little parcel of money tightly wrapped in the scrap of paper on which his bet was written. We would be instructed to keep it clutched firmly in the palm of our hand and not to let go of it until we passed it to one of the bookies. These men – invariably, in my memory, fat men with trilby hats on their heads and fags in their mouths, reminiscent of the famous silhouette of Alfred Hitchcock – would lurk in door-ways in St Ervans Road or Tavistock Crescent. We never knew their names, and the transaction, which was conducted in complete silence, was over in seconds. You'd hand over the bet and the bookie would give you a piece of paper, which Linda or I had to hand back to Steve to prove the bet had been laid. I do not recall ever collecting any winnings on Steve's behalf, which means either he wasn't very good at picking winners or that, on the rare occasions when he did win, the walk to find the bookie suddenly became less onerous for him.

When Lily won the pools in 1957, it wasn't enough to start a new life. I think she won about £90, which was a significant amount in the 1950s – the equivalent of two or three months' wages for a male manual worker. She used it to make down-payments on lots of things: a three-piece suite, a sideboard, a kitchen table, a Spanish guitar for me and a red and grey Dansette record-player for Linda. Inevitably, she couldn't keep up the HP payments, no matter how hard she worked. One by one, her acquisitions were seized or had to be returned, except for the guitar and the Dansette.

For Linda and me, that record-player brought a sense of joy that is difficult to articulate. We placed it in the middle of our room and spent ages just looking at it, admiring its sleek lines and absorbing the glorious smell of new plastic and rubber. While we were yet to acquire any up-to-date records, we could at long last listen to the old 78s, although I worried that the huge shellac discs would damage the delicate precision of the turntable. My favourites were the records by Arthur Tracy, 'The Street Singer', and his rendition of Frances Langford's 1937 hit 'Was it Tears that Fell or was it Rain?'

> Skies were grey that rainy day we parted in the lane,
> Was it tears that fell or was it rain?
> There we stood as lovers would;

Did parting bring you pain?
Was it tears that fell or was it rain?
I couldn't tell if your eyes were misty,
Or if you felt regret,
I noticed when you kissed me, that both your cheeks were wet.
Till we meet again, my sweet
The memory shall remain.
Was it tears that fell or was it rain?

I've never heard that record played on anything other than the Dansette in our damp room in Southam Street well over fifty years ago, yet I remember every melancholy word.

~

By the time she was in her early thirties, Lily seemed to be degenerating from a good-looking, petite young woman into a dowdy, prematurely middle-aged charlady. Her fresh, Liverpool-Irish prettiness was fading, the glamorous sheer stockings and bright red lipstick made fewer and fewer appearances and the hand-me-down fashionable clothes she acquired from various employers, or scavenged from the market on the Lane, remained hidden beneath the wraparound floral overall she'd once used only for work but now rarely took off. Her beautiful chestnut hair stayed bunched under her turban. Wounded by neglect and battle-weary, she began to put on weight as a result of the drugs she had to take for her heart condition, her legs became mapped with varicose veins and she developed bunions on her feet.

She was told to give up her cleaning jobs and rest. Any

exercise or activity that raised the heart rate, such as the nightly battles when Steve finally wandered home, made the symptoms worse. But Lily could not afford to stop working. When her increasingly frequent stays in hospital forced her to do so, we would be plunged deeper into poverty and debt and she had no choice but to work even harder when she came out.

When I was seven and Linda was ten, Lily was taken into hospital again just before Christmas. As usual, she'd been paying her few shillings into the Christmas club for a hamper, which was stashed in the pantry. She had also already bought and wrapped a *Hotspur* annual for me and a *Bunty* annual for Linda, placing them with boxes of sweets in two pillowcases for us to delve into on Christmas morning. I'm sure Linda must have abandoned any belief in Santa Claus by then. If I'd begun to doubt his existence, my suspicions were confirmed that year.

Steve went off on the afternoon of Christmas Eve and never came home. We were used to fending for ourselves but we'd never been on our own at Christmas before. We found our pillowcases and ate the sweets for breakfast while reading our annuals and waiting for Steve to return and cook our Christmas dinner.

When he failed to materialize Linda decided to take control. She put the chicken from the hamper in the oven, checking the instructions on the plastic wrapping carefully to make sure she cooked it for the recommended time. Lily had left a pile of shilling pieces to be fed into the meter so that there would be enough gas to cook the dinner. Unfortunately, the instructions said nothing about removing the wrapping, and while Linda prepared the potatoes and cabbage, the acrid smell of burning plastic filled the kitchen and eventually drifted into Southam

Street from the sash windows we'd raised to try to clear the air.

Alerted by the stench, Brenda, the young Irishwoman who lived with her husband and two young children on the next landing, tried to rescue the chicken but was forced to concede defeat. She showed us how the plastic had melted into the flesh of the chicken and explained that we wouldn't be able to eat it now. She asked where Steve was. Ashamed to admit he had abandoned us, we made an excuse for him and said he'd be back later.

We ate the vegetables and some more of our Christmas sweets before setting off on the long walk to Paddington General Hospital for visiting time. Steve was waiting for us outside the ward. His breath reeked of beer and cigars as he bent down to speak to us in confidence. 'Don't tell Mum that I didn't come home. Tell her we had a nice dinner together. If you say anything else it will upset her and she'll have a heart attack and die.' Hospital visiting times were very restricted then, even on Christmas Day, so we only had to keep up the pretence for half an hour.

When we left the hospital, Linda and I walked home while Steve headed off in the other direction. He didn't return that night or on Boxing Day. He must have come back very late on 27 December, while we were asleep, because he was there the next morning. Lily was due to be discharged the following day and he reminded us again of the reason why we must keep our little Christmas secret. I doubt Lily ever knew that we'd spent Christmas alone that year.

The stay in hospital did nothing to halt her decline. She picked up the cleaning jobs again just a few weeks after leaving hospital, contrary to doctor's orders. During school holidays she had to take us with her. We were quite happy to explore this alternative universe. Instead of individual gardens, the residents of the grand houses in Lansdowne Crescent, off Ladbroke Grove, where she charred for Mrs Dehn, had exclusive access to a private park at the rear, and we were allowed to play there. But it was Mrs McLean's, the refined boarding house off Church Street, that provided Lily's most regular employment. She had started there when Linda was at primary school and I was still at Wornington Road. On Lily's days at Mrs McLean's Linda and I would catch the 52 bus with her. We got off just before it turned into Kensington High Street, where she'd give us our instructions before sending us off to play in Kensington Gardens: 'Do not talk to strangers, stay together and shelter in the museums if it rains.'

Invariably she would spot a trace of dirt somewhere on my face (never on Linda's) and a huge handkerchief would be produced, spat on and rubbed vigorously at the offending stain, which no doubt added more bacteria than it removed.

We would carry sandwiches in the waxed paper wrapping from a Sunblest loaf and a few coppers for sweets. We had to report back to Mrs McLean's at 2.30pm, just before Lily finished at 3pm. We spent so much time in Kensington Gardens that we felt almost proprietorial. There was an invisible border with Hyde Park which we rarely crossed, although the two parks merged seamlessly. The little slope near the Church Street entrance seemed very steep to me at that age and our first ritual of the day was to announce our arrival by rolling down it. We loved the bandstand, from which we'd survey our territory, the statue of Peter Pan, the Round Pond, the

Orangery and the museum in Kensington Palace that contained a model of London at the time of the Great Fire. You could flick a switch and the scene would light up to replicate the spread of the fire from its source in Pudding Lane across the city. This effect was achieved by the simple use of tiny light bulbs, but it was the most exciting thing I'd ever seen – and I insisted on seeing it on every single visit.

Unlike the parks in Notting Hill – the Little Rec, the Big Rec and St Marks, where there were fights and thefts and tension – this was safe territory, and the many summer hours we spent in Kensington Gardens and Exhibition Road, away from the crumbling squalor of Southam Street, were a highlight of our childhood.

Linda, ever the mini-mum, always knew where the action was. There were regular Punch and Judy shows and, on occasion, films would be projected from a huge lorry with a screen at the back. This truck sometimes visited our area on a tour of 'play streets'. We'd watch the film sitting cross-legged on the dirty road. Here there would be much pushing and shoving in the battle for the prime spots at the front. The audience in Kensington Gardens was much gentler.

Whether it was raining or not, we would head off past the Albert Memorial to the museums in Exhibition Road. We went so often that we could have been employed as tour guides at the Science Museum, the Geological Museum and the V&A. But our favourite was the Natural History Museum, and the best exhibit of all was the blue whale that dominated the huge hall in which it was suspended. We adored that whale. Even at that age we worried about it being dead and on display rather than alive and swimming around in the sea. Lily told us we were all put on this Earth for a purpose and that the blue whale's was obviously to educate and inspire.

The whale would have admired Lily. Like the captain of a ship, ever alert to the dangers that surrounded us, she steered us through perilous seas. We might have been left alone but we were never neglected. She laid down few rules but we knew what was expected of us: to be polite and courteous and to help those less fortunate than ourselves. Lily swelled with pride when shopkeepers remarked on how well-mannered we were, and how we always remembered to say 'please' and 'thank you'.

In Southam Street, we were encouraged to run errands for elderly neighbours who lived alone, like Mrs Sudbury. Linda would do her shopping, while I carried her milk up from the doorstep. We were under strict instructions to accept nothing in return. When Linda once admitted that she'd been given a few pennies for helping with some task or other, she was marched off by Lily to take the money back.

In effect, Lily was a single parent. She compensated for Steve's lack of interest in us in the same way that she worked to make up the money that went to the bookies. Her belief in God, while absolute, was informal and unevangelical. She told us that He was everywhere but seemed to have greater faith in astrology and spiritualism than in the established Church. Every year she'd buy *Old Moore's Almanack* – a stubby little tome published on cheap paper – for a few pence. When she could afford it, a monthly magazine called *Prediction* would appear which she would pore over for hours, convinced of its integrity. Every morning, in the precious interval between getting us off to school and going out to work, she'd open her *Daily Sketch* at the horoscope page and sit with her varicosed legs stretched out in front of her, resting on a kitchen chair. While enjoying a cup of strong tea, a slice of toast and her first cigarette of the day, she would study the forecasts made for the entire family's star signs with the same intensity that Steve applied to picking winners (or more often losers) from the racing pages when he rose from his slumber later.

Lily's determination to stay with Steve was in part dictated by the times in which she lived. When couples got married they stayed together, come what may. Children born outside wedlock were stigmatized as 'illegitimate', single women were referred to as spinsters and a failed marriage was unusual and invariably deemed to be the fault of the wife. Divorce was rare outside the upper classes and 'living together' was practically unheard of beyond bohemian circles of artists and poets. Poor Lily: every woman close to her had married well – not in the material sense, but in the sense that their husbands were good men. Her sisters were happily married and so were most of the people we knew locally, which can only have increased Lily's feelings of isolation and sharpened her suffering.

Linda and I were certainly aware from an early age that our family was a poor example of what families were supposed to be. The father of Linda's lifelong friend Marilyn Hughes worshipped his wife in the most flamboyant, demonstrative way and the parents of my school pal Tony Cox were the most perfectly suited couple imaginable.

I met Tony when I moved up from Wornington Road Infants' School to Bevington Primary. He was tall and skinny with hair so blond it was almost white. With his blue eyes and fair skin, he looked positively Scandinavian. His sister, Carole, who was in Linda's year at Bevington, had similar colouring.

They took after their mother's side of the family. Their younger brother, by contrast, had inherited the dark, Mediterranean appearance of their father, Albert.

There are no surrogate fathers in this story. The lack of any meaningful relationship with Steve did not spur me to seek an alternative father figure. In fact it had the opposite effect: it made me mistrustful of men in general and uncomfortable in their presence. I much preferred being with women. But if I had been inclined to fantasize about the ideal father, as Linda was (she idolized her teacher at Bevington, Mr Freeman, and often voiced her wish that he was our dad), Albert Cox would have been my choice.

He epitomized the kind of steady, decent, hard-working man who had fought the war in the forties and delivered the peace in the fifties. He wasn't a striking figure: he was of no more than average height, his hair was thinning and, like many former soldiers, he was never seen out of the house without his army beret. The gabardine mac, buckled at the waist, teamed with the beret identifying the regiment in which the wearer had served during the war is a style we're probably more likely to associate nowadays with the 1970s sitcom *Some Mothers Do 'Ave Em*, whose gormless central character, Frank Spencer, clung on to a sartorial statement that had long since gone out of fashion. But it was a common sight on the streets of Britain twenty years earlier.

Steve never wore his beret. Having made an appearance at his wedding, it was never seen again. Perhaps his particular regiment didn't permit any part of the uniform to be retained on discharge; perhaps the beret was only available at a price he couldn't afford. More likely it was because he loved to show off his Brylcreemed red hair, combed tight to his scalp like finely raked soil.

Albert Cox, on the other hand, was proud of his beret, which I think bore the insignia of the Royal Engineers. At any rate, that was his trade in Civvy Street: he was an engineer with London Underground. The Coxes lived at 318 Lancaster Road in another house that no longer exists – that one became a victim of the Westway, the elevated section of the A40, which drove a huge concrete path through London W10 in the latter half of the 1960s. The Coxes rented two floors of the four-storey house, just round the corner from Latimer Road tube station. The buildings here were still in good condition and there was no trace of the squalor and debris that blighted Southam Street.

The Coxes' home was remarkable to me for boasting an entire room that you had neither to sleep in nor eat in. Compared to the numbing, incapacitating chill of our house, their two floors seemed gloriously warm all winter long, thanks to the paraffin heaters that burned on each landing and in the large, light, airy 'front room'. The Coxes had carpets, too – deep-piled, unfrayed and smelling of clean blankets and carpet shampoo – which added to the atmosphere of comfort and warmth. And in that gracious, cosy front room was another source of wonder: a beautiful glass-fronted bookcase. Inside were two sets of books, the *Encyclopaedia Britannica* and the novels of Charles Dickens, plus an assortment of second-hand hardback classics – *Treasure Island, Pride and Prejudice, The Moonstone.*

The carpet and the paraffin heaters, together with the break-fast Mr Cox cooked for everyone every morning – the Coxes believed in a proper big, hot breakfast, not a bowl of cereal or a slice of toast – spoke eloquently to me of working-class prosperity. Mr Cox provided for his family: not only did he dedicate all of his wages (supplemented by the money his wife Pat made working at a fish and chip shop on Shepherd's Bush Green) to ensuring their wellbeing, he devoted his spare time to the same cause. The tomatoes they ate at breakfast came from the allotment Mr Cox cultivated assiduously, spending every hour he could after his shift at London Underground planting and pruning and digging, tilling the city soil of North Kensington and bringing home boxes of its produce on his old sit-up-and-beg bike, balanced precariously on the front basket. Albert Cox: hunter, gatherer, provider, protector.

The bookcase, too, was a badge of Albert's benign paternalism: a signifier of his aspirations for his children's future – although it must be said the effect was undermined by the fact that, like Steve's piano, it was kept firmly locked. Unlike me, neither Carole nor Tony showed any interest in reading. Although I had been a regular at the library in Ladbroke Grove since Lily first took Linda and me there when we were toddlers, I possessed only a few books of my own, thanks mainly to the Cobden Club. When Steve hosted their Christmas party, we each received a gift and the gift was always a book. We must have gone to three such parties from 1954 to1957 and I clearly remember the three books I came away with – *Robinson Crusoe*, *Tom Sawyer* and a *Boy's Own* annual – and one of Linda's, *Little Women*. It was those three books that belonged to me, rather than the ones I borrowed, that I read and re-read, treasured and cherished.

I hinted to Mr Cox how much I'd welcome the opportunity to look at the gems in his bookcase, without success. Perhaps he felt they were too precious to entrust to a small, sticky-fingered boy.

I'm not sure what it was that cemented my friendship with Tony Cox, or even if that's how it could be properly described. We were complete opposites. He was a buccaneer, an adventurer straight from the pages of my favourite comic, *The Hotspur*. The thought of sitting indoors and reading a book was anathema to Tony. Just sitting indoors would be bad enough. This tall young Viking was a very good fast bowler, a half-decent footballer and the champion of our summer sport, known as Flick Cards. Although I was none of these things, we somehow forged a bond.

Most boys of that era collected the cards that came free with bubble gum and other sweets, as well as cigarettes and (I think) Brooke Bond tea. I was no exception. We were all desperate to acquire full sets, getting our hands on those that eluded us by bartering or swapping spares with our schoolmates. Some of the cards were educational (I still recognize the flag of Honduras from my 'Flags of the World' collection); others were military, featuring the uniforms of soldiers through the ages or the weapons they carried.

Those we liked the best were the strong, thick, laminated cards that bore the photograph of a footballer or cricketer. These were what we used at school to play Flick Cards. The obsession with this game among my primary school contemporaries was feverish, and yet, like so many childhood crazes down the years, it seemed to vanish almost overnight. Flick Cards could be played on your own or as a team sport. A card would be placed on its end against a wall with the players standing a prescribed distance away, usually ten paces, each holding his own stack of cards and taking turns to flick one at the target. The technique was to hold an edge of the card you were flicking between your first and second fingers and then throw out your arm as if you were slapping someone's face with the back of your hand. The boy who succeeded in dislodging the standing card would win all the others that had been flicked in vain. When there were several competitors, you could play with any number of cards lined up against the wall. The victor would be the boy who dislodged the final one.

At Bevington Primary our playground games were strictly segregated, as indeed was the playground: a thick painted line separated the girls from the boys. Flick Cards was for the boys. The girls' sporting seasons consisted of skipping in the winter and in the summer the game of Two Balls, which involved bouncing rubber balls off a wall with a level of skill far greater than was required for anything the boys attempted.

I kept my battle-scarred cards in an old Black Magic chocolate box, its shiny black quilted lid contrasting sharply with the sorry condition of the treasures it safeguarded. Although I joined in competitive games like Flick Cards in the playground, away from school I rarely ventured out to engage in the rough and tumble of the streets. I was a much more solitary child than my effervescent sister, who was usually to be found outdoors – often upside down, doing handstands against a wall with her dress tucked into her knickers to stop it falling over her face, or skipping with a rope hung ingeniously from the two little metal arms set high up on the lamp posts. I preferred playing indoors in our bedroom, where I created my own imaginary world.

As well as the boxful of records, someone – probably Steve – had brought home a huge stack of old greetings cards and post-cards. You could get all kinds of things for next to nothing down the Portobello Road that might well have fetched some much-needed income if we'd taken them to a collector. I used the greetings cards to build a cardboard city for my toy cowboys and Indians, standing them with their spines in the air and the two sides forming an open tent. My cowboys and Indians weren't separated into ghettos. The cardboard town centre and suburbs formed a peaceful, harmonious city with a grid system that would have impressed a town planner.

While Lily was happy to allow Linda to take her skipping rope out into the road, she was determined to make sure that I was not roaming the streets, principally, I think, because of a belief that while girls were safe, boys were likely to 'get into trouble' or to be attacked by other boys. In truth, preventing me from straying into dangerous territory didn't take much effort. Lily may have been over-protective, but her concerns were well founded.

Chapter 4

I HAD FIRST BECOME the victim of crime at the age of six. Still young enough to be fascinated by bright colours and shiny objects, I had built up an impressive collection of sweet wrappers and bus tickets. In the days before thin paper rolls were used to print tickets with the turn of a handle on a chunky silver machine, bus conductors carried an oblong board with a row of tickets in various colours which corresponded to journeys of different lengths. They would punch holes in these tickets, using a small contraption they wore slung round their necks, to prevent them from being used again.

I'd assembled my collection in the summer holidays when Linda and I rode the number 52 bus with Lily on her way to work at Mrs McLean's in Church Street. The sweet wrappers were purple and shiny and had once enclosed fruit bon-bons. I kept the tickets and wrappers in an old jewellery box Lily had given me, a navy blue tin with a cream interior and little compartments that opened out as the lid was lifted. I was so proud of this prized collection that I decided one day to take it to school and show it to my classmates.

My infants' school in Wornington Road wasn't far from

Southam Street and there were no roads to cross or traffic to navigate, which is probably why Lily, who watched over me so intently, allowed me to make the journey alone. On my way home that day I was accosted outside the ice-cream shop by an older boy called Stephen Kirk. With his badly cut hair, clenched fists and general air of malice, this kid spelled trouble. He didn't need to issue a formal request: I knew he wanted my navy blue box.

'What yer got in nair den?'

'Nuffink.'

'Less 'ave a look.'

'Nah.'

'Less 'ave a look or I'll wallop yer.'

I had no choice but to open the box and reveal the treasure. The boy snatched the blue box and ran off across the Golborne Road without so much as a backward glance.

Casting my mind back now, I don't think I ever felt safe on those streets. For while there was a genuine sense of community in our neighbourhood, the threat of violence that bubbled perpetually beneath the surface was a part of our everyday lives. It erupted frequently. Adult men would fight outside the pubs on a Saturday night and gangs of boys, keen to prove how tough they were, would attack if provoked. And it didn't take a lot to provoke them. Sometimes it was enough to make the simple mistake of looking at them. Having said that, sometimes not looking at them could be interpreted as weakness and lead to the same outcome.

When to look, when not to look and indeed how to look was a complex skill, acquired through trial and error. It was important to appear 'hard'. This could involve chewing gum or spitting indiscriminately and always required narrowing your eyes and adopting a jaunty gait. If you could carry this off in a way that made a potential adversary worry about the likely result of any attack, it was a useful deterrent. If you couldn't, it was best to keep your eyes averted to avoid the piercingly delivered question: 'Oi! 'Oo you screwin'?' (In the slang of that time and place, the verb 'to screw' had a less salacious definition than it does today: it merely meant 'to look'.) Fighting was an essential part of a boy's life and fathers regarded education in the arts of pugilism to be as important as learning to read (unfortunately, some thought it even more important).

Steve tried to teach me how to box. These little tournaments scared me and upset Lily, but he insisted they were necessary to toughen me up. He would be stripped to his string vest and trousers and we'd dance around aiming punches at the body, never the head. I was a very skinny southpaw and could duck and weave quite skilfully, but when Steve did land a blow, usually to my arms as I defended my body, it would be extremely painful and leave big bruises. Yet I had to carry on or risk humiliation.

Lily, who was used to taking his punches herself, was always hovering on the periphery like a demented referee trying to end the bout. If she thought I'd been hurt too much she'd push herself between us. I was too little and scrawny ever to hurt Steve but I punched with a venom that intensified over time, suppressing an urge to cry when his fists got through my defences and connected with my solar plexus, sucking the air out of me. I suppose it was as a result of those bouts that I began to see Steve as foe rather than friend. Someone who, to use a boxing analogy, wasn't in my corner.

Like Lily, many women were unconvinced of the virtues of teaching boys to fight, but this had more to do with their aspirations for their sons than any objections to them being 'toughened up'. To fight on the streets or in the playground was 'common'. Not fighting was a sign of gentility, of prosperity, of the different, more refined life they wanted for their boys. It's true that physical altercations in those days tended to involve fists rather than weapons and that they were required to be seen as 'fair'. There were quaint rules of engagement: you never hit a boy with glasses; you didn't kick; you never hit a man when he was down. But the Marquis of Queensbury was never around when you needed him, and it was rare, in my experience, that any adult sought to stop a fight, irrespective of how much kicking was going on, if it was between two boys of roughly equal size and age. It was thought to be healthy and natural to let them get on with it.

So there were playground fights, classroom fights and neighbourhood fights. Aggression wasn't confined to men and boys, either. Women fought in the street – hair down, sleeves rolled up, punching, biting, scratching, hurling themselves at one another, while spectators gathered round and shouted encouragement. Many men thought it quite acceptable to hit their wives. Mothers and fathers would beat their children in the firm belief that it was essential to good parenting. I can remember Lily giving me the occasional clump but Steve never beat me, apart from during the boxing matches. I don't think he was interested enough in me to care about 'disciplining' me, and Lily was the one who bore the brunt of his temper when he lashed out. But I had a friend further down Southam Street who was always being knocked around and our cousins,

Pamela and Norman, were terrified of incurring the wrath of Uncle George. At Bevington school, every male teacher was licensed to assault us. The most sadistic was Mr Hayes who, instead of bringing down the cane across the palm or upturned fingers of the hand, would strike us hard on the inside of our wrists. Cruel and unusual punishment indeed.

In the 1950s we were, of course, spared the influence of the unfettered violence depicted in films, computer games and other images that is so ubiquitous today. However, in a strange way, the fact that ours was a lesser, ostensibly more 'honourable' type of violence somehow made it more widely acceptable. The fights we saw on film were the showdowns between gunslingers and the saloon-bar brawls compulsory to every Western. It is perhaps significant that in those movies, the most contemptible anti-hero wasn't the 'baddie' but the man who refused to fight: the coward. We may not have had anywhere near as much violence served up to us as entertainment on screen, but because it was so accepted – indeed, institutionalized – it was an unremarked element of our day-to-day lives.

It's perhaps not surprising, then, that I was largely compliant with Lily's mission to keep me off the streets. But of course I didn't always obey. I still blush at the memory of the day she caught me on a box-cart with my cousin Tony Barker, Tottsy's son, and a gang of his friends from Southern Row. With bikes an unaffordable luxury where we lived, we would build our own transport, invariably involving a wooden plank lashed across two sets of wheels scavenged from an abandoned pram and steered using a rope or string. This particular Formula One model, featuring a little boxed-in seating area for the driver, had left its showrooms in Southern Row to be paraded in

Southam Street and I had somehow been persuaded to steer it while the other boys pushed me along.

When Lily turned into our street and saw me she yelled at me to stop. The emergence of a broad Scouse accent was a sure sign that I was in trouble. My 'car' underwent an enforced pit stop and the driver was removed to 149 Southam Street and subjected to some stern words along the lines of 'I never want to see youse tearing round the streets with a gang like that again.' And she didn't, because I wasn't. At least, not until I became friends with Tony Cox. If my adventures with him gave Lily greater cause for worry, on the plus side they were also responsible for introducing her to Tony's mum, who was to become her closest friend.

I don't know how it happened, but one minute I was alone and palely loitering, reading a book in the big, damp bedroom I shared with Linda, the next I was careering around on the saddle of Tony's blue bike, while he pedalled furiously, poised above the crossbar. It was a lovely bike: streamlined, modern, with a sparkle in its metallic blue paint.

One evening, Tony showed me a second bike he'd acquired from somewhere and challenged me to a race. The start was to be outside his home in Lancaster Road, following a circuit left into Brandon Road, left by Latimer Road Underground station and into Bramley Road, and then first left back into Lancaster Road, where Tony's neighbour, short, tubby Walter Curtis, would be waiting to declare the winner. What Tony's spare bike lacked in sophistication it made up for in size and I was not a proficient cyclist. He offered to give me an advantage by lending me his and taking the other one himself.

With the help of the state-of-the-art blue bike, glittering

faintly in the early-autumn dusk, I kept pace with Tony as we came to the final bend. But then disaster struck. I was going so fast that it was impossible to keep on track round the sharp corner of Bramley Road and Lancaster Road. I veered straight across the road and collided with a young woman who was just coming out of the little grocery store almost opposite the Coxes' house, carrying a pint of milk. Her leg was wounded, my front tooth was broken and the milk bottle was smashed to smithereens.

Such was the furore that Tony was dispatched to my house, ten minutes away, to fetch Lily, who arrived on the scene as I was being nursed by Tony's mother. I don't think the young woman I'd hit was too badly injured, though I can still remember her tender words of comfort: 'You fucking little idiot, why don't you learn to ride that fucking bike?' Strong words but well deserved. That 'fucking bike' needed a bit of attention after I'd finished with it. I was still in shock when Lily arrived – lapsing into Scouse as she scolded me only marginally less aggressively than my young victim. While Lily's tirade featured no swear words (we never heard Lily swear), it was equally bruising in its condemnation.

It was this incident that brought Pat Cox and Lily together. They discovered they had a lot in common. Two tiny, cheerful, funny women – Pat with her delicate, birdlike features and gold-rimmed glasses; Lily still petite and pretty before her heart medication made her put on weight – they had similar backgrounds, both worked every hour God sent and both cared deeply about their children's future. Like Lily, Pat was not a Londoner. She had come from her home in Nottingham during the war to work for the NAAFI, like Lily. She was even tinier than Lily but possessed the strength and energy of a person three times her size. The cups of tea they shared that afternoon became the first of many over the years, always in Pat's home because Lily was so ashamed of the conditions we lived in.

While they were alike in so many ways, they differed, of course, in one important facet of their lives: their marriages. At the end of every day – every single day – Albert and Pat Cox would sit together on their big, comfy settee. Albert would put his feet up on the small table in front of the paraffin heater; Pat would tuck her legs beneath her and lay her head on his chest, and he'd put his arm around her. In front of them would be two glasses of whisky. They separated only for Albert to roll an Old Holborn and Pat to light one of her small filter tips, or to take a sip of Bell's. Then they'd snuggle up together again. It mattered not who was in the room with them, they would sit like a courting couple, listening to the radio or, in later years, watching TV, uninhibited in their devotion to one another. Despite my tender age, the significance of this stark contrast between Pat and Albert and Lily and Steve was obvious to me.

∼

Along with his impressive sporting skills, Tony Cox had the fastest fists in West London. When it came to fighting, where other boys relied on their weight or their wrestling ability (or, like me, merely on their capacity to deter potential aggressors by trying to look hard), Tony was a whirling dervish, pummelling his opponents into submission: left, right, left, right. His height was an advantage. He might take the odd punch if his challenger managed to get through his flailing fists, but he'd dish out about six whacks for every one he received. Yet I don't remember Tony ever starting a fight. He only got involved when he was forced to react, which was frequently, probably because his Scandinavian looks made him stand out from the crowd and perhaps because his reputation encouraged other boys to have a go.

There were times when the dangers we faced were unpredictable, and when even Tony's exceptional talent was no protection. Walking home from school one day with Tony and our friend Dereck Tapper, I noticed, crossing into Chesterton Road, a man in his early twenties acting oddly. He was standing against a wall with a sheet of corrugated iron propped up in front of him. His weird behaviour grew weirder as we passed him. Lifting the metal sheet above his head, he suddenly bent his knees, bringing the edge of it down on our skulls. Clearly this was a man with serious mental health problems and we should have run away as fast as we could but, thinking the best course of action was simply to ignore him, we carried on walking along the street. We soon realized our mistake when he threw his corrugated iron away and swiftly grabbed me round the neck, announcing with a malicious smile that I was his prisoner.

Tony and Dereck could easily have escaped, but they stayed with me for the bizarre hour or so in which this man held me captive. As this strange quartet roamed the streets, a man with a boy in a stranglehold and two more in tow, my assailant plausibly and loudly proclaimed to passersby that he was a relative playing a game with me. Otherwise I can't remember what was said, either by him or by any of us in our attempts to persuade him to let me go. He kept Tony and Dereck at bay by threatening to cut my face open with a piece of broken glass, picked out of the gutter outside the notorious KPH pub, which he held against my cheek, just underneath my eye.

The grandly named Kensington Palace Hotel, on the corner of Ladbroke Grove and Lancaster Road, was where Irishmen drank (hence its other name: Keep Paddy Happy) and it was notorious for fights, both indoors and outside. They would usually begin in the pub and spill on to the streets. To be fair to the KPH, broken glass was a feature of North Kensington streets in general. It seemed to grow in the gutters like grass in a hedgerow.

The KPH was one of three places in my 'manor' that I took pains to avoid if I could possibly help it. The others were Isaac Newton Secondary Modern School (the blackboard jungle where I knew I would be sent if I failed my Eleven-Plus) and the Electric Cinema further up the Portobello Road, known locally as the Fleapit or the Bughole because of its derelict state. It never showed anything we would want to see and its clientele, we heard, consisted of nutcases who would carry us off to be mutilated and murdered.

The memory of being held against my will, with a jagged piece of glass hovering near my eyes, while people strolled past on one of the busiest thoroughfares in London W10, will never leave me. Nobody tried to intervene or asked if I was OK. In the end, our psychopath was distracted by something and Tony, Dereck and I seized our chance and fled as fast as our legs would carry us.

Tony and I belted into Cambridge Gardens, where the houses were big and expensive with ample front gardens, mostly hidden behind substantial hedges. We'd found a way to navigate the entire length of this long road without once appearing on the pavement. We knew all the gaps that allowed us to move from one secluded front garden to the next; indeed we'd created many of them ourselves, to the chagrin of the residents.

By the time we emerged 400 yards away at the junction with St Marks Road, there was no sign of our tormentor. I never told Lily or anyone else about this encounter. What was the point? It would only have worried her. For all his threats, I had only a scratch on my cheek to show for the ordeal, though for the remaining year or so of my time at Bevington Primary, I was constantly looking out for Mr Psychopath and had my escape routes planned in advance.

When Tony and I vanished into Cambridge Gardens, Dereck Tapper ran in the opposite direction, across Ladbroke Grove towards the room in Tavistock Crescent where he lived with his mother. Dereck was the only other boy who was with me at all three of the schools I attended. I'd first met him at Wornington Infants and we would go on to attend grammar school together. If my childhood was not exactly a bed of roses, Dereck Tapper had a much harder time of it. Dereck Tapper was black.

Chapter 5

THE 1951 CENSUS recorded that 12.7 per cent of the population in the area around Southam Street lived at a density of more than two people per room compared to a London average of 2.5 per cent. That figure must have risen as landlords like Peter Rachman exploited those arriving from countries such as Trinidad and Jamaica at the behest of a government keen to fill the many vacancies in public services, notably transport and the NHS. Most came alone, and at first they were mainly men: young men without family commitments or married men keen to establish a home before bringing over their wives and children.

As a result there can have been few, if any, other black kids at our school when Dereck Tapper began his education, along with me, at Wornington Road Infants. If there were others I don't remember them, and I can recall only two besides Dereck at Bevington, which we attended from 1957 to 1961. I have no memory, either, of any black people living at our end of Southam Street, although one house at the eastern end, number 27, was home to a large number of West Indian men.

With hindsight, it seems quite likely that it was one of the outposts of Rachmanism.

The West Indians came under an immigration policy that allowed free entry from Commonwealth and colonial nations. They saw Britain as the mother country and they were proud of it and loyal to its institutions. Theirs was a culture of relaxed conviviality, and they must have been expecting at least a welcoming hand. What they found, too often, was a brandished fist.

Into our decaying streets they came, useful scapegoats for the overcrowding, the appalling conditions, the poverty, the absence of hope and aspiration. One of Roger Mayne's 1956 photographs brilliantly captures the cultural collision. Four West Indian men are pictured sauntering into Southam Street (perhaps they were heading for number 27), relaxed but wary. One looks at Mayne's camera with amusement, two are half-smiling. But the man in front is on the look-out for trouble as they head towards a group of young guys gathered round the steps leading up to a front door. Youths with grey, pinched faces who don't yet seem to have noticed the quartet ambling towards them.

The black men are dressed in stylish jumpers and jerkins, baggy trousers and wide-brimmed hats, set at just the right angle. Four little white boys stare, glued to the spot as if they were witnessing a Martian invasion. I was six when that photo was taken, living in that exact location at that exact time. I remember very well the cards in newsagents' windows (we were instructed to check them on our way to school to see if anything interesting and cheap was being offered for sale). Those headed 'Rooms to let' were, like most of the rest, handwritten, but the legend 'No Blacks' could have been pre-printed, it was on so many of them. Often it was accompanied by 'No Irish' and 'No dogs'.

On stifling summer evenings, the little communities that gathered on the steps of the houses in Southam Street, their numbers swelled by the need of most inhabitants to escape the intolerable heat indoors, became a daunting challenge for any passing West Indian. The preferred method of provocation was to flick little missiles, usually rolled-up strips of the silver paper from their cigarette packets, at any black face that came within range. If their victim stopped to remonstrate there'd be a row, and often a full-blown fight. If he chose to ignore them and walk on, he would have to endure the catcalls that followed him down the street.

These black men were bus conductors, postmen and hospital porters and tended to be older, wiser and more self-controlled than their tormentors – young, thin Teddy Boys, either unemployed or still at school. But there was little doubt that those silver pellets conveyed the hostility of most of the community.

Maybe a year or so before Mayne encapsulated the simmering tension on our street, a young woman had hammered desperately on the door of 107 Southam Street. I have no idea who she was or why she ran to Lily for help. But I do remember why the Teddy Boys were chasing her. She had committed the ultimate sin in the eyes of her pursuers: she was a white girl who'd gone out with a black man. Lily went to the door and ushered her inside. Four or five Teds began to throw stones and junk from the streets at our window, shouting that the girl was a 'fucking wog-lover'. We cowered inside, transfixed by terror, until eventually they gave up and went away. This must have been around 1955, during the first stirrings of the rancour that would lead to the Notting Hill race riots three years later.

Was Lily different from most of her neighbours? That incident stays with me as evidence that she was. A kind woman, with instinctive Christian ethics, she was constantly exhorting Linda and me to see the good in everybody and did her best to instil compassion and tolerance in her children. I'd like to think that when the tensions exploded into the Notting Hill riots of August 1958, our three rooms in 149 Southam Street were a bastion of liberal values. And I believe that was in all probability the case, though I have no concrete evidence for it. I was too young then to grasp the complexities of the crisis; to absorb much more than the sense of fear and threat on the streets – and we already lived with that every day, to some degree.

I haven't the first idea what Steve's views were, either on politics in general or immigration in particular. I can't say I remember ever hearing him using what we would now call racist language, but by this time I barely saw him and wasn't privy to his conversations. Back then the complaint that immigrants were 'coming over here and taking our jobs' was practically a mantra – a soundtrack to our lives as familiar as moaning about the weather, or the filthy state of the streets or the absence of police on the beat (a common grievance in 1950s Notting Hill) – and given the prevailing atmosphere it would be remarkable if Steve was a non-conformist. There certainly wouldn't have been any black faces in the pubs where he played the piano, all of which had a saloon bar, a public bar and a colour bar.

The additional accusation that 'they' were taking over houses meant for us could have had a particular potency for Lily and Steve. But as well as being compassionate Lily was an intelligent woman, and would surely have been clear-sighted enough to observe that, far from 'jumping the queue' for one of the council houses for which she had been patiently waiting for ten years by then, black immigrants were being squeezed into the same sordid, decrepit buildings that we were occupying.

The August riots of 1958, so far as I know, didn't spread to Southam Street. Linda told me that there'd been fights in Bramley Road, where one of her friends lived, and the siege of Blenheim Crescent, during which white youths tried to burn down a house full of black immigrants, took place half a mile away on the other side of Ladbroke Grove. So even at eight years of age I knew that our little world was being discussed in every newspaper – variously described as Notting Hill, Notting Dale, Kensal New Town or North Kensington – and suddenly the focus of national interest.

I have no doubt that Lily would have stood up for the small, beleaguered black community who had come to live among us. I like to think that if we'd had any black neighbours, she would have been one of those Notting Hill women who did their shopping for them – black women didn't dare go outside during the riots. That she would have agreed with Justice Salmon's famous pronouncements when sentencing four white youths to four years' imprisonment for the part they played in the mayhem: 'Everyone, irrespective of the colour of their skin, is entitled to walk through our streets in peace, with their heads erect and free from fear. As far as the law is concerned, you are entitled to think what you like, however foul your thoughts; to feel what you like, however brutal and debased your emotions; to say what you like, providing you do not infringe the rights of others, or imperil the Queen's peace, but once you translate your dark thoughts and brutal feelings into savage acts such as these the law will be swift to punish you, the guilty, and to protect your victims.'

There were 108 arrests for offences ranging from insulting behaviour to grievous bodily harm. Mercifully, nobody was killed during the six days of rioting. But it would be only eight months before somebody was.

~

During 1958, the tensions on the streets were mirrored by increasingly strained relations at 149 Southam Street. Making ends meet was growing even more difficult. Steve had been out of work for months but continued to play the pubs and clubs, returning in the early hours, when he returned at all, and sleeping in until midday. His violence towards Lily was, for the time, at the mild end of the domestic abuse spectrum – many women put up with worse – but it's hard to express just how terrifying it was for a child to lie there at night listening to all the shouting and screaming, fearing for his mother; hard to convey the deep unhappiness it caused. Steve was a dark shadow in our life, and Linda in particular was becoming more and more contemptuous of him.

The pools win was a distant memory. The Rowe Housing Trust had decided to remove all 'pay-as-you-go' electricity meters from their Southam Street properties because they were being robbed so frequently, mostly by residents desperate for cash. That meant one more bill for Lily to struggle with.

One terrible day is etched on my memory: the day everything came to a head over a pet dog we had acquired after Linda passed her Eleven-Plus. Once my sister had persuaded Lily to let us have a dog as a reward, Linda and I had gone to Battersea Dogs' Home and fallen in love with a hairy, black mongrel with a sweet nature and bags of energy. We named her Cheeky and brought her back home with us. Our love for that dog was as fierce as Steve's hatred of her. He seemed offended by our devotion to Cheeky, and shouted at Lily for letting us have her in the first place. Lily shouted back and refused to upset us by obeying Steve's decree to return our pet to the dogs' home.

A compromise was reached. Cheeky was to be placed in the yard on a chain whenever Steve was at home. Given how rare this was, that didn't seem too unreasonable. In any case, Cheeky was terrified of Steve and would much rather not have been around when he was.

On that awful day, Steve came home early and drunk. It was around 6pm and he must have been drinking since lunchtime. Lily was cooking dinner on the gas stove on the landing. The stove, like the sink, was stand-alone, and when the oven was on the entire cooker was too hot to touch. Cheeky was in the kitchen. It was a bitterly cold day and when Steve insisted that she be taken down to the yard, Lily and Linda pleaded for her to be allowed to stay indoors.

Voices were raised and Steve moved menacingly towards the dog, which ran to the only shelter available and sat, petrified, in the space beneath the oven. There she remained, even though her back was touching the underside of the oven and being burned by the hot metal. While we cried, the dog howled and Steve yelled, Lily was on her hands and knees, trying to coax poor Cheeky to leave her refuge. When the dog was finally extracted, shaking with fear, there was a large bald patch where the heat from the oven had singed off her fur.

This was a watershed for Linda: the point at which her dislike and disapproval of Steve crystallized into hatred. From that day onwards, I watched my sister become a much more formidable opponent for Steve.

Linda had matured very early, both physically and emotionally. At eleven she was already bigger than Lily. The tone she used when speaking to Steve, even before the incident with the dog, was increasingly scornful. Steve was spending more nights away but when he did stumble in, drunk and abusive, he often found his daughter waiting to defend Lily and to remonstrate with him for his fecklessness.

On one occasion I saw Linda attempting to kick and punch Steve while Lily tried to restrain her. Linda marched down to our room and returned a few minutes later with her Girl Guide's penknife open in her hand. With a look of utter determination on her face, she launched an attack on her father. The knife would probably have struggled to cut butter but Steve's face was grey as he fended off and finally disarmed his daughter. Linda ran off with Cheeky. After several hours Lily found her sitting on a park bench in Wormwood Scrubs and persuaded her to come home.

One winter's day the year before, when Lily, Linda and I had been queuing to pay the rent at the cashier's grille in the Rowe Housing Trust offices, we had noticed a poster inviting applications to emigrate to Australia. A picture of an ocean liner sailing into a sunlit port, surrounded by images of kangaroos and koalas, promised 'a better life' for just £10 per person. Lily looked at it for a long time before saying, almost to herself, 'Shall we leave your father and go to Australia?'

She would have been almost thirty-six then, still a young woman but worn down with the pain and drudgery of her life. She carried her burdens cheerfully for her children, but she was desperate to improve our standard of living. Could we have joined the ranks of the emigrants known as the Ten Pound Poms? The Australian government, in a bid to expand the population and attract workers for their developing industries, offered assisted passage to adults, and children, in fact, travelled free. But however keen they were to have us, would we have been allowed to go without Steve? I don't know. All I can see, looking back, is a woman dreaming of 'a better life' feeling sorely tempted to climb into that poster and away from the slums of Southam Street. The response from Linda and me was firm and implacable. We didn't care about leaving Steve, but we were not prepared to leave London. 'No,' we said. 'We are not going to Australia.'

The moment passed, Lily paid the rent and we went home.

∼

As it turned out, it wasn't us who left Steve but Steve who left us. I knew immediately that he had gone when I noticed that his shaving equipment – the open razor, the stubby brush, the shaving soap, the jar of Brylcreem – had vanished from the shelf above the stand-alone ceramic butler sink in the kitchen. Lily was ahead of me. She was already rushing straight for the bedroom, emerging to tell us that all his clothes had disappeared, along with the battered suitcase that had accompanied us on our holiday to Liverpool. The first thing I checked for was the book of nudes at the top of the wardrobe. It had gone.

Steve left on a Saturday morning in the autumn of 1958, sneaking off while we were out. Lily, Linda and I had gone 'down the Lane', partly so that we wouldn't have to creep around to avoid disturbing him, but mostly to see if there was anything useful we could scavenge from the stallholders. We'd returned home expecting a normal Saturday afternoon. Steve would rise at noon and sit around in his string vest and trousers, studying that day's runners and riders in the *Daily Sketch*. Linda would go out with her friend Marilyn Hughes. I would play in our room and Lily would iron and clean and rustle up what she could to supplement our staple diet of bread and dripping.

But this was no normal Saturday. For me, it was a red-letter day; a Saturday I would always remember for the happiness I felt when I was sure Steve had really gone. The sense of exhilaration floods back every time my mind returns to that morning. It wasn't until I was much older that I understood why, while Linda and I were euphoric, Lily's reaction was to sit down at the kitchen table and cry. Life is very black and white to an eight-year-old and I was perplexed. Surely she should be as delighted as we were? The period before Steve's departure had been worse than anything we'd ever experienced. His idleness and our poverty had grown more acute, our lives more miserable.

Yet Lily sat at the table and sobbed. She wept for the wasted years, for the love that died, for the hardship that lay ahead. I'd never seen her cry before, but tears would come to her more easily from then on. She had always felt that Steve might change. Though she had shouldered the burden of supporting the family, while he was there, some small financial contribution was at least possible and she could nurture the faint hope that he might some day make more of an effort. Now even that was gone. She would also have been acutely aware of the stigma that attached to women abandoned by their husbands, irrespective of the circumstances.

I understood none of this on that Saturday in 1958. All I felt was joy and relief. My dread was not that Steve would be lost to me for ever but that he might come back. Linda, though even more ecstatic, was able to empathize with Lily. In my bewilderment and immaturity, I reacted only with impatience. Our response quite possibly made her feel even more wretched: the idea that her children could be so overjoyed at being abandoned by their father can only have added to the miasma of regret and failure swirling around in her head.

That evening Lily and Linda addressed the practicalities and resolved to try to track Steve down. There was probably little legal redress available to Lily and even if there were, we knew no lawyers and certainly couldn't afford to hire one. But they reasoned that if Lily at least knew where Steve was she could pursue him for financial help to raise their children.

Since the next day was a Sunday, Steve would surely be playing piano at the Lads of the Village at lunchtime. Lily decided to go there, taking Linda for moral support, but there was no sign of Steve. The landlord was brusque. No, he didn't know where Steve was. In any case, it was Lily's fault that he'd run off – 'You should have gone out with him more and not been so unsociable.' Their next port of call was the home of Steve's eldest brother, Wally. They got no further than the doorstep. After Lily had explained her predicament, he reacted angrily. 'We've all got our problems,' he retorted, closing the door in their faces.

Lily eventually pieced together what Steve had been up to (though not where he'd actually gone) from various conversations with local gossips eager to share salacious details. I knew little of what she learned. Linda often told me that the most-used phrase in Lily's vocabulary was 'Don't tell Alan.' But in the fullness of time I got to hear about Steve's affair with Vera, a barmaid at the Lads of the Village. How he'd spent Christmas with her when we were left alone in Southam Street; the hop-picking holidays in Kent with Vera and her son from a previous liaison; the child Vera had conceived with Steve, but miscarried. Now they were living together, but Lily didn't know where.

She had no one to turn to. Her sister Jean had by this time left Walthamstow to return to Liverpool, Uncle George having transferred there with the Post Office. In any case, Lily would have been reluctant to admit to her abandonment. Her sisters were never told of the problems when Steve was at home, so she was hardly likely to reveal what she regarded as her failure now that he'd gone. For Linda and me, Steve's departure marked the end of a terrible life and the start of a brighter future. We did not understand, then, why Lily felt that the bad old life was merely entering its next phase.

PART II
LILY

Chapter 6

IT WAS JUST PAST midnight on 17 May 1959, my ninth birthday, that Kelso Cochrane, a thirty-two-year-old Antiguan working as a carpenter to try to save enough money to study law, was murdered on the corner of our street.

The murder remains unsolved but Lily saw the beginning of the altercation that led to Kelso's death: five or six white men pushing and shoving one black man. As she shouted at them to leave him alone, one of the assailants looked up and their eyes met. She recognized him and she was pretty sure he recognized her, too.

I know this man's name, but will give him a pseudonym here. Let's call him Barry Dempsey. He was typical of the hollow-cheeked Teds who populated Roger Mayne's photographs. He lived at the other end of Southam Street, but was notorious right across the Town. Most of the young guys round our way swore and scrapped but few had Barry's reputation for unprovoked violence.

Poor Kelso Cochrane had the misfortune to encounter Dempsey and his cohorts at midnight on the Saturday of a warm Whitsun Bank Holiday weekend as he was walking back from Paddington General Hospital, where he'd gone to seek treatment for his hand after injuring it at work. Kelso lived in a flat in Bevington Road near my school and had presumably walked down Southam Street from Kensal Rise at the far end.

At the same time, Lily was walking up Golborne Road on her way home from serving and washing up for Mrs Dehn, who used to host a dinner party every Bank Holiday weekend. When Kelso Cochrane was accosted on the corner of Southam Street and Golborne Road, outside the bagwash, Lily had reached the Earl of Warwick on the opposite corner and was turning left into our end of Southam Street. After Barry Dempsey caught her eye, she took fright and ran home without a backward glance. Sadly, the sight of a gang of white Teddy Boys bullying a solitary black man wasn't unusual on the streets of Notting Hill. Lily hoped that by shouting at them she would let them know they had been seen and halt the attack. She must have been mortified to find out the following day that Kelso Cochrane had been stabbed once, in the heart, with great force and had died in St Charles's Hospital less than an hour later.

As my ninth birthday dawned on the Sunday of that sultry weekend, Southam Street became the centre of attention for reporters, police officers and politicians. The community was stunned and the atmosphere was heavy with suspicion and fear. A murder then seemed to create more shockwaves than it does today, perhaps because there wasn't anything like the saturation news coverage we are used to in the twenty-first century. Everyone tuned into the same few limited news bulletins on the wireless or on television, if they had a set. For those who did, having a choice between two channels was still a novelty: ITV had only been in existence for three years. Linda's friend

Marilyn Hughes' parents were the only people we knew locally with a telly – her father was also the only man we knew who owned a car – and they would occasionally kindly allow both of us to go round to their house in Wornington Road to watch *The Adventures of Rin Tin Tin*.

That day we didn't have to possess a TV to know that the camera crews set up outside the Earl of Warwick were broadcasting pictures of the streets where we lived to audiences around the world. Kelso's murder was the lead story in all the bulletins.

At lunchtime, the men got suited up as usual to go to the pub as the police began house-to-house inquiries, monitored by the women who habitually spent hours at their open windows on the upper floors of Southam Street, watching everything that went on. They would put pillows or cushions on the crumbling window sills on which to rest their folded arms, the raised sash windows poised above their necks like guillotines. The heavy activity that Sunday brought reinforcements to their ranks. They would all have seen the police come to our door, either that day or the next. The officers were mainly interested in talking to any men in the house to establish their whereabouts on the Saturday night.

There were, of course, no men in our home now and goodness knows what Lily told them, but she certainly didn't mention Barry Dempsey and I doubt if she told them about the fracas she had witnessed. Who can blame her? She would have been as appalled by the murder of Kelso Cochrane as anybody in Notting Hill, but this was where she and her children had to live. She had enough troubles without having to contend with the very real possibility of retribution by people who had killed at least once already. And with murder still punishable by the death penalty, the stakes were high.

The most reliable authority on Lily's frame of mind that weekend is Linda. It wasn't until some years later that Lily related the events of the early hours of 17 May 1959 to my sister. She told her how afraid she was that Barry Dempsey had recognized her and that the three of us might be in danger. When Linda asked why she hadn't told the police, she said it would have put us at even greater risk. So she said nothing.

Within five years Lily would be in Kensal Green cemetery along with Kelso Cochrane. Had she lived, I'm sure that one day she would have told the police what she saw that night. Many years later, I informed them of it myself. At the time Lily was convinced that they would find the murderers without her assistance. She was wrong. Fifty-three years later those killers have still to be brought to justice.

In the months after the murder, the febrile atmosphere in the area was palpable, even to us children. Bevington Primary, under the firm command of the strong and charismatic head-master, Mr Gemmill, evidently did its level best to ensure that the school – around 250 yards from the murder scene and in the road where the victim had lived – was a haven from the tension on the streets. Dereck Tapper must have felt par-ticularly vulnerable. Few of those in the habit of using openly racist language had any qualms about doing so in front of their children, and it was quick to filter through to the very youngest members of the community. I'm sure Dereck must have been subjected to the commonplace taunts and harassment. He was a bright and popular kid who could look after himself, but in the wake of Kelso Cochrane's murder he would have had far more to contend with than before: the issue of race was being deliberately ramped up on the street corners of our community.

This climate of antagonism was linked to one man, one word, one name: Mosley. Such was my youthful familiarity with talk of Oswald Mosley that I imagined him to be a Notting Hill local, known only in our part of London. To me he was indistinguishable from the other notorious villains or bullies in our area whose names were frequently heard on the streets. I had no idea, at the age of nine, that Mosley was infamous throughout the country and around the world as the founder of the British Union of Fascists, the politician who had campaigned to bring Hitler's policies to Britain before the war.

There are only four things I know about Lily's political opinions. She revered Emmeline Pankhurst, drumming it into Linda that she must always vote because Mrs Pankhurst had fought for her right to do so. She disliked Winston Churchill for reasons I'm not clear about. She loved Jo Grimond and voted Liberal because of her trust in him. And she detested Oswald Mosley.

Having been interned during the war along with most active fascists, Mosley had left Britain in 1951 to live in France. His attempt to re-invent a British form of fascism known as the Union Movement had failed dismally. He returned to Britain in 1959 for one reason alone: to exploit the racial tension in Notting Hill by standing as a Union Movement candidate for North Kensington in that year's General Election.

I heard Lily rail against this terrible man Mosley and picked up the name as it crackled on the Notting Hill grapevine that connected our phone-free homes. Leaflets announcing

Mosley's candidature had been distributed before Kelso Cochrane's murder. Their content fully exploited the absence of any laws against inciting racial hatred and he was therefore accused by many of being complicit in the crime.

The police laughably insisted that the motive for Kelso's murder was robbery rather than race, while Mosley defended himself by pointing out that his leaflets called for the race issue in Notting Hill to be settled by 'votes not violence'. This stance was totally undermined by the fact that he held a series of public meetings, both before and after the General Election, practically on the very spot where Kelso had been killed.

Lily laid down the law to Linda and me: she might well be out working when these gatherings took place but on no account were we to go anywhere near Mosley's meetings. He was a fiend who supported Hitler. His followers were bad people. We were made to promise we'd keep away. I think I kept my promise to Lily – I usually did. And yet I have this memory of Mosley, in a double-breasted suit, standing above a crowd of several hundred people on a grey, early evening outside the Warwick. He spoke in a rich baritone, his arms in constant motion, his face flushed, his large body turning this way and that to project himself to every part of his audience. Whether on that occasion I disobeyed Lily and actually did see Mosley in the flesh, or whether my memory has conflated my genuine recollections of his Notting Hill meetings with images I happened to see around that time or not long afterwards, I cannot say.

Mosley evidently had his supporters. In a community living in such overcrowded squalor, it would have been surprising if he didn't. Indeed, I suspect he had his supporters in the big houses at the other end of the Portobello Road as well. He had come to Notting Hill because he thought that our constituency of North Kensington offered him his best chance of being re-elected to Parliament. To do that he had to win over working people like Lily. He failed utterly. When the election was held on 8 October 1959, he came last, with under 3,000 votes. For the first time in his forty-one years of contesting parliamentary elections, he lost his deposit.

Claiming that the ballot had been rigged, he launched an appeal, but the result was upheld. After North Kensington sent him packing he would go on to stand in the 1966 election in Shoreditch and Finsbury, where he did even worse, putting an end to his political career.

~

Not long after Kelso Cochrane's murder we were moved to another Victorian slum at 6 Walmer Road, just off Latimer Road, which snaked its way from Wormwood Scrubs down to Shepherd's Bush. We were rehoused because Southam Street was being cleared for demolition and in acknowledgement of the fact that it was far from ideal for a girl and boy to be sharing a room at twelve and nine years old respectively. We were pleased when the Rowe Housing Trust found us four rooms – a kitchen plus a bedroom each for Lily, Linda and me. I'm sure Lily must also have been relieved at the opportunity to put some distance between us and Barry Dempsey.

The house was one of a small terrace linked by a frontage of dirty, dark green flaking paint, interspersed with doorways where a flight of steps led up to the front entrances. We had the ground and the first floor of number 6, beneath a young couple, the Thompsons, with a small baby and a collection of Shirley Bassey records. The basement, though only partially below ground level, was uninhabitable, but Lily persuaded the trust to install a bath and copper boiler in one corner of it. With the addition of some plain brown Formica boards, we created a bathroom: a source of tremendous excitement since we'd never had one before. It did not, alas, do a great deal to improve my low level of hygiene. We had to heat the water using the gas ring under the copper urn and a shilling in the meter produced only enough for one bath. As a result my baths were infrequent and to ensure we got our full shilling's worth, I would invariably have to use Linda's dirty water.

The rooms at Walmer Road were as damp and dreary as Southam Street and our toilet, shared with the Thompsons, was still in a crumbling shack outside. To reach the back door leading out to the small, concrete back yard you had to go through the basement, which had no lights. And Lily still hadn't attained her heart's desire: her own front door. But Linda and I were happy to have our own rooms, although for Linda this proved to be a temporary arrangement. Her room was immediately below Lily's, on the ground floor next to the kitchen on the landing, mine was next to Lily's. We could both hear her sobbing in the night. She tried to suppress the sound, taking huge gulps of air and holding her breath, but eventually, when she could contain herself no longer, the waves of her grief would break on the silence. It was almost worse than listening to the vicious arguments with Steve on his return from a night on the tiles.

After a few weeks spent witnessing this despair Linda had a

brainwave. If she slept in the double bed with Lily, not only could she comfort her during the night, but it would leave us with a spare room we could turn into a living room.

Linda was now a pupil at Fulham County Grammar School for Girls and if she wanted to bring her friends round they would have to sit in the kitchen, with its four battered chairs round a Formica table (we were big on Formica), one old armchair and the washing line slung across the room under the flyblown lampshade. Lily agreed and gave Linda's bed to the Salvation Army who, in return, found us a second-hand three-piece suite covered with brown plastic.

Steve had been gone a year by this time, and Lily had taken on yet more jobs. In spite of her illness, she never gave up cleaning. Her only concession to her GP's insistence that she must not work herself so hard was to try to find additional employment that was less physically demanding than yet more cleaning positions. Her CV soon incorporated the tobacco kiosk in Ladbroke Grove, a newsagent's in North Pole Road and Harry's Café on Wormwood Scrubs.

At Walmer Road she also took up 'home work' – painting and varnishing wooden figures to go on toy roundabouts. The pieces were delivered in large crates, which Linda and I would help to unpack. The extra money enabled Lily to rent a television, which took pride of place in our newly arranged living room alongside the Dansette.

Walmer Road was about a mile away from Southam Street, on the other side of Ladbroke Grove, and some distance from the shops and stalls of Golborne Road and the Lane. We still, of course, had a pub nearby – more or less everyone in London had a pub nearby then. Ours was the Latimer Arms, which was almost opposite our house on the corner of Latimer Road. A few doors down was an abandoned shop which an ancient woman had somehow commandeered. For a few hours every morning she would sell milk there across a makeshift counter. There were no other groceries available, and indeed no heat or light – just crates of pint bottles of milk.

Next to that was the newsagent's, run by Mr and Mrs Maynard and, on the corner of our row of houses, at the junction with Oldham Street, a traditional grocer's, Berriman's. Mr Berriman was a kind, cheery middle-aged man, with light brown wavy hair, red cheeks and glasses which he wore in a scholarly way on the end of his nose. He always had an immaculate brown buttoned overall over his collar and tie.

Berriman's sold virtually every kind of grocery and household product, which he and his assistants would dispense to customers with a dexterity aimed at preventing queues. But there was always a queue at Berriman's, particularly when I had to go with a list of things Lily wanted and the instruction to ask, once it was all packed and tallied, 'Mum says is it OK to put it on her bill?' I absolutely dreaded these moments. Irrespective of how often I had to do it, I always went red with embarrassment. I knew that Mr Berriman was being asked to provide groceries 'on tick' and that he would have to wait a long time before any of it was paid for – if it ever was.

There must have been other shoppers making similar requests but I never saw them. The people in front of me in the queue always produced crisp one-pound and ten-bob notes, while those behind me, or so it seemed to me, stood watching in judgemental silence as I threw myself on Mr Berriman's mercy. As far as I can recall, he never refused me.

Leaving Southam Street as it slid towards extinction, putting behind me the dirty old derelict houses, with their peeling plaster, rotten window frames and cracked panes and the streets that crackled continuously with the undercurrent of danger, seemed like a landmark event even to a nine-year-old. And if conditions at Walmer Road were only marginally better, all things considered, we saw the move as a significant improvement in our circumstances. I had my own room and lived closer to my friend Tony Cox; Linda was nearer to Latimer Road tube station, from where she needed to travel to Hammersmith every day to catch the number 11 bus to Fulham County, and there was a greater sense of community built around Mr Berriman's shop and the newsagent.

Lily liked sharing her bed with Linda and they would talk well into the night. It was during these confidential woman-to-woman chats that Linda came to learn more about our family history. Lily's unhappiness was compounded by her failure to track Steve down. He'd fled all of his old haunts in Notting Hill and we had no idea where his new ones were.

With no prospect of Steve returning, she had decided she wanted a divorce. As an abandoned wife she was, in effect, neither wife nor single woman, and trapped in a bureaucratic limbo between the two. As a result I doubt she had much access to help through the benefits system. The 'welfare state', established after the war to tackle the five 'giant evils' – squalor, ignorance, want, idleness and disease – identified by William Beveridge in his influential report, had brought us the National Health Service, an expansion of National Insurance and the Family Allowance, among other reforms. But in the 1950s any benefit entitlements would have been administered through the head of the family – the husband – and based on his tax allowance and the 'stamps' he paid. A divorce would formalize Lily's situation and lead to a court order for maintenance, but she couldn't even begin that process without knowing where Steve was.

Lily's motives weren't purely financial. She'd made up her mind that, at thirty-seven years of age, she was still young enough to start afresh with somebody else. Her other reason for finding him was one with which she annoyed me on a regular basis. 'He's still your father,' she would say. 'Whatever he's done to me, a boy needs a dad.' Given that neither Steve nor I had ever had the slightest interest in each other, this message was received with sullen resistance. I was managing perfectly well without a father and felt no 'need' for one at all. On the contrary, I'd been happy to see the back of him.

After over a year without a word, or a penny, from Steve, Lily was at her wits' end. She talked to Linda about borrowing money to pay a detective. Her health was deteriorating and she was due to go back into hospital for another lengthy stay, which meant there would be no money coming in at all.

It was during this spell in hospital that Lily's heart condition was at last accurately diagnosed and explained. She was suffering from mitral stenosis, which meant that the mitral valve, which separates the upper and lower chambers on the left side of the heart, wasn't opening properly and the blood flow was being restricted. This causes the upper heart chamber to swell as the pressure builds up. Blood may flow backwards into the lungs, with fluid collecting in the lung tissue, making it hard to breathe. Lily was told that, in her case, the condition was in all probability a legacy of the rheumatic fever she had suffered as a girl. Though I, of course, knew nothing of this, the doctors must have made it clear to her then that she would not have long to live, particularly if she continued to drive herself so hard.

At a point where her prospects couldn't have seemed much bleaker, to Lily's surprise and delight, she was given some real help from some qualified professionals.

Chapter 7

ONE DAY, ALONE in one of the comfortable bedrooms of the flat in Notting Hill where she cleaned for the trio of brothers, Lily was overwhelmed by sorrow and exhaustion. With everyone out and the door shut, she sat down on the edge of the bed and began to sob uncontrollably. Unbeknown to her, one of the three 'young professionals' – the journalist – had come home and heard her crying. Having coaxed her into telling him about Steve's moonlight flit with Vera from the Lads of the Village, he asked Lily to give him the most recent photograph she had of her errant husband. He worked for a local newspaper in Kensington, he told her, and he was sure he would be able to track Steve down. For Lily, just being able to talk to somebody about her plight was a help. She didn't think anything would actually come of this man's generous offer.

She was wrong. After various fruitless inquiries around the Town, our determined reporter rang The Lads of the Village and asked to speak to Vera. The landlord said she hadn't worked there for a while and no, he hadn't a clue where she'd gone. The journalist, assisted by his modulated, plausibly authoritative tones, commented that this was a shame, because he represented an insurance company and he was trying to find Vera because she had some money coming to her. They had found her workplace but the address they had for her was out of date. The amount was significant and it would be so unfair if they were unable to pay it out.

The landlord made an excuse about needing to ask his wife and when he returned to the phone, he provided the address of a house in Dulwich. The journalist then went to the trouble of making the trip to south-east London with Steve's photograph in his pocket and knocked on the door of the Dulwich address. The man who answered was Steve, all right. He gave a false name, but when he was confronted with the photograph and a press card, he was forced to admit that he was Stephen Arthur Johnson: pianist, painter and decorator, philanderer and absent father.

Lily was overcome with gratitude. The journalist's efforts had been more than she'd ever hoped for and thanks to him, she now knew where Steve and Vera were living. For Linda and me, Dulwich fell into the same category as Walthamstow: it was some far-off place about which we knew very little. Its only relevance to us was that it meant Steve was living a long way away and we didn't have to worry any more about bumping into him on the streets of Notting Hill.

The brothers' kindness didn't end there. Journalist brother spoke to solicitor brother and he offered to help Lily, pro bono, to secure a divorce. I've never seen the divorce papers (though years later, my Auntie Peggy told me that she had, and had been shocked and enraged by what she'd read) and so I have no idea how long it all took. Given that it was a straightforward case of desertion, I presume the divorce was granted more or less automatically. I have no recollection of Lily going to court: all I remember is that she was very pleased with the outcome. Steve was ordered to send her a postal order every week for £6 10s – £1 10s for her and £2 10s each for me and Linda. There were no custody or access issues: Steve never asked to see his children and his children certainly didn't ask to see him. Lily had her decree nisi and we had some money from Steve – for a while.

To begin with, at least, the postal order would be delivered every Friday through the letterbox of 6 Walmer Road and Lily built a little ritual around its arrival. Friday's tea would be fish and chips from the shop in Latimer Road and I would be sent to Berriman's to choose a cake in possession of the money to pay for it. Lily's slate at the shop was in any case no longer the source of anxiety and embarrassment that it had been, for it was in the process of being wiped clean.

When Linda had gone to the shop one day to get some sugar 'on tick', Mr Berriman had taken her to one side and told her that unfortunately he couldn't allow any more credit until Lily's bill was paid. My ever-resourceful and industrious sister asked if she could work off the debt by helping out in the shop. Mr Berriman agreed and thus it was that Linda started her first job aged twelve, working two evenings a week after school and at weekends, stacking shelves, cleaning and occasionally serving customers.

Lily did her best with whatever food she could afford, but although she had many talents, cooking wasn't one of them. She didn't enjoy it, either, and given the inadequate facilities she had, who can blame her? At least the gas stove at Walmer Road was in the kitchen, and not on the landing like the one at Southam Street. The kitchen was also where we ate (our redesigned front room, with its Salvation Army three-piece suite, was reserved for visitors and special occasions, and certainly not to be used for eating), and where Linda and I did our homework, on a 'desk' created by placing a piece of hardboard across the armchair. In summer, Lily would have the sash window wide open, which allowed the bluebottles to circulate freely.

Linda has always claimed to like burned toast. She may well have made a virtue of necessity. Since Lily didn't so much cook as overcook, we were used to eating burned food and were in no position to be fussy. And for some strange reason she always used batter mix for pastry, so on the rare occasions when she had the time and energy to bake, we would have laid before us a kind of incinerated Yorkshire pudding with meat or apples in it.

However, she couldn't be faulted on her two specialities: bread pudding and roast potatoes (or 'roasties', as we called them). The bread pudding, made from stale bread donated by the people she cleaned for, might have been a little overdone but it was beautifully moist with a crunchy coating and we'd eat great slabs of it sprinkled with sugar. For the 'roasties', she put the potatoes straight into a pan of dripping without parboiling them first. They were nearly always perfect, miraculously escaping the fate of so many other elements of the Sunday roasts Lily tried to produce every week.

When our finances didn't stretch to such a feast, we'd have left-over potatoes and greens mashed together as bubble and squeak and cold Yorkshire pudding, smeared with jam, or our staple diet: bread and dripping. Potato fritters would be produced from a more conventional use of batter. We'd drink tea and, during our exotic phase when Steve was ponying up the maintenance payments, Camp coffee – ersatz, treacly black stuff from a bottle with a colourful label. In the bad times we'd be given a bowl of Oxo with bread floating in it, or have corn-flakes for tea as well as breakfast.

The few years from the end of 1959 until the early 1960s were the best of times for us. There was no more shouting, no violence, no arguments and Steve was at long last making a regular contribution to the household income without actually being there. Lily seemed much happier: she'd come to terms with losing Steve, and obtaining the divorce and securing the court order were major achievements. She was now receiving more money from him than she ever had when they were together. Though Steve's exit had lifted a shadow from my life and Linda's, Lily's despair had cast another. Now that she was so much more cheerful the approach of a new decade seemed to herald a better life for all three of us.

Lily had high hopes of Linda and me. She had been thrilled when Linda was accepted by the Fulham County Grammar School for Girls, even though she had to rely on welfare pay-ments to acquire the school uniform with its neat little velour hat. Linda was focused and always knew where she was going: she had declared her intention to become a children's nanny from a very early age.

Lily expected me to follow in my sister's footsteps by passing my Eleven-Plus. There were no inducements or repressive demands, just an unwavering awareness of her ambitions for me. Lily wanted me to become a draughtsman. She told me it was a skilled profession and, like Uncle Tottsy, I would go to work in a suit. To be a draughtsman I had to go to grammar school, and to get there I had to pass the exam.

In the meantime she persuaded me to join the Cubs, where every week we'd chant our mantra – dyb, dyb, dyb, dob, dob dob. Do your best, do your best, do your best. Done our best, done our best, done our best. And I was doing my best, believe me.

My incentive to pass the Eleven-Plus was twofold: to please Lily and to avoid the dreaded Isaac Newton Secondary Modern. In those days the type of education you received would be decided, and therefore your academic prospects more or less mapped out, at the age of eleven, when all children in their last year of state primary schools were tested and streamed for secondary education. Those who passed the Eleven-Plus – approximately 25 per cent of pupils, though this varied around the country – would be offered grammar school places, a more academic education, O-Levels and A-Levels and a springboard to better opportunities in the job market or for joining the tiny elite that went on to university. All the rest would go to a secondary modern, where the broader curriculum embraced practical skills (woodwork for the boys; cookery for the girls).

This separation of sheep from goats seems ruthless now (though there are still some politicians who long for its return) but it was in fact introduced as one of a series of progressive educational reforms that emerged from the wartime coalition government. The 1944 Education Act (known as the Butler Act after the Conservative president of the Board of Education, 'Rab' Butler) was also responsible for free and universal education, raising the school leaving age from fourteen to fifteen and the provision of free milk for schoolchildren. As part of the new tripartite education system, it enshrined a commitment to establishing technical schools alongside the grammars and secondary moderns. These, however, failed to materialize on the scale envisaged.

The teachers at Bevington Road Primary School seemed just as aspirational for their charges as Lily was for Linda and me, none more so than the school's motivated and motivational headmaster, Mr Gemmill. I'm not sure whether Lily and Mr Gemmill ever met. Parental involvement seemed to be minimal then, and I don't remember there being such things as parents' evenings where the children's progress was discussed. We would simply bring home our school reports (or not bring them home, in the case of some of my classmates, who'd boast in the playground about how they'd destroyed them) at the end of each term and that was the extent of the contact. Lily was generally pleased with my reports, which she studied closely before storing them, in date order, in a cardboard suitcase that had once contained a hamper from the Christmas club.

Mr Gemmill was a hands-on headmaster, interrupting our lessons at random in order to dispense slices of his cracker-barrel philosophy. Thanks to him, I never began a sentence with 'and'. Nor did I ever put 'i' before 'e', except after 'c'. I knew better than to pronounce the letter 'h' as 'haitch', or to expect thirty-one days in September, April, June or November. At school assemblies, Mr Gemmill would tell us about the discovery of the planet Pluto a few decades before and how, one day, man would colonize the moon. Before school holidays, he'd recommend radio programmes to listen to in order to improve our minds.

Unfortunately, it was also thanks to Mr Gemmill that I acquired a lifelong fear of water. When I was eight he decided to take all the boys in my year to Lancaster Road swimming baths to teach us to swim. His method was simple. He would stand like Neptune, up to his chest in the water, his arms out-stretched, and beseech us to jump in one at a time. He boomed reassuringly that we had nothing to be afraid of because he would catch us. The first barrier to learning to swim, he said, was fear of the water, and he was there to help us overcome it.

Soon it was my turn to throw myself in the general direction of Mr Gemmill's hairy torso. We failed to connect and my journey to the bottom of the pool is one I still relive every time I get a whiff of chlorine. After what seemed like an eternity, though it must only have been a few seconds, Mr Gemmill's huge hands located me and I was pulled to the surface to be restored to dry land. There was no sympathy for my near-death experience but I was never taken swimming again, and that suited me fine.

Swimming apart, at Bevington school I was, if I say so myself, a model pupil, ending up as a prefect and an official dinner monitor. As a prefect I was required to stand on the landings at break time and when the classes finished for the day to prevent fellow pupils from running down the stairs too quickly. At dinner time the dinner monitors would be responsible for clearing up the dirty plates collected by the table monitors.

My general good behaviour and these responsibilities were not enough to spare me from Mr Hayes' enthusiasm for the cane. I wish I could remember what he caned me for, but I struggle to come up with a single significant transgression. I do recall a minor incident one dinner time, when I was collecting the plates from the table where my first true love, Linda Kirby, was table monitor. I loved Linda so much that I befriended her unctuous brother, Russell, even though he was in the year below me, in an attempt to weave my way into her affections. It failed. Linda Kirby was totally indifferent to my good looks and natural charm. My cause wasn't helped when on this occasion I took the plates she had piled up and handed to me and, in response to some light-hearted banter, playfully brushed her cheek with my hand. Unfortunately, I hadn't noticed that on the edge of one of the plates was a mound of mashed potato into which I had inadvertently stuck my thumb. The sight of Linda glaring at me as the whole table laughed at the huge blob of half-eaten mash I'd accidentally transferred to her nose has haunted me ever since.

Showing off to girls might well have had something to do with me falling victim to the attentions of Mr Hayes. It certainly didn't take much effort to get yourself caned. Some of my schoolfriends endured it on an almost daily basis. We all feigned nonchalance but in truth it was a petrifying experience.

～

'Who can tell me which record is at Number One in the Top Twenty?' Miss Woofendon asked. She was our music teacher but this was the first time she had ever remotely touched on the kind of music I was passionate about. I imagine that if you asked that question of a class of ten-year-olds today, plenty of hands would go up. Even more would have done in the golden years of the 45rpm disc from the mid-1960s to the end of the 1970s. But this was January 1961, pop music was in its infancy and youth culture had yet to spread to primary-school pupils.

I was still a painfully shy boy and blushed profusely if ever I found myself the centre of attention. But I knew the answer and nobody else did. My hand went up. '"Poetry in Motion" by Johnny Tillotson,' I announced confidently. If Miss Woofendon had asked for the rest of the Top Twenty, I could have reeled those off for her and I'd have had a fair stab at naming the 'B' sides as well.

By this time, Steve's regular postal orders had enabled Linda and me to add to the collection of shellac 78rpm relics that he had left behind. I remember the excitement of the Saturday morning trip we made to the Lane to buy our first two records. After much deliberation, we plumped for 'Fings Ain't Wot They Used T'Be' by Max Bygraves and 'Theme From a Summer Place' by the Percy Faith Orchestra. Not the most tasteful choices, I concede, but back then people of all ages bought singles and the charts reflected this diversity.

With our new-found affluence – supplemented by some of the money Linda began to earn from other jobs she took on in addition to the Berriman's debt repayment plan – we purchased records by Emile Ford and the Checkmates, Jimmy Jones and Johnny Kidd and the Pirates. We kept them pristine, each in their paper sleeve, and they would be catalogued before being stored in an old shoe box. When we couldn't afford the original we'd go to Woolworth's in the Portobello Road to buy cover versions released on their own Embassy label. A record then cost about 7/6d (37½p) whereas the Embassy cover would only be about five bob (25p).

Lily indulged our passion for music as far as she could. She entered Linda for a competition which resulted in her winning tickets to see Cliff Richard and the Shadows at the London

Palladium in 1958. The same year she took me to the Chiswick Empire, where my hero Lonnie Donegan was appearing in pantomime along with the top-of-the-bill singer Joan Regan. She displayed a patient appreciation of our efforts to replicate The Marcels' version of 'Blue Moon' as we walked back to Walmer Road after picking Linda up from Girl Guides on a Wednesday evening.

I'd been writing my own songs since I was six or seven. I was too shy to sing them to anyone other than Lily and Linda (I found even that something of a challenge). So they'd be subjected to 'When the Wagons Keep on Rolling' or my rock classic 'Fed Up' ('We had a date/You were late/And when I tried to kiss you/Baby you hesitate/Well I'm fed up – ooooh'). As always, Lily would offer encouragement though the closest she got to liking pop music was a penchant for the Bachelors (known then as the Harmonichords – they changed their name in 1962) and Elvis singing 'Old Shep'.

Seeing how besotted I was with the Top Twenty, one Christmas she bought me a tiny crystal radio set so that I could listen to music on my own in my room. It had a metal clasp and a string aerial that led me into the Promised Land of Radio Luxembourg, with its three or four hours of pop music every evening, preceded by Horace Batchelor advertising his 'Infra-Draw' system for winning the pools and the American evangelist Garner Ted Armstrong, who would preach in a thunderous voice throughout his programme *The World Tomorrow*. Armstrong's message, shouted in capital letters, had to be endured in order to get to the music, which thrilled me, despite the snap, crackle and pop of the continuous static.

Steve's piano had come with us to Walmer Road and Linda

used a screwdriver to break the lock and open it. Either Steve had taken the key with him, or he'd hidden it amazingly well, because we never managed to find it. Although I now had access to the 'joanna', the only instrument I wanted to play was the guitar. Happily, the Spanish one Lily had bought me, like the Dansette record-player, had continued to survive the process of down-payment followed by repossession that befell most of the purchases Lily had made with her pools winnings.

I acquired Bert Weedon's *Play in a Day* instruction manual, first published in 1957 and still going strong today, which is renowned for inspiring so many apprentice guitarists in the 1950s and 1960s. I should have lodged a complaint under the Trades Descriptions Act because it was ages before I began to master even the basics. Sitting alone in my room at 6 Walmer Road, with no heat and a bucket of urine in the corner, I tried my best to imagine I was in the Deep South with Lonnie and his Dixie Darling, fighting the Battle of New Orleans.

But I got there, and by the time I was able to answer Miss Woofendon's question, I already considered myself to be a singer-songwriter. And I knew in my heart I would never be a draughtsman.

Chapter 8

IT WAS BETWEEN the ages of eight and eleven that the three great passions of my life – music, books and football – began to impose their grip on me. Although Steve was no longer around to influence me, I need to acknowledge the important role he played in sowing the seeds of all three of them.

A little of his musical talent passed through the Johnson genes to Linda and me. Lacking his instinctive genius, I could never play by ear so I needed Mr Weedon's help. But I would do the kinds of things I can imagine Steve doing had he decided to take up the guitar rather than the piano: retuning the strings so that I could more easily shape major chords, for example. While that instilled habits I'd have to unlearn eventually, my long periods alone with the guitar, finding out for myself the joys of composition and chord progression, might well have echoed Steve's approach at my age as he taught himself to play the piano.

As for football in general and Queens Park Rangers in particular, Steve was a Rangers fan. That was hardly remarkable because everyone in Notting Hill seemed to be a Rangers fan. With nothing like the huge media coverage of football that exists today, most boys supported their local team. And for us that meant the club right on our doorstep: I knew of no Chelsea, Fulham or Brentford fans on our manor, even though all three clubs were within easy reach.

As Brentford, like Rangers, were firmly entrenched in the Third Division, they were our main West London rivals. Fulham spent most of the 1950s in Division 2 and Chelsea, a seemingly permanent fixture in the top flight, were literally out of our league. The Rs, though, had tasted success – just the once. In the 1947–48 season QPR had been champions of Division 3 (South) and for the first and, at that point, only time in their existence they had been promoted to the Second Division.

Every football league team used to produce a handbook at the end of each season recording their results, goalscorers and so on. There were photographs and profiles of the players, lots of information on the reserve and youth teams and a little potted history of the club, updated every year.

Steve had the QPR handbook for that gilded 1947–48 promotion season. It was small and stubby, with the photographs printed on shiny paper that felt more expensive than it probably was. It had lost its cover and been knocked about a bit by the time he passed it on to me, but passed on to me it was.

He never actually took me to a match, but to be fair, I'm not sure that he ever went himself. We never talked about football, not even about that glorious pinnacle of success (QPR were back in the Third Division by 1952), but no matter. This precious record had been passed from father to son and I treasured it. I read and re-read everything that had been written about the manager, Dave Mangnall; about the only

QPR player ever to have won an international cap, that season's skipper Ivor Powell, who played for Wales; and about our magnificent goalkeeper, Reg Allen, who had moved to Manchester United in 1950 for £11,000 – a record transfer fee for a goalkeeper.

I pestered Lily constantly to let me go to see Rangers play at Loftus Road, which was not far from Hammersmith Hospital in Du Cane Road, where she was spending an increasing amount of time. In the end she gave me the few shillings I needed for admission and a programme. I would be going with Tony Cox and Lily was content that his dad, the ever-reliable Albert, would be there to keep an eye on us.

It was the 1959–60 season and we were playing Bournemouth and Boscombe Athletic. Like a camera, I stored away my first images of a real football ground, its open green space marooned in a sea of concrete like a small coral island. I soaked up the atmosphere of excitement and expectation, the smell of hot dogs, Bovril and tobacco smoke. Bournemouth were led on to the pitch by their mascot, a man dressed entirely in red and white and known as the Candyman. But he couldn't hope to compete with the blue and white hooped shirts of the Rangers' players.

Lily needn't have worried about any crowd trouble. There was hardly a crowd worth speaking of. Albert Cox stood sentry at the spot he occupied for every home game: leaning on a crush barrier at the Loftus Road end, about thirty steps up the terrace from the pitch. Pat had provided him with a flask of tea and a couple of rounds of sandwiches wrapped in waxed paper.

Tony and I were free to go anywhere we liked. We settled for standing at the front, behind the wall that separated the terraces from the pitch, and running up the steps every so often to take a swig of tea from Albert's flask. Watching the QPR heroes and especially their new signing, the prolific goalscorer Brian Bedford – I tumbled immediately into the grip of an allegiance from which I will never escape. It must have helped that Rangers won 3–0.

From then on I went to Loftus Road as often as I could to marvel at the exploits of Bedford, Tony Ingham, Jim Towers and the rest. Steve's gift of that tatty handbook is where that allegiance began.

As for books, Steve's influence is, admittedly, more tenuous. It was Lily, so cruelly deprived of the scholarship she coveted, who had read widely as a young girl; Lily who had signed us up at the library in Ladbroke Grove before we could even read ourselves. But I struggle now to remember the books I borrowed, or to recall Lily ever having the leisure to sit down and read as an adult. The truth is that Lily, Linda and I became less assiduous about making the trek to the library as time went on and the routine of borrowing, reading, returning and collecting the next book lapsed into long periods when our library tickets lay dormant.

To actually possess your own books was different. Being able to pick them up and dip into them or re-read them whenever you liked lifted the pleasure of reading on to another plane. No wonder I was so in awe of the treasures in Mr Cox's glass-fronted bookcase. And it was through Steve that we began to acquire our own books. Those Cobden Club gifts – *Robinson Crusoe, Tom Sawyer, Little Women* and my *Boy's Own* annual – formed a tiny library which would never have existed if he hadn't taken us to those Christmas parties.

It was expanded by two books that followed them into the house, again as presents, I think. One was an Enid Blyton 'Famous Five' story. I can't recall which; what I do remember is the wonderful escapism of immersing myself in the adventures of those children: the delicious-sounding things they ate and how happy their lives were. When the good times gave way to the dark days of the 1960s, I would lie on my bed covered in coats, cold and hungry, drooling over the sausages, pies and cakes and lemonade scoffed by the children of Blyton-land. Their school summer holidays seemed endless, and each day as warm and cloudless as the one before. Well-fed contentment oozed off the page and provided me with genuine comfort for an hour or two every evening.

But it was the other book that, more than any other, instilled my love of reading: *Shane* by Jack Schaefer, a slim Western that I first read when I was nine and to which I returned at least twice a year until I was able to add further to my library.

It's a simple story of good and evil, set in nineteenth-century Wyoming and told through a boy of about my age then, Bob Starrett, who lives on his parents' ranch. Shane is a former gun-slinger trying to escape his violent past who is hired as a ranch hand and eventually has to return to his fighting ways in order to protect the Starrett family from the powerful landowner trying to drive them from their homestead.

The book had a profound effect on me. I wanted to be like Shane, to be admired like Shane, to carry an air of mystery like Shane and to impress gullible kids, as Shane had impressed Bob Starrett (and me). The 1950s was the era of the Western, which dominated both the cinema and imported television drama; a time when *Gun Law*, *Wagon Train* and *Rawhide* created stars like James Arness, Robert Horton and a very young Clint Eastwood; when Hopalong Cassidy, the Lone Ranger and the Cisco Kid held us in thrall for half an hour most evenings, once Lily eventually managed to rent a telly as well as a wireless from Radio Rentals. (It was, incidentally, *The Lone Ranger*, which used the thrilling *William Tell* overture as its theme tune, that introduced me to classical music.) But Shane, created by Schaefer in 1949, was different from them all. He was darker, more textured; an anti-hero unsuited to the clean-cut innocence of 1950s television.

Music, books, Queens Park Rangers. We had a telly at last, 45rpm discs for our record-player, an embryonic library and I had a guitar. So Steve had played his part in making my life more fulfilling and was now sending money on a fairly regular basis. Credit where credit's due.

~

My enthusiasm for the Cubs didn't last and I hung up my woggle well before the age that a Cub was meant to mature into a Scout. I'd learned to light a match (although I persisted in striking it towards me rather than away from me, as Baden-Powell advised), to use a public telephone and to chop wood. I played in goal for the Cubs football team and Lily would come to watch our games at Wormwood Scrubs and Hyde Park. My role model was Ray Drinkwater, the QPR goalkeeper, and I was never happier than when I trooped home covered in mud at the end of a match.

But I lost interest in the kind of organized fun offered by Akela and her colleagues, preferring the disorganized fun to be had with Tony Cox (for whom the Cubs had never held the slightest allure) and our band of brothers – and one sister, Carol Smith, the archetypal tomboy.

Because of her friendship with Pat Cox, Lily now had fewer qualms about me going out on to the mean streets of Notting Hill, away from her protective gaze, whenever Tony knocked for me. We would play football, either in St Marks Park, where we set up a five-a-side mini-league, or thundering around a disused car park on Bramley Road, or cricket, usually on the wickets to be found painted on the walls of so many of our streets, bowling from one pavement across the road to the one opposite, where the batsman would stand. Occasionally our game would be rudely interrupted by a passing car or van but not often: there still weren't many cars around, even as the 1960s approached.

We knew our own streets in London W10 so well that sometimes we liked to wander further afield to the sunlit uplands of W11, where we knew no one and no one knew us. Holland Park, at the far end of Portobello Road, was unlike anything we had in the Town. It seemed to me more exotic even than Kensington Gardens. For a start, it had peacocks, which strutted around as if they owned the place. It had statues and water features, tennis courts and a Japanese garden. Best of all, it had wild woodland and something called an adventure playground that looked like a film set for a Western: logs positioned deliberately for hiding behind, rickety bridges across a real stream and shrubs and bushes everywhere.

Strangely, whenever we went there after school, there would be no other children around. We could swing and climb and jump and roll for hours in this outpost of our little empire as if it were our own private fiefdom. Holland Park produced conkers on an industrial scale and Carol Smith, who could beat most boys at most things, was always particularly keen to stock up for the season.

At the other extreme, geographically, culturally and aesthetically, was Wormwood Scrubs. There were very few trees on the Scrubs and certainly no peacocks. Just flat, barren land used for football pitches at weekends and overshadowed by the dark, hulking mass of Her Majesty's prison on the far side. This was London W12 at its most desolate, and it stretched for what seemed like miles. When Lily worked on the White City side, at Harry's Café, cooking eggs and bacon for the truck drivers heading up to the North Circular or down to Shepherd's Bush, I'd go to meet her there sometimes and wonder what it must be like to be lost on the Scrubs after dark.

Tony Cox persuaded me to find out. He'd heard there was a derelict army camp way over towards the prison and talked us into going to investigate it. A tenuous grasp of history was only to be expected in a bunch of ten-year-olds, but even that doesn't fully explain why we were convinced that the camp had been run by the Japanese and that they had baked British soldiers in the ovens. But apparently that was the word on the street. This alternative Famous Five – Tony, Dereck Tapper, Walter Curtis, Carol Smith and me – set off in the late afternoon of a winter's day.

By the time we reached our destination the prison walls were still visible in the gathering gloom. Tony had brought the front lamp off his bike to use as a torch. The site had indeed been an army camp of some description. There were turrets and concrete bunkers overgrown with grass and weeds. We played a few half-hearted war games, pretending to be soldiers, but as the prison walls faded into the descending darkness, all we really wanted to do was to lay down our arms and head for home. Tony, our leader, was scathing. What was the point of coming all the way out here if we didn't go down into what looked like a concrete subway and find the ovens in which our brave boys had been incinerated?

We stood nervously contemplating the slope leading down to what had once been a tunnel but was now open to the sky. It contained a complex array of walls and alleys that looked as if they had been the living quarters. Tony switched on his lamp and pointed the way. The rest of us followed meekly, staying very close together. When we reached the bottom, Tony moved the beam of his bike lamp around to properly illuminate what we'd already discerned by the light of the moon: there was a row of three or four openings that looked very much like ovens.

I froze but Carol insisted on poking about inside these large metal canisters, searching for bits of charred remains – a bone or a tooth that might have survived the flames. Convinced that we were the first to make this discovery, we vowed to ensure that it remained our secret. This was fine by me, particularly as Lily would have been extremely cross if she'd found out where I'd been. We returned to the 'death camp' once or twice more in daylight but it was always deserted and the only people who might have been aware of our investigations were a few dog walkers and any lost souls peering out of the tiny, barred cell windows above the walls of HMP Wormwood Scrubs.

The camaraderie I shared with Tony and our mates was the nearest I got to Blyton-land during my time at primary school and its days were already numbered. The band of Bevington brothers (and one sister) would be scattered once we followed our own paths through the secondary education system and my close friendship with Tony did not survive puberty.

I passed my Eleven-Plus. Given how momentous the exam was, I wish I could recall even one of the questions. I do remember the day of the exam itself, with Mr Gemmill in attendance and my final year teacher, Mrs Leadsford, super-vising. Tall, slim and very attractive, she'd been an enormous help in those all-important last twelve months. When the results arrived, Lily was ecstatic, although I don't think she ever really doubted that I'd succeed.

Dereck Tapper also passed the Eleven-Plus, becoming the first black child at our school to do so. He must also have been one of the first to take it. Given the hardships he must have endured, it was a remarkable achievement.

Carol Smith failed. Walter Curtis was in the year below us so had a year to wait for his ordeal; he, too, would fail. The big surprise was Tony, my resolutely unstudious friend. I think he would actually have preferred to have gone to Sir Isaac Newton Secondary Modern, along with the majority of the boys in our year at Bevington, but instead he found himself destined for grammar school. A few others also passed, including a boy named Peter Hayward, whose parents declined the opportunity of a grammar-school place because they couldn't afford the uniform. Peter wore glasses and I remember feeling really sorry for him because I knew he'd be bullied as a 'four eyes' at Isaac Newton. Lily couldn't afford the uniform, either, but she would never have contemplated for a second not sending me to a grammar school.

On that single day, the day of the exam, Tony Cox did well.

Others in my year who were bright enough and worked much harder happened to do badly. Yet our performances on that day alone would largely determine our futures. The arbitrary nature of this test, and the traumatic effect of its importance on the lives of small children, was already the subject of fierce political debate.

There was, in fact, already another alternative: a new type of secondary school had just opened in Holland Park which was neither a grammar nor a secondary modern. Ironically, for some of the well-heeled parents at the other end of the Portobello Road, it would have been *de rigueur* to send their Eleven-Plus successes to this innovative 'comprehensive' school, which was open to all children, whether or not they had passed the exam. But for working-class Lily, there was no point in passing the Eleven-Plus if it didn't lead to a grammar-school place, which she saw as her children's escape route from the kind of life to which she'd been condemned. Ironically, Holland Park Comprehensive was to become a hugely successful and fashionable school, and even at that early stage the kids who went there were more likely to be mixing with the offspring of diplomats and politicians than the Bevington Road Primary School diaspora.

So Lily and I set out to find a grammar school that would take me. The nearest was St Clement Danes in Du Cane Road, but they didn't even call me in for interview. Our next choice was Sir Walter St John's in Battersea. They at least granted me an audience, which Lily attended with me. This consisted of the pompous, begowned head teacher putting a coin on one end of a ruler, balancing it across his fingers and asking me a question about the weight needed to counterbalance it, or some such nonsense. I was nervous enough being interviewed; having to subject myself to more tests struck me as perverse. I gave the wrong answer and was rejected. It began to dawn on Lily and me that passing the Eleven-Plus might have been the easy part. These head teachers were sizing me up to see if I was good enough for their schools and I was not, it seemed, coming up to scratch.

Sloane school was our last roll of the dice. There were no other grammar schools within reasonable travelling distance. As it was, Sloane was a forty-minute tube and bus ride away in Chelsea, well beyond my stamping ground. It had five hundred boys and a famous headmaster, Guy Boas, who'd been in situ for thirty years and was known nationally for his schoolboy Shakespearean productions during the 1950s. When Lily and I arrived there seemed to be hundreds of boys sitting in the school hall, all waiting to be interviewed by two teachers stationed at desks on the stage.

Guy Boas wasn't there but his avuncular deputy, Mr Bailey, was and it was he who beckoned me towards him for a five-minute discussion from which Lily was, to her chagrin, excluded. I reassured her that the interview had gone well. At any rate, there had been no silly tests and no trick questions, as far as I could tell. A few days later, I was offered a place, as were Tony Cox and Dereck Tapper.

As well as free school meals, I qualified for a free tube and bus pass because I lived more than three miles from the school. Lily was able to purchase a second-hand uniform, which included a belted navy blue mac I never wore and a cap which I'm proud to say never went anywhere near my head. The 'Social' provided shoes, but there were still books to buy and 'amenity fees' to find, which meant Lily taking on still more cleaning jobs, in spite of the doctors' warnings.

Why had Sloane taken me when two other schools hadn't? Perhaps it was less discerning than the others; maybe there was some kind of 'baby boomer' drought in London SW3, or more wealthy families than in other boroughs who eschewed the state system altogether and sent their offspring to public schools.

Whatever the reason, on 5 September 1961, Tony Cox and Dereck Tapper and I set off, on separate routes from our respective homes, to begin our grammar-school education in the unfamiliar environs of the King's Road, Chelsea.

Chapter 9

I WAS DEEPLY UNHAPPY at Sloane Grammar School. I hated the journey, the teachers, the lessons. I had few friends. Tony Cox was in a different form and in any case I'd grown less fond of wandering the streets with him in the evenings, preferring solitary confinement with my guitar, my burgeoning collection of second-hand Matchbox cars – which could be had for a few pence down the Lane – a book or *Charles Buchan's Football Monthly*. Dereck Tapper was in my class but, like me, he seemed to have become more introverted in the scholarly environment of 'the Sloane', as it was known. We'd be subjected to dense and wordy lectures every morning at assembly by the gowned and mortar-boarded Guy Boas who, in our first year, was seeing out the final months of his distinguished career.

We 'one-ers' would be placed in the gallery, looking down at the imposing figure of our headmaster, holding centre stage, leaning on his walking stick and regaling us with his reflections on over thirty years at the school. The only plus point was that assembly would overrun and eat into the timetable of, typically, double maths, French and Latin.

Guy Boas was succeeded by Dr Henry, a small, thin man with

sharp, pointed features and wire-framed glasses which encouraged our depiction of him as the Camp Commandant. Our form master was a young Welsh geography teacher, Mr Woosnam, who collected the dinner money every Monday morning by calling each boy's name and waiting for them to approach his desk with the required cash. Every week he'd call 'Johnson' and I'd be forced to respond by shouting, 'Free, sir.' It was an embarrassment akin to asking Mr Berriman to put Lily's groceries 'on tick' in front of a shop full of customers.

Unlike me, Dereck was a PE star. Also in our class was the nascent footballer Malcolm Macdonald, who went on to play for Fulham, Newcastle United, Arsenal and England, and the two of them developed a fierce rivalry in our well-equipped gym (we had wall bars, a trampoline and ropes which we were required to climb at the end of every PE lesson). Malcolm lived in Fulham, between Bishop's Park and Craven Cottage. It goes without saying that he was an exceptional footballer but he also excelled at cricket and athletics, and carried off the prize in every event he entered at our annual sports day at Hurlingham Stadium. But Dereck matched him as a gymnast – if such a term can be applied to the practitioners of the PE we were forced to endure every week.

At breaks I would avoid the playground, preferring to go to the geography classroom where Mr Woosnam or one of his colleagues would show reel-to-reel film documentaries about Africa or India, or the Monte Carlo Rally. Or I'd go to the excellent library where, on my first visit, I had picked up a paperback and borrowed it on the strength of the cover. *A Damsel in Distress* by P.G. Wodehouse launched a lifelong love affair with the work of the great man.

There were other cultural pursuits. The music teacher recruited me to the school choir, in which I sang Verdi and Bizet's *Carmen* for a school production. There was also a film club that showed proper movies one evening each month. I had no interest in this until I noticed that the film to be shown in November was *Shane*, starring Alan Ladd (yes, him again). I was thrilled by the prospect of seeing the book I knew practically by heart brought to the big screen (or to be accurate, the flimsy, portable screen, stretched to its full height of about ten feet in the school hall). I decided to pay my tuppence and go.

I know this may sound like hyperbole, but that evening was one of the biggest disappointments of my life. Shane's appearance in the first pages of the book is a moment of dark foreboding. He wears dark clothes, a black silk handkerchief knotted loosely around his throat and a plain black hat with 'a wide curling brim swept down in front to shield the face'. As Bob, the young boy watching his approach, records: 'The eyes were endlessly searching from side to side and forward, checking off every item in view, missing nothing. As I noticed this, a sudden chill . . . struck through me there in the warm and open sun.'

As I took a seat in the front row of the school hall, I was anticipating this dramatic opening and all that would follow as if I were Bob Starrett sitting on the upper rail of his father's corral in Wyoming. The film kept to the sequence of the book, beginning with Bob watching Shane's approach – but the man who came into view wasn't dressed in dark clothes with a black hat, riding a black horse. He was a diminutive, blond man with a white hat on a grey horse. He was dressed in bright colours and seemed to have a cheery disposition. Paramount Pictures had turned my Shane into Roy Rogers.

~

While Lily had pulled herself out of the depths of despair, she remained in the shallows: sad, regretful and, above all, lonely. As she cooked dinner on Sundays the Bakelite switch on the radio would be set to number 1, the Light Programme, for *Two-Way Family Favourites* – as much a part of Sunday dinner in my memory as the smell of roast lamb. The successor to the wartime *Forces Favourites*, the programme played records requested by soldiers stationed overseas for their loved ones at home, and vice versa. When that week's 'bumper bundle' (the most-requested record) was one of her own favourites – 'True Love' by Bing Crosby and Grace Kelly, for instance – she would leave the vegetables boiling to a mush and sit down in the little kitchen armchair, dabbing her eyes with a tea towel. Lily liked Bing and adored Grace Kelly. She'd light one of her razor-cut cigarettes and gaze up to the ceiling singing softly, 'For you and I have a guardian angel/On high, with nothing to do/But to give to you and to give to me/Love for ever true.'

Not so much a lone parent as a lonely one; still young, still pretty, still hoping that someone other than Bing and Grace would bring true love into her life.

The mother–daughter relationship between Lily and Linda was by this time beginning to reverse: Lily was becoming dependent on Linda rather than the other way round. At night, I'd hear them talking in the bedroom next to mine. Linda's sacrifice of her own room had had the desired effect and there were now more conversations than tears emanating from the big double bed. They talked of the past, of Lily's childhood, of her hopes and dreams, of her illness, and of how she might meet a man who would care for her.

Lily's 'three young professionals' had suggested that she look through the ads in the lonely hearts section of the local paper. Linda sanctioned this idea and eventually I was told that a man called Henry would be visiting us one weekday evening. A plan of action was devised. He was to be shepherded straight into the front room, with its small television set, the Dansette, Steve's honky-tonk piano and the Salvation Army three-piece suite. On no account was he to see the less salubrious kitchen-cum-dining room-cum-study at the back. I was to be home from school, reasonably clean and presentable, to meet Lily's 'friend'.

Unbeknown to me, she'd answered an advertisement from Henry and met him one evening the previous week in a pub. The first date had gone well. Lily liked him but it was essential to her that we did, too. I made it obvious that I was unhappy about this disruption. Leaving aside my acute shyness, the thought of having to try to impress a strange man who may one day take Steve's former role in our lives filled me with dread.

Linda, who'd been in on this from the start, chivvied and nagged me. This was Lily's chance of happiness after the dreadful time we'd all had with Steve. She knew that my disapproval would be fatal for Henry's prospects. But she was the extrovert, mature way beyond her years and in absolute empathy with her mother. It was easier for her, I thought in my childish, resentful way. I liked things the way they were and couldn't understand why Lily didn't feel the same. But I subdued my protests and followed Linda's strict instructions to be on my best behaviour.

So there we were, on parade, clean and smiley, like two children from the Von Trapp family in *The Sound of Music*, when Henry knocked on the door. Lily behaved like a nervous schoolgirl. She spoke in the pseudo-posh accent she reserved for special occasions, fussing and clucking round the small, balding, rotund, middle-aged man who stood in our hallway clutching a bunch of daffodils. His thinning hair had been arranged carefully to cover his bald patch. When he spoke it was in an accent that belonged in South rather than North Kensington. This was proper posh – as refined and crystal-clear as Guy Boas's tones at Sloane school assembly every morning.

Henry was ushered into the front room, where the sight of the piano sent him into spasms of joy. Since Linda's intervention with the screwdriver, it had been accessible to all and Henry asked for a chair to be brought in so that he could 'tickle the ivories'.

And he could play. Not the stuff that Steve played to order, such as 'Heart of My Hearts', 'On Moonlight Bay', and 'Maybe It's Because I'm a Londoner'. Henry played hymns and sang in an uninhibited, impeccably phrased tenor voice. He asked if Linda and I could sing and insisted that we perform, red-faced with embarrassment, in front of him. I was red-faced, at any rate – Linda didn't do blushing.

We fetched a copy of the *Record Song Book*, which published pop lyrics on cheap paper every month for 3d, and sang 'Take Good Care of My Baby' a cappella (Henry obviously hadn't heard of Goffin and King and didn't have Steve's ability to play by ear). There followed Henry's stirring rendition of 'Onward Christian Soldiers', which we joined in while Lily fluttered between the front room and the kitchen with tea and biscuits. Henry told us he was a music teacher and asked me to sing to his accompaniment. He said I had a lovely voice and was obviously very musical. He would recommend me to the choir at Westminster Cathedral, where he worshipped.

I did have rather a sweet voice (before it broke) but I wasn't a Catholic. At that age I didn't have the first idea that Westminster Cathedral was the country's leading Catholic church or that it mattered, but Lily, of course, was well aware of the implications. Although she was pleased by Henry's appreciation of her children, it may well have been her very polarized view of religion, stemming from her Liverpudlian upbringing, that did for poor Henry.

His visit had been truly memorable, like someone dropping in from another planet. There was nothing to dislike about him, his jollity and enthusiasm were infectious, the worst I'd had to suffer was a mild dose of embarrassment and I'd been flattered and pleasantly surprised. And yet, as the door closed behind him, Lily had already made her decision. She announced with some solemnity that though he seemed a nice man, they had nothing in common. She had his address and would write him a nice letter thanking him for his kindness but saying she didn't think they were suited to one another. Nevertheless, she was glad she'd taken her employers' advice and answered that lonely hearts ad. Next time, she would place her own advertisement and she promised that Linda could help her to sift through the replies and choose another candidate.

By 1961, Linda herself was ready to become involved in the dating game. She was fourteen, but looked eighteen; more significantly, as a result of the adult responsibilities she had taken on she was mature far beyond her years on every level. Having toiled away at Berriman's until she had paid off Lily's slate, she was now working there one evening a week and on a Sunday for wages. She also had a Saturday job at Woolworth's and a job in a chemist's two evenings a week after school. During Lily's frequent stays in hospital, it was Linda who took care of us and dealt with officialdom. Having opened letters from the likes of the Provident, the Prudential and the Electricity Board to discover other debts, she was now working to try to clear those as well.

Linda had taken to frequenting a youth club in Sutton Dwellings where, years before, she'd discovered Steve and Elsie in flagrante. Lily allowed her one night out a week but she wangled a second by persuading me to join a boxing school there so that she could go again on the pretext of escorting me to and from my boxing sessions.

The boxing was short-lived but Linda managed to retain her second night out. She would spend ages getting ready, back-combing and lacquering her hair into the required beehive. Her clothes, like mine, had always come 'off the barrow', the second-hand stalls in Portobello market, but now she was managing to set aside some of her wages to buy the occasional new item for herself. Her liberty bodice had long been replaced by a bra and life at 6 Walmer Road had become more fraught for me, with two women constantly screaming for me not to come in as I opened the back-room door. One or other of them would invariably be engaged in some feminine ritual such as a strip wash, the purpose of which I failed to appreciate.

One day, Linda came home from school and announced that

she'd been asked out on a date. An Italian man named Antonio had approached her on her tube journey between Hammersmith and Latimer Road, told her how lovely she looked, given her his address and asked if he could take her out. The news exploded in our little back room like a hand grenade. The interrogation swiftly followed. How old was Antonio? He'd told Linda he was twenty-four or twenty-five. Couldn't he see by her uniform that Linda was a schoolgirl? Lily wanted to know. What kind of depravity motivated a twenty-five-year-old man to chase after schoolgirls? Linda wasn't old enough yet to go out with any boy, let alone a man of his age. Linda protested that he was a young student living alone in a room at the other end of Walmer Road. He was tall, handsome, courteous and respectful – a real man.

As she always did when she was angry, Lily lapsed into Scouse. 'Youse wouldn't know a man from a shirt button!' she yelled. Her daughter, by contrast, was controlled and determined. She knew that the extra responsibility she'd shouldered gave her greater licence to stand her ground.

A compromise was reached. Lily and Linda would visit Antonio's lodgings so that Lily could meet him and, more importantly, speak to his landlady to get a third-party appraisal of the handsome Italian. It all seemed to go well and Lily reluctantly agreed that Linda and Antonio could step out together, but with strict conditions attached. She must know where they were going (the cinema), what route they'd take there and back (they'd be going on foot to the Royalty in Lancaster Road) and a strict curfew (9pm) was applied. Antonio was to walk Linda straight home and there was to be no kissing. Lily would have chaperoned them if she could. As it was, she paced around all evening, patrolling the front room as 9pm approached, peering out of the window up the road for the first sign of Linda's return.

Since Lily was either working in the evenings or in hospital, she wasn't in much of a position to apply her strictures consistently. But she never lost her power over us and the thought of upsetting her was probably as effective in controlling Linda's hormones as it had been in getting us both through the Eleven-Plus. Antonio wasn't around for long anyway, though as Linda grew older, inevitably more boyfriends materialized.

~

In early December, three months after I'd arrived at Sloane Grammar School, I was granted a temporary escape from it. It was an accident in the gym that brought about my reprieve.

I had been given the job of putting the ropes away after our PE lesson, which involved sliding them to the side of the hall to be tethered against the wall bars. Each rope was weighed down by a heavy metal ball – one of which was sent swinging around by a boy as I approached, hitting me in the eye.

Our sports master, Mr Alder, over-dramatized the incident and so I did as well. What was a simple bang in the eye became sight-threatening – there was even talk of calling an ambulance, but it was decided (with my encouragement) that I'd be better seeing my own doctor. So I was sent home to visit the surgery, walking slowly out of the school, holding my head as if in agony.

By the time I'd arrived at the little tobacco kiosk in Ladbroke

Grove where Lily was working that day, I had entered into the spirit of my wounded soldier role and was clutching my bruised eye like King Harold at Hastings after the arrow hit him. Lily took me to see our glamorous American GP, Dr Tanner, whose basement surgery was close to Lancaster Road Baths. More like a movie star than a medic, Dr Tanner had thick, copper-coloured hair and was just about the most exotic person in our bleak West London landscape – not only a foreign doctor but an attractive female foreign doctor at that. She must have chosen to work in our part of Notting Hill out of a sense of public duty.

Owing to her heart condition, Lily spent a lot of time with Dr Tanner, who took a great interest in our welfare. Having examined my eye, she said I must stay away from school until after the Christmas holidays, when she would reassess the situation. In the end, a combination of what must have been some genuine eye damage, a bout of conjunctivitis and my ability to persuade Lily that the effort of prolonged study would make me feel desperately ill kept me off school until the following April.

I never recovered academically, and by the time I returned to Sloane, things at home had changed for the worse, too. Steve's money had begun to arrive more infrequently and then stopped altogether.

Chapter 10

THE DAWN OF the new year of 1962 saw me off school, Lily off work and the little income we had to supplement Steve's increasingly rare postal orders being brought in by Linda.

Lily had been in and out of hospital, either for check-ups or because of illness, throughout the previous year. At least she and the doctors now knew exactly what they were dealing with. But she had another heart complaint in addition to the mitral stenosis: the continuing absence of a man in her life. There were two main topics of conversation in her big double bed every night. Linda would be telling Lily that she had to do something about Steve's failure to honour his commitment to send us money every week. Lily would be telling Linda how she was planning to put her own advertisement in the lonely hearts column of the local paper.

The two issues were related. Lily's planned adventure wasn't just a quest for companionship. Her only regret about breaking with Henry was that he was obviously reasonably well off and, while she wasn't a mercenary woman and money wasn't her prime consideration (we occupied that position), these were days when women were much more heavily dependent on the income of their husbands.

The 'three young professionals' she had cleaned for had moved on by this time and were no longer available for advice and guidance. Linda was. She argued that as we had Steve's address in East Dulwich, Lily must write explaining how desperate we were. To Lily this seemed like begging, but she swallowed her pride and wrote to Steve. There was no reply. And there were no more postal orders.

Early that year Linda began to go out with Jimmy Carter, a fifteen-year-old lovable rogue, one of seven children in a family renowned for being 'hard'. They lived in St Anne's Road, on the cusp of Notting Hill and Shepherd's Bush, and the patriarch was a rag-and-bone collector – a totter (Jimmy always swore that Hercules, the horse in the TV series *Steptoe and Son*, had belonged to his dad). Jimmy had already left school and worked with his father selling on the scrap metal and second-hand tat gathered on the cart. Unfortunately, his dad also dealt in manure, which meant that Jimmy sometimes arrived to take Linda out carrying a certain aroma that was noticeable even in our unsanitary conditions. Lily would heat up the copper in our cobbled-together basement bathroom and insist that he had a bath.

Although she liked Jimmy, she never saw him as being remotely suitable for her daughter. In the end neither did Linda, but his big smile and tall, gangling frame were part of our lives for over a year before they split up. It was an eventful year for us and Jimmy Carter, who became a regular breezy presence in the house, played a part in it.

Jimmy would give me the odd cigarette on the understanding

that I wouldn't tell Lily. But when she eventually went back to work later that year at the kiosk next to Ladbroke Grove station, she was allowed free cigarettes to supplement her wages and used to bring home a packet of ten Rothmans King Size for me every week.

The health implications of smoking had yet to be widely understood. Back then everyone smoked, and everyone smoked everywhere. On the Metropolitan line tube I took to school, there was just one carriage on each train for non-smokers, and that was usually empty. I don't think Lily's many hospital clinicians, or Dr Tanner, ever advised her to give it up. As for me taking it up, Lily saw that as a rite of passage.

I certainly considered it to be a badge of manhood. As Lily and I passed each other cigarettes or (once he knew it was OK with Lily) I accepted one of Jimmy's Player's tipped, I felt I was forming an adult bond with them. The ever-sensible Linda, on the other hand, became devoutly anti-smoking – thanks to an early advisory lesson at Fulham County, which included the scrutiny of the blackened lungs of a dead smoker, preserved in a glass container. 'I want to keep my lungs pink,' she'd say.

Lily was surprisingly relaxed, too, about all the lessons I was missing. It must have been a strain on her finances, since she had to provide a meal for me that I would have got free at school. Having pushed me so hard at Bevington, she didn't seem concerned about my absence from Sloane. It was as if the fact that I was a grammar-school boy was enough in itself to secure my future.

She certainly believed my eye problem to be worse than it was. She had absolute trust in Dr Tanner but being well aware that I was miserable at Sloane it seems unlikely that she wouldn't have suspected some degree of exaggeration, if not downright malingering. Maybe she had bigger worries on her mind; perhaps – just perhaps – she liked having me with her while she prepared to go back into hospital for more tests. This time she was not going in for diagnosis of the complaint but to work out what to do about it.

If that was the case, I must have provided scant comfort or companionship since I spent almost all my time alone in my room, following the pop charts, playing my guitar and reading (and re-reading) my books. By now my interest in football had become an obsession and I invented my own league, featuring teams like London Rovers and Haden Park and over-populated with players going by the names Alan or Johnson. Lily paid for my *Charles Buchan's Football Monthly*, ordered from Maynard's, the newsagents, and preserved in good condition, apart from the double-page centre-spread team line-ups that I pinned on my damp bedroom walls. I produced my own magazine every month, too, called *Soccer News*, full of team news and 'photographs' (my shaky attempts at drawing and colouring in). Lily indulged me by reading it and taking out a monthly subscription. A *Soccer News Annual* was also produced in a hardback ruled notebook Steve had left behind.

I was constantly hungry. I've never forgotten that emptiness and craving for food. As always, Lily did her best with what we had, but she was feeling very low and on drugs that made her listless. Her stale bread floating in Oxo speciality appeared regularly on the menu.

Once Lily had gone into hospital, Linda made a momentous decision for a fourteen-year-old. One evening, as she, Jimmy and I sat in our little back room, cold and hungry, Jimmy and I flicking fag ash into the fireplace as we huddled round its fading glow, she made up her mind that she needed to confront Steve herself, face to face.

~

Using an *A to Z* and the London Transport maps in her school library, Linda devised a route by tube and bus to the address we had for Steve in Dulwich. If there had been no alternative, I'm quite sure she would have gone there on her own. As it was, Jimmy volunteered to accompany her. There was no question of me going, and I wasn't asked. While I admired my sister's bravery, I couldn't match it. She didn't want to see Steve again any more than I did, but she felt she had to force him to face up to responsibilities he was obviously keen to forget. Lily was not to be informed until after the event. For once the 'Don't tell Alan' policy had been overruled. This time it was 'Don't tell Lily.'

Linda and Jimmy set off one Sunday afternoon when they reckoned Steve was most likely to be at home. He and Vera were living in a street of tall, highly desirable Victorian houses off Lordship Lane. It was a world away from the slums of Southam Street. Linda and Jimmy found the right house, where Steve and Vera evidently occupied the two upper floors. At the top of the flight of steep steps climbed by our intrepid reporter when he first discovered Steve's whereabouts there was now a bell marked 'Johnson' which Linda pressed. They waited.

It was Vera who answered the door. Small and round with swollen legs – very different from the woman we had imagined – she spoke precisely, in a Home Counties accent. Linda told her the purpose of the visit and Vera invited them in, calling up the stairs to Steve that his daughter was here with her boyfriend. Steve may already have seen Linda from the upstairs window, but she felt that Vera's advance warning suggested he hadn't, and therefore needed to be prepared for the shock.

As Jimmy stood uncomfortably by the door to the flat, Linda marched in and went straight on to the attack. She had no intention of engaging in polite conversation or of staying for a minute longer than she had to. The room, she told me later, was neat and clean, carpeted and warm. In the corner sat a boy of around Linda's age: Vera's son, Michael, who gazed quizzically at the visitors trying to work out why they'd come. He lived with Steve and his mother and apparently had no contact with his biological father.

Steve had been sitting in his armchair by the gas fire. His ginger hair was, as always, combed and Brylcreemed straight back from his freckled forehead. He looked shaken and pale.

'You haven't sent us any money for weeks,' Linda announced. 'Mum's in hospital and can't work and we've got nothing.'

Steve tried to make excuses. 'Things haven't been easy . . .' he began.

'They've not been easy for us either and we need money badly,' Linda cut in defiantly.

She stood her ground and in the uncomfortable silence that followed Steve crossed the floor and disappeared into the bedroom, returning a couple of minutes later with two £10 notes. Three weeks' money, much less than he owed but more than Linda expected. She relaxed a little.

Vera brewed some tea. Jimmy offered round his cigarettes and they sat talking awkwardly for half an hour. From what Linda gleaned, Steve was a changed man. There was a piano in the corner but he no longer played the pubs and clubs. Painting and decorating now took precedence.

He invited Linda and Jimmy to visit again and to bring me with them. Linda rose to leave, thanking Vera for the tea. As she and Jimmy headed to the door Steve said: 'By the way, Vera is having a baby. You're going to have a new brother or sister.'

Only once the mission had been accomplished was Lily informed. As soon as she was out of hospital and got me on my own she laid into me about going to see Steve. In what must have been an extraordinarily difficult commitment for her to make, she promised she'd come with me if only I'd agree to visit him.

I was adamant. I refused to see Steve in any circumstances, whether it was with Linda or with Lily. Linda was more accommodating. She told me that although she had felt like a traitor sitting there drinking tea with Steve and Vera, she would go back when the baby was born to see our half-sibling. She and Lily both possessed an exceptional courage that I lacked. As far as I can recall, my obduracy wasn't rooted in any heroic principle of loyalty to Lily. It was about me, and it was simple. Steve was a stranger to me. It would be embarrassing to have to meet him again and I was afraid that if I wasn't careful, I might end up having to live once more with this man I neither knew nor liked. My greatest fear was not losing a father; it was having one.

Lily didn't let up. Steve was my dad, she reminded me; a boy needed his father; I'd grow up regretting this missed opportunity. With hindsight, I can see that she was worried about what would happen to me if the heart condition killed her. Steve would need to take responsibility for me, and for that to work I had to be reconciled with him. After the misery he'd inflicted upon Lily and Linda, who'd sought to protect her, they would have been far more entitled than I was to vehemently oppose the re-establishment of contact. Their magnanimity was remarkable, but it was lost on me.

Linda did go back to East Dulwich a few times, primarily to extract further funds from Steve – despite her appeal, the postal orders were few and far between. I never went with her, much to Lily's chagrin. Our half-sister, Sandra, was born later in the year. Steve was, by all accounts, a model father this time around. As I say, credit where credit's due.

~

Apart from helping Linda to prise some cash out of Steve, Jimmy Carter's other main contribution to our family fortunes was introducing me to his older brother, Johnny.

Johnny was the eldest of the seven Carter siblings. He was in his mid-twenties and married with two small children. Tall and handsome – except when he laughed and revealed his bad teeth – he retained the look of the Teddy Boy he'd recently been. Johnny's hair was a work of art. The style he wore was known as a Tony Curtis with a DA (duck's arse, for anyone unfamiliar with the term, owing to the tapered shape of the hair at the back). He might once have shared his brother's breezy good humour, but having become a father himself he took his position as eldest son very seriously. In fact he was a very serious man, quietly spoken and mature beyond his years. He could have been taken for Jimmy's father rather than his brother.

Johnny had a reputation as a fighter and a man you'd be foolish to cross, though he was now pursuing a respectable occupation as a milkman in Notting Hill – a milkman in need of an assistant. I was given the job, for which I was to be paid 10 shillings (50p) to work all day Saturday (the busiest day of the week because that was when the money was collected) and until midday on Sunday, when the round was completed more quickly. I'd wait in the pre-dawn gloom for Johnny to fetch me in his Express Dairies milk float, which he'd pick up from the depot in St Charles Square.

Saturday was a long, arduous slog – delivering the milk, collecting the empties, knocking on people's doors and waiting for them to answer, telling them how much they owed, running to Johnny for change from the big leather pouch he carried around his waist like a gunslinger's belt. In some of the more prosperous streets on the round, money would be left wrapped in a note jammed into the neck of an empty bottle. Johnny would stop periodically to light the roll-up that rarely left his lips and open the huge black ledger to record who'd paid, who hadn't and which orders had changed. When he'd finished, out would come his comb and he'd carefully reconstruct the 'Tony Curtis' that never seemed to me to have deconstructed in the first place. Lunch was a Swiss roll from the little produce cupboard on the milk float, torn in half and shared between us, washed down with a pint of silver-top, full-fat milk.

The worst houses to service were the overcrowded, multi-occupied ones with an open front door and no bells with which to summon the occupants. We'd have to go in together and take a floor each, banging on the two or three (or even four) doors behind which a family or a group of single West Indian men were squeezed in appalling conditions.

There was one of these places in Ruston Close, a cul-de-sac of twenty houses off St Marks Road. Number 10 was in particularly bad repair and there were two customers on each of the three landings. Johnny always sent me in alone while he lit a fag, removed the pencil he kept lodged behind his right ear and commenced an unusually intense scrutiny of the ledger.

No matter what the time or season, 10 Ruston Close was always dark. There was no natural light on the landings or bulbs in the light fittings. An awful smell of decay and mould, stale food and detritus seeped from the walls. Each room contained several young West Indian men for whom existing in these conditions was the price they paid for coming to the motherland. It took me ages to collect the money, run to Johnny and return with the change. I could never understand why my streetwise boss, my Shane on a milk float, never came in with me to lend a hand.

It was some time later that I discovered the truth about Ruston Close. The cul-de-sac had been renamed. It had previously been Rillington Place and number 10 was the house where, over the course of ten years, the infamous serial killer John Christie had murdered at least seven women, including his own wife, and the baby daughter of one of his victims, concealing their bodies in the garden and behind the walls of that gloomy, forbidding house. He had committed his final murder there less than a decade earlier. After a badly mishandled police investigation, Christie had finally been caught, tried and hanged for his crimes in 1953 – but not before innocent fellow resident Timothy Evans, the man whose wife and baby girl

Christie had killed, had been wrongly convicted of their murder and sent to the gallows. No wonder even tough Johnny Carter was loath to set foot in the place.

I actually began working on the milk round before Dr Tanner declared me fit to return to school. The 10 shillings a week brought me some money to spend. Desperate though she was, Lily would never take a penny from me, insisting instead that I began to save in a Bible-shaped piggy bank she gave me for the purpose. Neither did she question why I was able to work but not to study. Dr Tanner had provided the sick certificate and that was good enough for her. Eventually I had to bite the bullet and go back. The anticipation was probably worse than the reality, but I'd still have preferred not to have been there if I could have avoided it.

The Saturday milk round restricted my chances of getting to Loftus Road to watch Queens Park Rangers, but I attended as many home games as I could manage or afford. When I couldn't go I had to content myself with my football magazines and books. Lily had trained us to keep our eyes on the pavement and the gutter whenever we passed a pub or one of the newly legalized betting shops, because that's where men were most careless with their cash and most likely to drop coins from their pockets. One day I struck lucky outside a betting shop on my walk home from Latimer Road station, spotting an array of coins scattered on the ground, which I pounced on and quickly pocketed. When I inspected my haul I found I had about 10 shillings' worth in all, including three half-crowns. I ran all the way to Shepherd's Bush market to buy the one thing I desired above all others: *The Topical Times Football Annual.*

Although I lived and breathed football for a long while, I

wasn't much good at actually playing it. I made the Danvers House team at Sloane no more than a couple of times, and even then only as goalkeeper. Malcolm Macdonald demonstrated his footballing genius early on for Turner House, scoring five against me in the Danvers goal.

The Sloane playing fields were a bus ride away in Roehampton, where we had to trek one afternoon a week. I might not have shown much prowess on the park, but I looked forward to those afternoons. They were a break from the schoolwork I hated. And at Roehampton there was fresh air and extensive grounds. Another attraction was the presence of pupils from the Carlyle Grammar School for Girls, situated right next door to Sloane in Hortensia Road, who shared our Roehampton sports ground. The walls of Carlyle Grammar were high and we never mixed with the girls apart from at Roehampton. As we matured, that window of opportunity was welcomed more and more eagerly by the boys from Sloane.

Chapter 11

ALTHOUGH 1962 WAS a difficult year, it was not all gloom and doom. That summer I was to be taken away on holiday by the Children's Country Holidays Fund, a charity that provided seaside or country breaks for inner-city slum children who would otherwise never have the chance of any respite. Originally established in 1884 by the Reverend Samuel Bartlett and his wife as the Children's Fresh Air Mission, the charity is still going strong today, known in its current incarnation as CCHF All About Kids and focusing on children of primary-school age.

I don't know how this opportunity came about: I imagine Lily or Linda must have put my name forward as Linda had been on a CCHF holiday herself, in 1956, when she was nine. I remember waving her off at the coach station with Lily.

Linda had gone to Guildford, a mere forty miles from Notting Hill, though at the time it seemed to us a long way away. I was going somewhere more exotic than Surrey, to another country: Denmark. It was to be a ten-day adventure at the end of the school summer break. We would be staying at an agricultural college about thirty kilometres from the port of

Ejsberg, taking the train from Liverpool Street to Harwich and sailing from there to Denmark. From the day the trip was arranged, I spent hours lying on my bed thinking about the voyage and anticipating the thrill of arriving in a foreign country. I could not begin to imagine what it would be like. With our visits to Coventry, Hull and Liverpool now a distant memory, I could hardly comprehend not being in London, let alone not being in England.

When the time came, Lily removed my school reports and other papers from the cardboard Christmas hamper case and packed it with everything she thought I would need. Before waving me off on the train at Liverpool Street, she managed, as she invariably did whenever taking her leave of me, to find a mysterious patch of dirt on my face that required the spat-on hankie treatment.

Our party comprised about seventy of us waifs and strays of secondary-school age, a small officer corps of university students who had volunteered to supervise us and a couple of adults in overall charge. The crossing to Ejsberg was terrible. An almighty storm had the North Sea heaving and rolling like a fairground ride and practically every one of us was seasick. I abandoned my bunk in the humid cabin below deck where I was supposed to be sleeping. In the crew's quarters nearby, sailors were chatting, eating, drinking and smoking, oblivious of the turbulence. Green with sickness, I eventually found some relief sheltering under blankets on a deckchair in the open air. There I spent the rest of that long night, dozing fitfully.

The dawn of a beautiful summer's day transformed everything. The rising sun revealed a wondrous sight. I gaped, utterly dumbstruck, as Ejsberg harbour came into view under an impossibly clear, piercing blue sky. This was another country where people spoke a different language, watched different television programmes, followed different football teams. It seemed incredible that I should be here.

We were taken by coach to our accommodation at the college, a fine old building in good repair which the students had left neat and tidy for us before departing on their own summer break. We were all given an information pack, a small ring binder full of notepaper on which to record every day of our adventure, and £2 worth of Danish kroner. I was allocated a room with two brothers named Ozorowitz, who were of Eastern European extraction – Russians, I assumed – and who would spend the entire holiday arguing and fighting with one another. I was often called upon to adjudicate, which was something of a thankless task. On one occasion I got into a fight with Alex, the elder Ozorowitz, after I tried to defend his brother.

As we all gathered together, boys and girls from all over London, I spotted a familiar face I hadn't seen for years: Stephen Kirk, the boy who had stolen my precious blue metal box, the one with the cream interior containing my collection of bus tickets and sweet wrappers, when I was six. Although a few years older than me, he hadn't grown very tall and wasn't as big as I might have expected. He still smelled of trouble, though. He was surrounded by a little gang of which he was obviously the leader. He looked in my direction but with no sign of recognition.

I focused my attention on the delights that awaited us, which were being outlined by one of the adults in charge. There were to be organized excursions to the seaside, to the Lego factory and to the Lurpak dairy to see how butter was produced. On most days, however, we would be free to do what we liked: to explore the grounds of the college, to walk in the surrounding farmland and to make use of the extensive sports facilities. The undergraduates would be supervising us and if there were any problems we should go to them in the first instance.

The leader of the students, a young man called Raymond, was introduced to make a little speech to us assembled tykes. Tall, with shoulders even broader than his smile, he was also what Lily would have called 'well-spoken'. Raymond told us that he and his colleagues would be available whenever they were needed, day or night.

The next morning I was enjoying a hearty breakfast and chatting with the eight or nine kids at my table when Stephen Kirk walked by. 'Watch out for him,' I advised my new brothers-in-arms. 'He's trouble.' I told the cautionary tale of how he'd stolen from me (though I failed to mention what I'd kept in my blue tin box, for fear of ridicule).

After breakfast we all wandered outside to play for a few hours before our first trip. A boy approached me and asked me to come with him as he wanted to show me something. He took me to the back of an accommodation block where nobody in the college grounds could see us. There stood Stephen Kirk, surrounded by his acolytes. So much for brothers-in-arms: somebody had told him what I'd said at the breakfast table and he was not at all happy about being called a thief. He grabbed me by the throat. 'You bin talking abaht me, 'ave yer?' I was frightened but also angry – too angry to feign ignorance. I said that he had indeed stolen my tin box, but then struck a conciliatory note, telling him it really didn't matter now.

He ordered me to empty my pockets. I had on me some of

the kroner we'd been given the previous day. Aggrieved to have been labelled a thief, he apparently saw no contradiction in demonstrating that this was exactly what he was. He took the money and said he wanted the rest as well, otherwise he and his gang would 'get me'. I was pushed to the ground as they strolled off, laughing.

What to do? We'd been split into two groups for that day's trip and neither Kirk nor any of his gang was in mine, so I had a little time to consider my options. I could hand over my remaining kroner and spend the whole holiday being terrorized by him. I could fight him to get back what he'd taken already. Or I could report him. I wasn't keen on ten days of misery, and I didn't have a hope of beating him in a fight. The last option was a risky one and would break the great unwritten rule: thou shalt never grass to a teacher. But the students weren't teachers and Raymond had been insistent that any problems should be reported to him.

When we got back to the college, I found my way up to the office where the students were based. Raymond was there. I explained what had happened. He thought for a while, and then asked me to come at 7pm to the main lounge, where the students were responsible for us in the evenings. He told me he would get Stephen Kirk there as well so that the grievance could be sorted out.

As the main lounge was the principal thoroughfare between the TV room and the table tennis and snooker room there were lots of other children milling around when I arrived at seven o'clock. The adult leaders largely left the students to it, so neither of them was around. Stephen Kirk had evidently been summoned as Raymond had promised – he was already standing there, smirking, with some of his gang dotted around him. A flock of girls was in the corner dressing a doll. Raymond sat in a huge armchair, looking cheery and benign. He had four or five of his male colleagues with him. He called Stephen over and asked him if he'd stolen my money. 'Nah, sir,' said Stephen emphatically. There was a pause before Raymond stood up and delivered the most horrendous clump to the side of Kirk's head, knocking him sideways.

Still smiling sweetly, Raymond asked again if he'd stolen my kroner. This time Stephen owned up. Two of the other students grabbed his arms and lifted him up so that his face was level with Raymond's. There followed the kind of battering that may well have been normal in the public schools these students would have attended. We inner-city urchins were used to violence, so it was nothing startling to us, either. It was the methodology that was unusual.

Stephen Kirk was humiliated in front of his peers. He wasn't cut or bleeding but he'd been made to crawl around on all fours, he'd been slapped and pushed repeatedly, held in a head-lock, kicked and finally held upside down by his ankles while the coins were shaken from his trouser pockets.

Raymond gave me back my kroner and, still smiling, told the children present how much he and his friends looked forward to repeating this process every evening if any of us bullied, robbed or interfered in any way with another child. Seven o'clock would be punishment time in the lounge, and anyone called before them should be aware that the ordeal would increase in severity every time they were obliged to administer it.

In an age when disputes were resolved with fists and

corporal punishment was synonymous with discipline in homes and schools across the class divide, this behaviour was less shocking than it sounds from the vantage point of the twenty-first century. And in the case of my nemesis, it certainly did the trick. He never so much as looked at me for the remainder of the holiday and while even at the time I felt his punishment was a bit excessive, I couldn't help thinking it was a shame Raymond hadn't been around when I first met Stephen Kirk.

The remainder of the holiday was a pure Enid Blyton idyll. Just as in the book I'd read and re-read, the sun shone every day, there was plenty of good, fresh food and for once my stomach was full. The Brothers Ozorowitz and I formed our own Famous Three and Lily wrote to me with all the news from West London. She added that she was going into hospital for a couple of days and told me that Linda would meet me off the train on my return. Her letter was sent in reply to mine – on our first day, all the children had been instructed to write home to let their parents know they had arrived safely. Mail travelled faster in those days and the fact that none of our families had phones didn't make them any less anxious to hear how we were faring.

I hadn't told Lily about Stephen Kirk in my letter, and I didn't when I arrived home, for that matter. Neither did I tell her something else that happened on that trip to Denmark. I met a girl. Her name was Edna, and she lived in the Whitechapel Road in the East End. She was pretty in a tomboyish kind of way, with short, curly hair, nice teeth and bright blue eyes. And she told me that she loved me.

I'm not sure how it all started. After the Stephen Kirk

incident, the Russian brothers and I played a lot of football. The Danish boy whose parents ran the college brought in a crowd of his friends and we played Denmark versus England internationals, over and over again.

I was very impressed by how polite and friendly these big, blond Danish boys were and how perfectly they spoke our language. They won practically every match as well, and we had to mix the teams to even up the contest. Edna and some of the other girls would watch us play. I encouraged her interest. Having failed in my attempts to impress Linda Kirby at Bevington (not to mention Jennifer Shepherd and Maureen Langton, two more girls for whom I harboured affections I was too shy to reveal), this was the perfect opportunity to pursue my burgeoning interest in the opposite sex.

By the end of the holiday, I barely saw the Ozorowitzes except on the organized trips and at night in our room. I was devoting almost all of my time to Edna. She was the same age as me, had never known her father and lived with her mum and four siblings in a council flat. Whitechapel was as much of a mystery to me as North Kensington was to her, but we were both well aware that neither side of London, East or West, was anything like the paradise in which we found ourselves now.

Edna and I would go for long walks in the Danish countryside, holding hands, and I would inflict my songs on her, along with my interpretations of recent hits, the lyrics of which I'd memorized from the *Record Song Book*: 'Picture of You' by Joe Brown, 'Hey Baby' by Bruce Chanel, 'Things' by Bobby Darin.

This will sound like a case of the rose-coloured spectacles, but it's absolutely true. On one of our many strolls through the quiet country lanes that weaved through the green fields, we came across an open barn. We took a peek inside. Beside the farm equipment stored there, lit by the sunbeam shining in through the open door, we saw three kittens frolicking in some straw. We were sitting there playing with them when the farmer walked in. Startled, our first thought was that he'd be angry with us for trespassing, but he immediately put us at our ease with his wide smile and fetched some milk so that Edna could pour it into an empty saucer to feed the kittens.

We explained where we came from. He knew the college well and was pleased that it was being used to show children from London the glories of the Danish countryside. He told us how much respect the Danes had for the British. This was only seventeen years after the end of the Second World War and its horrors were still fresh in the minds of adults across Europe. He asked us if we were hungry. We politely demurred but he insisted we followed him into the farmhouse, where Edna and I were astonished to find a sturdy kitchen table groaning with ham, cheese, pickles, pies, herrings and a freshly baked loaf. His wife had prepared lunch for her sons, who worked on the farm, but was pleased to welcome two unexpected guests. The warm breeze fluttered through the open window as we feasted.

It was on one of these country walks that Edna and I kissed, and that's when she told me she loved me. Addresses were exchanged and promises made to write and meet again; promises that were never kept.

The voyage back from Esjberg seemed just as choppy as the incoming one, but I reckoned I knew now the best way to ride the waves – al fresco, huddled under my blankets and gazing at the stars – and passed on this seafaring tip to the Ozorowitzes. Since the girls and boys were, of course, in

Left: My mother Lily as a teenager, working for the Co-op in Liverpool.

Bottom left: My mother in the back yard of 107 Southam Street in the early fifties.

Bottom right: Linda and me celebrating the Coronation in 1953.

Roger Mayne's photograph of
Clarendon Crescent, taken in
1957, a few streets away from
Southam Street.

Right: On the beach at New Brighton during our trip to Liverpool.

Left: With Lily in our matching blazers at Mr and Mrs Ireland's in Liverpool.

Left: With Linda in the toy car that had belonged to the Irelands' grown-up son.

Below: A Southam Street scene as captured by Roger Mayne.

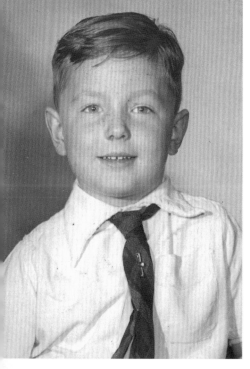

Above: Wornington Road Infants' School, 1955.

Below: Bevington Primary School, c. 1958.

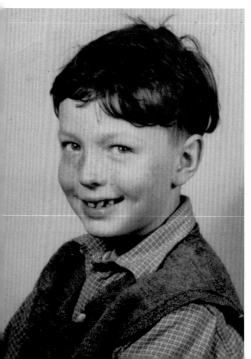

Above: One of Mayne's most memorable photographs of Southam Street in 1956.

Right: My teacher at Bevington, Mrs Leadsford, on the right, together with Mrs Gryf.

Above: Christmas 1968 at the night-shift Christmas dinner in Barnes Postmen's Delivery Office. My daughter Emma was born on Christmas Eve, a week after this photograph was taken.

Below: Wedding line-up, 1968. From left: Andrew Wiltshire, me, Judy, Linda, Judy's grandmother and our daughter, Natalie.

separate sleeping quarters I couldn't sing to Edna (much to her relief, no doubt). So instead the brothers and I spent a while talking and laughing with the crew below deck before retiring to our deckchairs for the night.

When I stepped off the train from Harwich at Liverpool Street the following day, Linda was waiting for me. She wanted to know why every kid except me was carrying a Lego set. I confirmed that we had visited the factory and yes, we had all been given a box of Lego as a present when we left. I was obliged to confess that I'd traded mine with a sailor on the ship – for forty Senior Service untipped.

~

If returning to unlovely North Kensington and the dreaded autumn term at Sloane was dispiriting after the glories of Denmark, I had the new football season to cheer me up. In 1962–63, QPR decided to relocate to the larger White City Stadium, and I was among the thousands of supporters who flocked there on a wet Wednesday evening in anticipation of their first match at their new home. It was cancelled due to a waterlogged pitch – an outcome that set a trend for that ambitious, if ultimately disastrous move. Cheering on the team amid a crowd of 4,000 at cosy Loftus Road was exciting; with those 4,000 dedicated souls transplanted to an Olympic-sized, 70,000-capacity stadium it was like crying in the wilderness. Rangers moved back to their old ground at the end of the season.

And I had missed Lily and Linda, of course. I'd arrived home to find them in a state of high excitement: Lily had finally prepared her advertisement for the lonely hearts column of the *Kensington Post*. For one reason or another Lily hadn't got round to it all year. But now, with Linda's help, the advert had been placed, pared down to its shortest possible form because it had to be paid for by the word. I never actually saw it, but it should have read something like this: 'Divorced woman, early forties, petite, dark-haired, 5ft tall, seeks dependable man of similar age or older for companionship. Good sense of humour essential.'

Lily received five replies, which she and Linda sifted and inspected as if they were precious vellum scrolls. The one that most appealed to Lily was from Ron, a builder from Romford, who'd picked up the *Kensington Post* while working in the area. Lily liked that. It chimed with her interest in what was written in the stars. She felt that destiny was bringing her and Ron together.

Ron's letter explained that he was divorced, his wife having left and taken their two children with her. He'd kept the family house and was a man of means; he was keen to enjoy Lily's company; he had a car and he could drive over to meet her as soon as she liked. He had provided his telephone number. This man not only had his own house and car, he had a telephone as well. We were impressed. We didn't, however, have a clue where Romford was. Somewhere near Southend, Lily thought. After writing back to tell him more about her situation, she walked to a telephone kiosk one evening with Linda to speak to him directly. The conversation went well and arrangements were made for a meeting. There followed at least two cinema dates before he was allowed to visit 6 Walmer Road.

Lily was rejuvenated. The money was found for a perm. She

rarely visited a hairdresser, usually styling her collar-length hair herself with grips and clips and curlers. Mostly it remained hidden under her turban anyway. Now the turban came off more often and the pink Bri-nylon overall she'd taken to wearing was consigned to working hours only.

If things worked out with Ron, there was a chance of escaping all the drudgery and poverty. She certainly seemed to like him, and when he eventually came to meet us, we could see why. He was very personable: about fifty, of medium height with a wiry frame and a shock of greying hair. There were deep lines on his face, tanned by constant exposure to the elements. His two daughters, he told us, were teenagers, the younger one the same age as Linda.

Lily revealed that Ron was appalled by the conditions we lived in. Although we weren't that over the moon about them ourselves, Linda and I took offence. We felt this smacked of snobbery. Lily assured us that Ron wasn't looking down on us; he was just appalled by what we had to put up with and wanted to make our lives more comfortable. Perhaps we were being unfair in privately labelling him 'flash', but it had to be said that he was for ever going on about his lovely house, his car and how successful his business was. Although we didn't tell Lily what we thought about him, she sensed we weren't enthusiastic.

Poor Ron. I don't think we were receptive to being captivated by him. Linda and Jimmy Carter took against him early on and I would have been sceptical about any man courting Lily. However, we didn't have to see Ron very often, Lily loved being taken out and it was good to see her happy. The relationship flourished throughout the latter part of 1962 and Lily, Linda, Jimmy and I were all invited to Ron's house to spend Christmas with him and his fifteen-year-old daughter, Sheila. We were to stay from Christmas Eve until Boxing Day, travelling by bus and train to Romford station, where Ron would pick us up in his Vauxhall Velox.

It had been decided that Ron would supply the food if Lily agreed to cook it. This arrangement worried Linda, given Lily's limitations in the culinary arts. Her present from Lily that Christmas was to be a cookery book, already ordered from Maynard's and unwrapped by Linda a few weeks before the day itself. The plan was for Linda to take this with her to Romford and help Lily to prepare a Christmas feast that would cement the relationship.

Ron's house was everything he'd led us to expect. It was on a smart new estate in Harold Hill, rather than Romford itself: a large four-bedroomed, detached bungalow with a substantial lounge separated from the well-equipped kitchen by a glass partition. Lily and Linda were to have one bedroom and I was to share with Jimmy, with Ron and Sheila occupying the other two.

Jimmy, with his six siblings, was used to big family gatherings at Christmas (although he'd never spent one anywhere this spacious). For us, though, it was a novel and exciting experience. Christmas Eve went well. Lily was pleased to be with Ron, Linda was pleased because Jimmy was there and I was – well, I was enjoying what promised to be a proper Christmas. And I liked having Jimmy around. His cheeky good humour and his fags were dispensed generously. He didn't like Ron and Ron didn't like him, that much was obvious, but with the help of a few beers the two of them mellowed and the prospects for the next day looked good.

Ron's daughter, Sheila, may have been the same age as Linda but she lacked her maturity. That was hardly surprising, considering how fast Linda had had to grow up. In fairness, Sheila was a normal fifteen-year-old whereas Linda was already more of a woman than a girl. Blonde and annoyingly coquettish, Sheila seemed to me to consider herself the bee's knees. I caught her eye as she glanced meaningfully at me on several occasions that evening, whereupon I blushed and she smiled.

Jimmy and I got up the next morning to a fried breakfast prepared by Lily and Linda. Ron was very satisfied. He rather tactlessly told us what a great cook his wife had been and how important good food was to a man's happiness. He'd already presented Lily with a challenge. When we arrived the previous day, he had shown her the Christmas fare he'd provided. For Christmas dinner there was a goose, complete with head and feathers and so fresh it might have flown into the kitchen that afternoon.

Lily and Linda had been conferring in their room during the night. Linda was having cookery lessons at school but she knew nothing about how to cook a goose. Lily had never seen a goose before, let alone cooked one, but she could handle a chicken and reasoned that it couldn't be all that different. The main problem was the preparation – how to chop the head off, pluck the bird and remove the innards. When this was mentioned in the general chit-chat over breakfast, Ron grew imperious.

He couldn't understand how anyone could live as long as Lily without tasting goose. His family always had goose at Christmas and this was the most expensive one he'd ever purchased. It was clear that, to match up to the departed Mrs Ron, not only must Lily cook this bird, she must cook it to perfection.

Ron was going to the pub to have a few pints with his friends and would return shortly after 2pm when dinner needed to be on the table so that it could be finished as the Queen's Speech came on the telly. Despite being under-age, Jimmy was invited to go to the pub with him. I was left trying to read in the lounge while Sheila flitted around. Every time I looked up from my book she'd be staring at me disconcertingly, quickly looking away as our eyes met.

The tension on the other side of the glass partition was palpable. Linda had scoured her cookbook but while it had much to commend it and offered a wealth of advice on baking a cake, it had nothing on gutting a goose. Ron had chopped the head off before going out, but defeathering it took the two women ages. Poor Lily wasn't to know that geese are notoriously difficult and time-consuming to pluck. This was a job that should have been done in advance – and preferably outside. Evidently Ron didn't know this, either, never having been obliged to participate in the cooking of his Christmas dinners in the past.

As so often, I made a bad situation worse by announcing pompously that I couldn't possibly be expected to eat the poor bird and that although I'd never tasted goose, I just knew I wouldn't like it. I could hear Lily speaking more loudly and sounding more Liverpudlian as the clock ticked away.

By the time Ron and Jimmy returned, Linda had laid the table and the dinner appeared to be cooking nicely. Lily confirmed that it would be on the table at 2.15pm. Ron had sunk a few pints which made him a little over-jolly. He lit the open log fire and went to sit at the head of the table, ready to carve. Suddenly, thick smoke began billowing out of the oven. The copious goose fat had caught fire. The oven door was pulled open and the goose rescued from the flames. Ron called Lily a stupid woman, which was a big mistake. Lily might have been small, she might have had a weak heart, but she could stand up for herself. 'Who are you calling stupid?' she demanded.

I buried my head in my book as the recriminations flew. As always, Linda rushed to defend her mother while Jimmy went outside for a fag. Eventually Ron calmed down, Lily rescued what she could of the goose and we sat down to dinner. As always, Lily's vegetables were overcooked but her roast potatoes were perfect. The goose tasted like lumps of congealed, burned fat and when we got round to the Christmas pudding, as Ron was heard to mutter, the custard was lumpy.

If we'd had any means of getting home we'd have left immediately. Lily was in high dudgeon, sitting all afternoon with her arm around me. She never normally did that. It must have been a defence mechanism, designed consciously or subconsciously to show Ron that to her, he was not the most important male in that house. I was at an age when such displays of motherly affection could be acutely embarrassing and Lily had never had to cuddle me to let me know she loved me. But unusual though it was, it was somehow appropriate to the circumstances on that tense Christmas afternoon in Harold Hill. Ron dozed off, as did Jimmy. Linda and Sheila cleared up. We were trapped overnight until Boxing Day, when Ron drove us to the station. We never saw him again.

Something else happened that Christmas that I didn't tell Lily, Linda or Ron about. After Jimmy and I went to bed that night, a note was pushed under the door. It read: 'Dear Alan, I hope you've enjoyed your time with me. I like you very, very much. My room is opposite. I'd love it if you came to see me. Love Sheila xxx.'

Jimmy read it over my shoulder. He laughed so much I thought he would choke. I just sat there bemused, flattered that Sheila was attracted to me but with no intention whatsoever of crossing the hall to experience whatever delights lay behind that door. I turned out the light and, as Jimmy continued to chuckle away quietly, drifted off to sleep. I woke up in the night. Although it was pitch-black I soon ascertained that Jimmy wasn't on his side of the double bed we were sharing. Perhaps he'd just gone to the toilet but he didn't come back in the ten minutes it took me to fall asleep again. I'm not suggesting that he padded over the hall to Sheila's room, but then again, I can't be sure that he didn't.

Chapter 12

IT CANNOT HAVE been long after that disastrous Christmas that Linda decided to sit me down and explain the facts of life. I was twelve and Lily was in hospital. Linda and I were alone in the back room of Walmer Road, me in the little armchair, Linda perched on the kitchen chair. 'Do you know how babies are made?' she asked. I suspect that Lily had put her up to this. Too embarrassed to tell me herself, she'd subcontracted the task to Linda. Or, knowing my sister, Linda had volunteered.

I can see with hindsight that Lily was worried about me reaching puberty without knowing the things a father was meant to pass on to his son. I recall how, when I visited her in hospital and sat by her bed with my hands out of sight resting on my knees, she'd say: 'What are you doing down there?' As I blushed and remonstrated with her, she'd justify her concern by elaborating, 'I don't want you playing with yourself.' Lily had learned the Ten Commandments off by heart when she was at school and she was fond of quoting all ten to us. 'Thou shalt not play with thyself' had lately become the eleventh.

'Do you know how babies are made?' I was confident I had the answer to Linda's question. It had all fallen into place a couple of years earlier, when I'd watched the wedding of Princess Margaret to Anthony Armstrong Jones on television. Up until then, I'd never been able to figure out why a woman could not have babies before she was married. During the Royal Wedding service, after the couple were pronounced man and wife, the cameras had focused on the altar while the bride and groom went somewhere with the Archbishop of Canterbury, out of sight of the congregation and the cameras.

It came to me in a flash that this must be the point at which a bride was injected to enable her to have babies. It all made sense. Princess Margaret had been injected and the following year she'd had a child.

I relayed this information to Linda with a knowing smile, proud that I'd worked this out all by myself, and sat back awaiting confirmation of my theory. Linda looked carefully at me to see if I was joking. When she realized I was not, she dismissed my theory disparagingly, pointing out that one of our cousins who'd had a baby had not been married. Then she told me exactly how babies were made.

I listened with mounting horror. How could a man do that to a woman? It was so brutal and indelicate. If the woman I married wanted a baby, I would have to make sure the wicked deed was performed swiftly and sensitively, inflicting what I had no doubt would be my unwelcome attentions on her for as short a time as possible – in the dark. A simple injection seemed, to my twelve-year-old self, to be preferable in every respect.

It was also early in 1963 that Lily saved my life. In my second year at Sloane, I was beginning to hate school less. The indignity of being a 'one-er' was over, I was adjusting to the grammar-school environment and had started to enjoy the lessons that interested me and not to bother too much about those that didn't. I did what little homework we were given on time and received moderately good reports. I'd picked up a knack for making myself anonymous, keeping my head down, staying quiet, avoiding trouble.

My favourite subject was English, taught at that time by Mr Smith. He must have been in his late twenties but dressed as if he were much older. Unlike the other young teachers – Mr Bollard, for example, who drove a two-seater sports car and wore sunglasses – Mr Smith could have been born in brogues and turn-ups. His face, beneath a fringe of severely cut fair hair, bore a permanent expression of anxiety. Small and shaped like a bowling pin, he walked with tiny steps, as if his shoelaces were tied together. We were constantly expecting him to topple over any minute. A committed Christian, he also taught Religious Education, a role that did not always sit easily with the fierce temper he tried, but often failed, to suppress. He was once seen hitting a boy over the head with a rolled-up newspaper yelling: 'Christ is love, you little bastard!'

What I most admired about Mr Smith was that he spent a part of every single RE lesson railing against the evils of apartheid in South Africa, a regime that was far from universally decried in the early 1960s. His moral outrage was infectious and while he never converted me to Christianity, he converted me, and, I suspect, many other boys, to the anti-apartheid cause. My limited – and obviously indirect – experience of what people in West London had to suffer merely because of the colour of their skin was troubling enough. The idea that racism could be enshrined in law was truly shocking.

Mr Smith had been given permission to put on a school play to be staged on two evenings in January 1963. It was a production of *Emil and the Detectives*, Erich Kästner's children's adventure set in 1920s Berlin. I was cast as one of the gang of detectives and had about four short lines to learn. I had practised them throughout our Christmas sojourn in Romford and felt confident of giving a masterly performance. Lily couldn't come to the play but Linda dragged Jimmy Carter along on the first night. I travelled home with them afterwards, my coat covering the blue and white matelot shirt I'd worn on stage and my face still smeared with dirt to reflect my character as a street urchin who had been recruited to Emil's cause.

The following evening, a Friday, the school hall was packed for our final triumphant performance. As I made my way home alone afterwards, I began to feel unwell. Lily and Linda were already asleep by the time I got in. I collapsed on to my bed and endured a night of delirium. Lily found me sweating and shivering the next morning and transferred me to her big double bed while she pondered what to do.

Dr Tanner had a Saturday morning surgery and Lily decided that instead of waiting for a home visit that afternoon, I must be taken to see her straight away. Unable to stand unaided, I wanted to stay in bed and refused to budge.

Lily grew agitated, shouting at me to get up and finally recruiting Linda to help fling the covers back, drag me to my feet and into some clothes and half-carry me out of the house.

It was about three quarters of a mile from our house to Dr Tanner's surgery. At twelve, I was already taller than Lily and Linda and they struggled, slinging one of my arms round each of their necks, to take my weight and haul me along the pavement. By the time we arrived I looked so ill that the receptionist ushered me straight in to see Dr Tanner, who immediately called an ambulance to rush me to St Charles' Hospital.

It turned out I had acute appendicitis. I went from ambulance to operating theatre in ten minutes to have my appendix removed. I was told later that if there had been any delay it would have burst and I'd have died from peritonitis. It was only thanks to Lily that I didn't. Had she waited for the doctor to visit I wouldn't have been here to tell the tale.

I thoroughly enjoyed my fortnight on the large Nightingale Ward at St Charles' among men of all ages, including a few who seemed to be more or less permanent residents, though they were far from bedridden. There was a communal room with a TV where we could go whenever we liked during the day and every bed had its own radio set on which I could pick up the three BBC stations I was used to. I was able to read as much as I wanted to and was brought three substantial meals every day. My hospital bed was much more comfortable than my own, with clean bed linen and warm blankets.

Visiting was tightly restricted to half an hour every weekday evening, an hour on Saturdays and none at all on Sundays. Lily came on all six days she was allowed, occasionally with Linda and Jimmy. We went through the familiar ritual, usually played out around Lily's hospital bed rather than mine, of trying to find things to say to fill in the time. The long silences were punctuated by Lily barking in a loud voice: 'What are you doing down there?' every time one of my hands slipped under the covers.

I was the only child on the ward and the nurses and my

fellow patients made a great fuss of me. One young nurse in particular commanded my devotion. She was French and the loveliest woman I had ever seen. She worked nights and was responsible for bringing my Ovaltine, checking I had removed the earpieces from my radio set and that my pillows were plumped and positioned ready for sleep.

I'm not sure if the adult patients were given the same treatment. In the more regimented NHS of the time, they might well have been. For me, it was the highlight of the day. The French nurse would chat and smile and cast her tender spell. As she bent over me to straighten the bed covers, I would catch a whiff of her perfume. She made her rounds at about 9pm and one evening she found me listening to a brilliant science-fiction play on the Home Service, which was only halfway through. She agreed that I could continue to listen, provided I kept my earpieces out of sight by putting the sheet over my head. The glorious experience of listening to a radio play in the dark was matched only by the warm sense of complicity with the woman I'd fallen for.

It was through those little plug-in earpieces on the Nightingale Ward that I first heard 'Please Please Me' by the Beatles. The Fab Four themselves weren't new to me – 'Love Me Do', their first single, had been a minor hit the previous year and I'd seen a photograph of them in a music magazine to which Linda subscribed. We liked the fact they came from Lily's home town and noticed that the drummer had a grey streak in his hair, which seemed to disappear as Ringo's fame grew.

Linda never went beyond this early interest but for me hearing 'Please Please Me' on that hospital radio began a passion I feel just as strongly fifty years on. It is difficult to describe the impact the Beatles had on me, a young boy approaching puberty who had always been enthralled by pop music. It's no exaggeration to say that they became one of the most important elements of my life. Their songs came soaring out of the sea of mediocrity and imitation that was British popular music at the time, leaving our other home-grown rock stars, all second-rate replicas of US artists, floundering.

They would all succumb, one by one, to the Beatles' influence – Marty Wilde, Adam Faith, Billy Fury and eventually even Cliff. Their Elvis Presley pompadours were de-greased and cut in the new style – the moptop. From slicked-back hair to floppy locks; from a music culture driven by middle-aged men in Tin Pan Alley to something fresh and new introduced by four young Liverpudlians who wrote their own songs. Once, as I sat on a number 11 bus on my way to school, I overheard a conversation between the bus conductor and some adult passengers on the conspiracy theory of the moment: those two kids in the Beatles couldn't possibly have written those songs. Unable to deny their talent, they doubted its source. John and Paul had to be a front for accomplished older musicians and songwriters. I burned with resentment at the outrage of the old misappropriating something that belonged to the young. At least, that was how it looked from my side of the generation gap.

Happy as I was in my cosy hospital bed that January listening to 'Please Please Me', I didn't realize quite how fortunate I was to be there at that precise moment. The outside world to which I would shortly return was in the grip of the bleakest, coldest winter since the seventeenth century.

~

Apart from a brief reappearance at Sloane after Christmas the appendicitis was responsible for me beginning 1963 as I'd begun the previous year – off school. The Big Freeze made the house even colder than usual and I'd stay in bed, dressed in layers of threadbare jumpers and buried under as many old coats as I could muster, until lunchtime, when Lily came home between jobs to see how I was. After two weeks in hospital, I had more or less fully recovered from the operation but I cultivated an air of fragility to draw out my freedom from school for as long as possible.

My main task during the freeze was to fetch coal in Lily's old pram. Those in better houses and with greater resources had their coal delivered, often in bulk to last the entire winter. While some coal merchants had acquired trucks by this time, most still used a horse and cart, lifting the sacks on to their backs and tipping them into the coal cellars through a manhole cut into the pavement.

Their horses vied with those of the totters for space at the water troughs, great stone structures placed on convenient corners by animal welfare charities. Huge, magnificent carthorses were also a regular sight outside the Earl of Warwick and the Latimer Arms, patiently chomping from a nosebag full of hay while their masters sank a couple of pints at lunchtime.

That winter it was difficult for Lily to follow the route of the coal trucks, as was her custom, to pick up the precious lumps that fell on to the pavement or into the road. She and I tried it once or twice but the weather was appalling, with ice and snow making all the surfaces perilous to walk on. Besides which, with the hours she was working, Lily didn't have the time to scavenge for coal.

Our two-bar electric heater in the front room had to be used as sparingly as possible because of the amount of electricity it consumed. When it was switched on, the little wheel in the middle of the meter accelerated to an alarming whizz and its appetite for coins became insatiable. So we relied on the coal fire in the back room, which also benefited from the heat generated by the cooker. During the winter we spent nearly all our time there and the front room was rarely occupied.

Linda was spending less and less time at home anyway. I had come out of hospital to find she'd dumped Jimmy Carter after learning from his father that on Saturday nights, once he'd bid her goodnight at around 10pm, he'd head for Soho. There he was frequenting the dives and strip joints, taking purple hearts (the fairly innocuous but notorious recreational drug of choice in the early 1960s) and mixing with shady characters of both genders. In the post-Jimmy period, Linda and her best friend, the slim and attractive Cheryl Roberts, had become Mods and took to going out with a bunch of like-minded friends most evenings.

As there seemed to be a rule that Mods didn't fetch coal, the job devolved to me. I had to queue outside the coal merchants', about ten minutes' walk from Walmer Road, with my battered pram every day except Sundays, when it was shut, because our budget didn't stretch to buying it in anything other than small quantities. We never had supplies of anything in reserve, let alone coal. I would wrap up as warmly as I could and try to time my visits to be near the front of the queue when the merchant opened after lunch.

He'd spend his mornings delivering and the afternoons dispensing, like a GP holding surgeries and then making home visits, only in reverse. My task would have been onerous once a week in that terrible weather; as a daily chore it was debilitating, particularly as Lily insisted that on every occasion I must ask if we could have our coal on tick. In a normal winter, Lily wouldn't light the fire until the evening, particularly if nobody was in. But during the Big Freeze, and with me at home, she was having to spend far more on coal than she could afford.

The merchant was a small man with no teeth. Every exposed part of his body was ingrained with dust from the product he traded in. His huge and imposing wife helped to shovel the coal into sacks and weigh it on a set of rusty old scales. Both of them were clear: there would be no credit. There was already a roughly chalked sign on the wall to that effect, as I explained to Lily, to no avail. She insisted that I made the attempt regardless. Her theory was that the more often I asked, the more I would wear them down and the more likely they would be to concede a credit arrangement. Thankfully, I was at least always able to pay when I was knocked back. Lily would give me the few shillings I needed for the single bag that would see us through to the next day, with a few lumps set aside for Sundays. Having tried and failed several times to get credit and being acutely embarrassed in the process, I took the unusual step of ignoring Lily's instructions.

I'd wheel the pram back through the treacherous streets, keeping an eye out for pieces of orphaned coal on the ground. If I found any I'd force them into the bulging sack, taking care to ensure that none of my precious cargo was spilled for others to scavenge.

The snow and ice lasted from December to March, and that January proved to be the coldest month of the twentieth century. There was no football so a pools panel had to be established to predict the results, thus ensuring that this great Saturday evening institution continued uninterrupted. The thaw had arrived before Dr Tanner considered me fit to return to school, and by the time I did I was even further behind.

At school a majority of the boys were Chelsea supporters – Stamford Bridge, the club's ground, was barely 500 yards from Sloane. The contempt I attracted for supporting QPR instilled a lifelong antipathy to Chelsea and I tended to avoid Stamford Bridge but in the late spring of 1963, when they were vying for promotion from the Second Division with Stoke City, I made an exception. Chelsea were due to play Stoke at home on Lily's birthday, 11 May – and the visitors would be fielding the legendary Stanley Matthews on the right wing. I was determined to get there to see the man who, as far as I was concerned, was the greatest footballer who ever lived. As usual, I went alone. Unfortunately, another 66,198 people went as well, and I was very lucky indeed not to have been crushed to death. Incredibly, in spite of periodic tragedies at soccer stadia in Britain and around the world, the potential perils of having vast numbers of supporters crammed into football grounds were not addressed in any significant way until the terrible Hillsborough disaster of 1989 led belatedly to the introduction of proper safety measures and all-seater stadia.

At Stamford Bridge in 1963, my main concern was that I wouldn't be able to see any of the action. Squashed against the big men around me I had only one small area of the pitch within my vision. Happily, it turned out to be the particular patch of grass patrolled by the great Matthews during the first half. He was forty-seven years of age by then and had been brought into the Stoke side for his crowd-pulling ability rather than his fading skills. The Chelsea left back, Ken Shellito, seemed frightened of Stanley's venerable status – in truth, I think nobody wanted the dubious honour of accidentally injuring him and putting an end to his long and illustrious career – and as a result, I saw the famous Matthews body swerve take him past the Chelsea defender two or three times. In the second half I saw nothing of Stanley Matthews and not much of anything else. Stoke won 1–0 and I struggled to get out of Stamford Bridge in one piece.

Six days later, I celebrated my thirteenth birthday. In the space of a week, I had become a teenager and Lily had turned forty-two – the age at which both her mother and her grand-mother had died.

Chapter 13

I DON'T REMEMBER HIS name, if I ever knew it. He'd come to our house with a crowd of Linda's friends when Lily was in hospital for a few days of tests.

He was older than my sister, about nineteen, and the most impeccably dressed of all her friends. Indeed, I'd never seen anyone dressed like him. This was no apprentice Mod, like Linda and Cheryl: he was the genuine article.

It was a Sunday afternoon and I'd just got back from my milk round. Whisper it softly, but I suspect my sister had been at an all-night party. She'd borrowed some of my precious records to take with her. By now, I'd discovered Chuck Berry, Bo Diddley and Muddy Waters on the Pye International label. There was a record shop in Roehampton, close to our school sports ground, which sold less mainstream music unavailable on the high street. My milk-round money would be spent on these exotic rarities with their distinctive red and yellow labels. The Beatles and the Rolling Stones had sparked interest in the middle-aged, black American artists whose songs were now being recorded by white English boys and would soon be sold back to American kids during the Beatles-led 'British invasion' of the US charts.

At Sloane, among those of us who were 'aware', a form of oneupmanship developed based on who could discover the most obscure American blues artist nobody else had heard of. Thus a liking for Howlin' Wolf would be countered by John Lee Hooker, only to be trumped by another boy with Blind Lemon Jefferson.

Chuck and Bo and Muddy were soon old hat, although my fondness for Chuck Berry was enduring, enhanced by the fact that he was serving a sentence in a US penitentiary for smuggling a girl across the state border. I had no idea what this meant (which was, of course, that the girl was under the age of consent in her own state and had been taken to a neighbouring state where it was lower), but it sounded romantic and rebellious and added to Chuck's allure.

When I arrived home that Sunday lunchtime, Linda, her friend Cheryl and six or seven others were draped around our small front room drinking tea, listening to records on the Dansette and recovering from their party night. Linda insisted on introducing them all to 'my little brother' and they talked to me in the patronizing tone so often adopted by adolescents to address those younger than themselves. Linda and her girl-friends wore skirts cut above the knee and their hair was in transition from beehive to bob. The lads wore Ben Sherman shirts and jeans, apart from the Real Mod. He was exquisitely turned out in a pale grey suit and white shirt with little silver cufflinks. His hair was short but thick on top with a high part-ing and neat fringe. His Italian shoes were polished to perfection.

The Real Mod was interested to learn that the Pye International records Linda had taken to the party were mine.

Following me out to the back room (from which Linda had tried to keep her friends away), he talked to me normally, as if I were his equal.

I was annoyed to discover that Linda hadn't brought my records back with her. The Real Mod said he would take me in his car (in which they'd all arrived, packed together like a box of dates) to pick them up.

So it was that we left Linda and her friends lounging at Walmer Road and journeyed a few miles across West London to Kilburn, where the party had been held, to retrieve my precious 45s. My new hero obviously worked and earned. This was only the second or third time I had ever been in a car but I knew a lot about them, not least from my old collection of Matchbox toys. His was a 1950s Cortina with a bench seat and column gear change.

We talked all the way there. The Real Mod told me how much he liked Chuck Berry and Bo Diddley and asked if I'd heard Sonny Boy Williamson or Lead Belly, Elmore James or Mose Allison, providing me with valuable ammunition in the battle to be top dog in the musical knowledge stakes at school. He told me about the clubs he went to and the bands he heard. Best of all, he passed on his own maxim: the philosophy, in a nutshell, of the West London Mod. 'You may be poor, but don't show poor.' These were kids from the slums, like me. Infatuated with Italian style, they saw no reason why they couldn't match it. Scooters were cheap to buy and run; the clothes could be expensive but if you saved and bought wisely, you could look good with fewer clothes of better quality. Decent second-hand suits and ties could be picked up in the Portobello Road or Shepherd's Bush market.

At the Kilburn party venue the Real Mod left me in the car and went in to collect my records, returning with each one neatly replaced in its paper sleeve. He assured me he'd wiped them carefully with a tea towel and he was so meticulous about everything that I believed him. On the way home I listened as he relayed sacred advice about the beauty of a tonic suit with five-button cuffs and six-inch vents; how cufflinks must only be worn on shirts with double cuffs, never in single cuffs; how important it was to wear long socks so that you didn't show acres of bare shin between sock and trouser leg when you sat down.

Although he'd progressed to a car, the Real Mod still revered the scooter and spoke of the joy of riding a Vespa through London on a sunny day, wearing a Fred Perry with Levi Sta-Prest trousers (never, never, jeans, which were a nasty American garment worn by greasy Rockers) and a pair of brown Hush Puppies.

I soaked it all up, every word. Here was a role model with whom I could identify: a young man from the slums who dressed with a style and confidence that personified his attitude. By the time he dropped me back at Walmer Road, the others had dispersed and Linda had gone with Cheryl back to her home in Sutton Dwellings. I sat alone in the front room pondering a new approach to life: 'You may be poor, but don't show poor.'

I'd known since primary school I wouldn't be a draughts-man. I might be a musician. I would certainly be a Mod.

～

While Linda continued to take care of me during Lily's spells in hospital, I needed less and less looking after as I got older. With Tony Cox in a different class from me at school, and our interests diverging outside it, we had completely grown apart by this time. Instead I'd become friendly with Colin James, a classmate who lived in Elthiron Road in Parsons Green. Colin came from a middle-class home but was doing his damnedest to rebel against his background. His father, who was a senior officer with Hammersmith and Fulham Council, would plead with me to exert a calming influence on his errant son.

The courtesy Lily had instilled in me often gave the parents of my friends (and later my girlfriends) the mistaken impression that I was more sensible and virtuous than I was. In truth, I didn't have a great deal to rebel against, but I had certainly emerged from my shell and Linda didn't have to worry that I was moping around at home on my own when she was out.

Colin badly wanted to be so many things he wasn't. For a start, he wanted to be a tough street kid. It was becoming fashionable to be working class. On the London stage, aristocratic drawing rooms were giving way to kitchen-sink dramas as the spotlight was turned towards ordinary lives. On television, politicians were being lampooned and the workings of the Establishment held up for public scrutiny by *That Was The Week that Was*, which brought satire to viewers for the first time. The city was starting to swing and the cultural explosion of the 1960s was catapulting talented role models from humble backgrounds into the limelight. From East London came the photographer David Bailey and the actor Terence Stamp, the son of a Thames tugboat captain. West London produced the hairdresser Vidal Sassoon, scion of an immigrant family and pioneer of the iconic geometric cut.

At thirteen, none of this registered with me and I doubt it did with Colin, either. But in keeping with the spirit of the times, he resented the stable, middle-class lifestyle his mother and father had provided and his resentment seemed to increase with every dirt-poor blues artist he discovered. Worst of all, try as he might, he found it impossible to upset his kind and loving parents. When he grew his hair his mother said it looked 'nice'. When he informed his father that he and I (aged fourteen and thirteen respectively) would be hitchhiking around the south coast that summer, his dad merely offered to give us a lift to the station. He told both parents of our intention to spend Saturday night in Soho and they were unworried, saying only that we should be home by midnight. I could stay over and Mrs James would leave out a couple of glasses of milk and some biscuits in the kitchen for us when we got in. The more Colin attempted to rebel, the less inclined his parents seemed to give him a cause.

Colin longed to emulate his heroes, the Rolling Stones, but had no ear for music. There were three boys in our year at Sloane who could play the guitar, and he wasn't one of them. As well as myself, there was Paul Swinson, whose father wrote comic songs for the Parlophone label, recorded by the likes of Peter Sellers, and a tall lad whose Mod stylishness was rather spoiled by Hank Marvin-type horn-rimmed spectacles. His name was Stephen Hackett, or Steve Hackett, as he was better known later, when he became famous as a guitarist with Genesis and GTR.

Stephen hung out with the toughest kid in our year at

Sloane, Terry Lawrence. Colin wanted to hang out with him too, but Terry considered him a wimp, unworthy of his patronage. Colin reacted by constantly seeking fights and improving with practice. He was tall and well built, but his major asset was his sheer bravado. He enjoyed walking on the wild side. If we were heading for somewhere in Fulham, for instance, and saw a crowd of rough-looking kids horsing around way off our route, he'd insist that we change direction in order to walk through the middle of them looking 'hard'. Nine times out of ten it would be OK and our chutzpah would carry us through. As for the tenth time ... well, we were very fast runners.

The fact that Colin could neither sing nor play any instrument didn't deter me from making him bass guitarist in my band, the Vampires. The line-up was me on my Spanish guitar, Jimmy Robb, a Sloane pupil who was small, blond and good-looking, on drums (or, to be accurate, on Tupperware bowls) and Colin, thumping away on an old acoustic guitar to which I'd affixed four bass E-strings. We played in the cellar retreat Colin's parents had kindly put at the exclusive disposal of their eldest son and his friends.

Those friends included two from the hitherto alien species commonly known as girls. Yvonne Stacey and Pauline Bright were in the corresponding year at Carlyle, the girls' grammar next door to Sloane. They were also Colin's neighbours. Pauline lived almost opposite him in Elthiron Road and Yvonne in a huge house overlooking Waltham Green.

The concept of having girls as friends was novel to me. Although Carol Smith had been in our little Bevington gang in the days when I knocked around with Tony Cox, she had been such a tomboy that we never really thought of her as a member of the opposite sex. Now that I was a teenager, girls had become more interesting – and more frightening. After my trysts with Edna in Denmark the previous year my shyness had dissipated but the first time I went round to Colin's house and found two girls in his cellar, it still came as a bit of a shock.

Colin introduced this duo – both dressed in identical slacks (as they used to be called), royal blue cotton and polyester stretched tight by stirrups at the ankle that had to be secured under the arch of each foot – as his friends. I think they'd all been to primary school together, but unlike Carol Smith, Yvonne and Pauline could hardly have been described as tomboys. We played records on the sleek, polished wood gramophone that was another excellent feature of this refuge. As was the cushioned seating area that Colin had arranged on the floor against the rear wall and under the stairs, out of the line of vision of any prying adult who might open the door to peer in and check up on us. Any uninvited guests would have to walk halfway down the wooden steps and look over the banister to see us, thus giving us plenty of warning of their arrival.

After a while, Colin suggested that we sit on the cushions. The four of us lined up with our backs against the wall: me, Pauline, Yvonne and Colin. The light from the single naked bulb that hung from the centre of the cellar failed to penetrate our shadowy corner.

Seeing Colin put his arm around Yvonne, I put mine around Pauline, tentatively, taking care not to pause or alter the tempo or subject of our inane conversation; trying to make it seem as if it were a natural reflex, like scratching an itch or blowing your nose. Inside, however, my stomach fluttered and my heart pounded. We didn't kiss or cuddle or go any further than that simple caress. Two boys' arms around two sets of girls' shoulders.

We never were anything but friends with Pauline and Yvonne. Pauline had a boyfriend Colin didn't like and so wasn't in our company often. Yvonne became a close friend of mine but our relationship was entirely platonic. That's not to say she was not attractive. She was a lovely girl: slim and pretty with long, fair hair and an effervescent personality.

When Colin, Jimmy Robb and I got down to what was laughingly known as 'band practice', we were inspired by the marvellous musicians we saw playing live. Colin and I were frequent visitors to Soho, to the Marquee Club in Wardour Street and the 100 Club in Oxford Street. There must have been age requirement for admittance but we were never refused entry. Such regulations were far less rigorously observed in those days. We saw the Yardbirds, the Pretty Things and Georgie Fame and the Blue Flames. We went to the Crawdaddy Club in Richmond – where the Rolling Stones had played twice a week until they became too big for little local clubs – to catch Gary Farr and the T-Bones. We saw the Stones, believe it or not, at the Wimbledon Palais (twice). The raw excitement was exhilarating and although I was a confirmed Beatles fan, I had to confess that the Stones were more attractive in terms of their anti-establishment rakishness.

We'd heard a rumour that the band drank every lunchtime at the World's End pub just down the King's Road from our school and took to hanging around outside in our customized uniforms – by now we had cut six-inch vents into our black school blazers. Such modifications attracted the unwanted attention of 'Doc' Henry, our headmaster, who was for ever sending Colin and me home to get our hair cut or to change various bits of our attire. When he tired of sending us home he began caning us for these misdemeanours.

At Sloane, I had found the methods of Bevington Primary's resident sadist, Mr Hayes, replaced by a much more sophisticated brutality. There only the headmaster and his deputy were authorized to use the cane and instead of being beaten in front of their classmates, as had been the case at Bevington, boys would be caned across the backside in the privacy of the headmaster's office.

To Colin, getting the cane meant so much – he'd achieved respectability as a rebel at long last. Even Terry Lawrence began to acknowledge him and agreed to join us once or twice as we posed outside the World's End every lunchtime for months on end, never catching so much as a glimpse of the Stones.

As for Colin's plan to hitchhike round the south coast, his parents eventually persuaded him to join them and his four siblings for a holiday in Burgess Hill, where they had arranged a house swap with friends. Colin's mum invited me to go with them. We had a marvellous sun-kissed week and I remember spending one idyllic day sitting in the beautiful garden of this huge house reading the James Bond novel *Goldfinger* from cover to cover while Colin and his family went out for the day. For me it was a great holiday but Sussex didn't quite provide the rock 'n' roll adventure Colin had envisaged.

Earlier in that summer of 1963, before the school holidays, Lily had received a letter from her heart specialist at Hammersmith Hospital asking to see her to discuss a possible cure for the disease that had blighted her life. Ever since mitral stenosis had been diagnosed, she'd spent half her time in hospital having fluid removed from her lung tissue to make it easier for her to breathe and the other half being a guinea pig for the heart specialist, who was seeking a cure. From the moment this letter arrived she began to fret. What kind of remedy would this be? What would it entail? What were the risks?

In my memory this worrying period for Lily is intertwined with the fall-out from the Profumo scandal that was dominating the news. It had emerged that the secretary of state for war, John Profumo, had conducted a brief relationship with a call girl, Christine Keeler, at the same time as she was involved with a senior naval attaché from the Soviet Embassy. Having initially assured the House of Commons, under parliamentary privilege, that there was 'no impropriety whatsoever' in his relationship with Keeler, in early June Profumo was forced to admit that he had lied and to resign from the Cabinet and the Privy Council.

The sexual liaison at the root of the scandal was something that in those days would probably have been brushed under the carpet had it not been for Profumo's cardinal sin – lying to the House of Commons – and Keeler's association with the Soviet attaché, an alleged spy. As it was, at a time when the Cold War was at its peak, the spies Burgess, Maclean and Philby had only recently been outed, the Establishment was being challenged and the media were becoming less inclined to show deference to politicians, the scandal rocked the nation and would lead, by the end of the year, to the toppling of Harold Macmillan's Conservative government. For many it remains a powerful catalyst in the seismic social changes of the 1960s.

As well as the fall from grace of the Establishment archetype John Profumo, educated at Harrow and Oxford, the story featured minor characters from London's underbelly, including a society pimp and a Jamaican drug dealer, as well as the good-time girls Christine Keeler and Mandy Rice-Davies. Some of its sub-plots unfolded close to Walmer Road in Notting Hill and Marylebone, where both these women had at one stage or another been kept as mistresses by none other than our local slum landlord, Peter Rachman.

I can picture Lily on the morning of her hospital appoint-ment, sitting down for her treasured fifteen minutes of self-indulgence after getting me off to school. Feet up, a cup of tea and a cigarette in her hand, the *Daily Sketch* on her lap and *Housewives' Choice* playing quietly on the radio. She must have found it hard to concentrate on the latest shocking revelations in her newspaper. She said nothing within my hearing about the scandal itself – it involved too much sex for her to feel com-fortable discussing it with me. Profumo's resignation did, however, give her a chance to reiterate one of her favourite homilies: 'A liar is as bad as a thief,' she'd say as Jack de Manio, or one of the other presenters of the *Today* programme, pontificated on the latest developments as I ate my morning cornflakes (or, if I was lucky, Scott's Porage Oats). It was all far too complex for me to understand. I was just mesmerized by the beauty of Mandy Rice-Davies.

Lily's appointment was at noon, which meant she would have to leave her job at the newsagent's early to be there on time. Linda had offered to go with her and they'd agreed that she would leave Fulham County at morning break to meet Lily at the hospital. Lily relied so much on Linda, confiding in her, consulting her; she knew she couldn't face this ordeal without her daughter's support.

The previous week, Dr Tanner had written to the council's Housing Department to say that, given her illness, Lily could not go on living in such terrible conditions. Neither should she be climbing stairs. After seventeen years on the waiting list for a council house, she would, Dr Tanner assured her, be given medical priority. Lily's dream of opening her own front door into a house that was all hers was at long last tantalizingly close to being realized.

Linda had decided to leave school that summer and begin training as a nursery nurse. Her weekly pay would be only £5 but that was more than she earned from her various evening and weekend jobs. She had promised Lily £3 a week to help with the housekeeping. Lily should have been feeling happy about all this good news: she was going to be rehoused, receive some regular income and a cure for her weak heart was in prospect. And yet . . .

Lily and Linda sat silently side by side as the heart specialist explained what he had in mind. Hammersmith Hospital was pioneering an operation to cure mitral stenosis by inserting a replacement plastic valve. The procedure had only just been developed and Lily would be one of the first patients to benefit from this breakthrough. He warned that without an operation to replace the mitral valve, she would not live for very much longer.

As this operation was so cutting-edge there were obviously

risks involved but if it was successful it could add ten years to Lily's life. If she agreed to have the surgery, she'd need to give up work and take things easy. She would have to be as fit as possible before they could operate. She would be in hospital for at least three months, probably six. Lily listened, her eyes focused on the specialist's desk. An old-fashioned clock on the wall ticked loudly. Beneath the desk, out of sight of the consultant, Lily's hand reached for Linda's.

When the doctor had finished, Lily frowned. She thanked him and said she needed time to think about what he'd said. As they left the hospital, Linda sensed that Lily had already made her decision. She was going to refuse the operation.

Chapter 14

LINDA LEFT SCHOOL as planned in July 1963, at fifteen years of age. She studied for two days a week at Brixton College and worked in a nursery at Brook Green in Hammersmith for the other three days in pursuit of her National Nursery Examination Board Certification (NNEBC) to qualify as a nursery nurse.

As predicted, Lily refused to countenance the radical heart surgery she had been told would extend her life in spite of Linda's attempts to persuade her that it was the best option. 'Don't you want to see your grandchildren?' she'd ask, exasperated at Lily's Taurean stubbornness. But Lily wasn't being stubborn. She was scared. Scared of the operation, scared of having to stop work when we were poorer than ever and scared that the dreaded age of forty-two had brought with it the spectre of death, as she had feared all her life it would. She was finding it difficult to carry on working, there was no money from Steve any more and no sign of any offers of a council house, despite the medical urgency.

All of this was discussed by Lily and Linda long into the night, their conversations whispered in case I overheard. I was meant to believe that all was well and Lily was fine, and I played the role expected of me, preferring to hide my deep sense of foreboding than to attempt to break into their secret dialogue and have my fears confirmed.

When Linda started work she found to her consternation that her travel costs from Notting Hill to Hammersmith and Brixton ate into her modest wage so extensively that she could only manage to contribute £2 to the housekeeping, rather than the £3 she'd planned. Another heavy blow was dealt by the Rowe Housing Trust, which decided to remove all gas and electricity 'pay as you go' meters from their Walmer Road properties, too. We knew from having to switch to fuel bills at Southam Street that this would only make life even more difficult. Lily had already begun to fall behind with her debts in the summer and the bills would now be much higher in the winter.

She spent most evenings alone. There were no trips to the cinema any more. Her only nights out were spent on her own in the new bingo hall, where she hoped to win the jackpot that would transform our lives. There had been no man on the horizon since the debacle with Ron and her children were spending more and more time away from the squalor of Walmer Road.

I was usually to be found with Colin James or Andrew Wiltshire, another schoolfriend, who lived close to the newly built BBC TV Centre in Wood Lane and was part of a completely different musical scene. Unlike Colin, Andrew was proficient at playing an instrument – the drums – and he was keen that we should play together. So I would be either in Fulham, or Shepherd's Bush, or going to see bands in Soho and all over south-west London. At weekends I was delivering milk and now, some evenings, paraffin.

As the summer waned, Johnny Carter had decided to boost his milkman's income by delivering paraffin oil two nights a week and asked me if I'd help. My wages were 3 shillings a night plus free pie and chips on the way home. I set aside some old clothes for handling this awful stuff. They reeked so much of oil that Lily insisted I store them in our decrepit basement.

The paraffin round was in Barnes and Mortlake, following the flow of the Thames. We had a van – a kind of souped-up milk float with the same type of door-free cabin at the front to make hopping in and out easier. I would knock on designated doors on cold, dark winter evenings, collect a metal or plastic container, take it to the tank on the back of the van, fill it up, return it to the customer and collect the money. We had a monopoly on pink paraffin – our only rival traded in the blue variety. The livery on our respective vans was coloured accordingly. Don't ask me what the difference was. All I know is they both smelled the same.

In the depths of winter it was hard to motivate myself to go out for four hours in the evening. It was only the thought of that hot pie and chips afterwards – purchased from a shop on Hammersmith Broadway and transferred from the newspaper in which it was wrapped to our mouths by paraffin-soaked fingers as we drove back to the depot – that spurred me on. That and the money. Those 3 shillings, plus tips, enabled me to buy more Pye International records, or back copies of *Charles Buchan's Football Monthly* from a second-hand shop in Hammersmith Road, or some of the detective novels I'd recently begun to read. It also meant that as well as free school meals, I had a hot dinner twice a week. Both Linda and I ate much better than Lily, who hardly touched anything alone in that cold, damp house every night.

Indeed, Linda now had a new boyfriend who, on their first date, actually took her to a proper restaurant for dinner. She tried to pretend she was used to it although Renee's Pie and Mash Shop was the closest either of us had ever come to such an experience. Her boyfriend's name was Mike Whitaker and he was the cousin of her best friend Cheryl. She'd gone with Cheryl to a family wedding and by the end of the evening had been asked out by two different suitors: the drummer from the band and Mike. She did what any girl in her right mind would do and turned down the drummer.

Mike would probably have been rather disconcerted if he'd had any idea how much we already knew about him by the time he came to Walmer Road to pick up Linda for that first date. She had given Lily chapter and verse, as she was required to do before going out with any boy. Mike was in his early twenties, with a car and a profession. The car was a sky-blue Ford Zephyr and he worked as an electrical engineer at Henry's Radios in Praed Street off the Edgware Road.

He was only about 5ft 8ins tall, but taller than Linda (a pre-requisite on which she insisted), blond with dimples in his cheeks when he smiled and pale blue eyes that matched the colour of his car. Lily liked the sound of him. On the night of the date she kept watch from the shared upstairs front bedroom while Linda got ready. When she saw the big blue car driving slowly down the road she rushed downstairs and out into the street, waving her arms and shouting frantically: 'Are youse luking for Linda?' in her most excited Scouse. There was to be no prospect of this excellent catch slipping through the net.

Mike was ushered into the front room to wait. I'd made sure I was already in there. I shared Lily's curiosity – this was a man of means and he was taking my sister out. Jimmy Carter had been fun but he was too young and too immature to be suitable as a serious contender for Linda's affections. Mike was an adult with a car and a good job. I needed to do a full appraisal.

He was dressed smartly in an Italian suit (though the jacket was cut too short for my liking). He wore Chelsea boots with Cuban heels and elasticated sides which made him look taller than he was. Goodness knows what he made of that house (he told Linda much later that he couldn't believe anyone still lived in such conditions). Mike had been brought up in a neat semi in Watford, which his parents owned. His father was a manager on the railways and his mother was a housewife who idolized her son and had difficulty accepting that he was no longer a child. Although he was in his twenties, she'd take his wage packet each week and hand him back an allowance she determined to be sufficient for his needs.

If, when Mike walked into our front room and took off his coat, he'd revealed a pair of angel's wings it would merely have served notice of what he was to become to us. I have never met anybody as kind or gentle or more generous than Mike Whitaker. Neither have I ever met anybody I admired more – not in the same way I had admired the Real Mod, with his double cuffs and streetwise philosophy. Mike wasn't a Mod. If truth be told he was a bit of a Rocker, but in those days, by the time you were in your early twenties, you were neither. You were an adult, and adults weren't Mods or Rockers, they were just adults.

I respected Mike in a much more fundamental way. He engaged me from that first meeting. Softly spoken with impeccable manners, within about ten minutes he'd captivated

Lily as well. For me the attraction was simple: he was someone who knew a great deal but carried his wisdom lightly; somebody I could look up to, perhaps even emulate. Mike had left school at fifteen, against his parents' wishes, to do the only job that interested him: working with valves and circuit boards, repairing radios and TVs, advising and consulting on electrical systems, making amplifiers and loudspeakers. The family that owned Henry's Radios, which had been established for many years, treated him like a son. He'd gone to work for them as a Saturday boy when he was thirteen and spent a lot of time in there when he should have been at school, too. I don't think Mike had any formal qualifications. He had learned his trade by working at it and he was now not only the chief electrical engineer at Henry's but managing the shop as well.

One of Mike's eccentricities, as far as I was concerned, was his fondness for folk music. He had every LP ever made by the Kingston Trio, and others by Peter, Paul and Mary and Pete Seeger, but it was an artist with a more contemporary sound that he eulogized the most. He introduced me to the music of a little-known young American folk singer called Bob Dylan and lent me his latest LP, *The Freewheelin' Bob Dylan* – the one with the cover showing Dylan, shoulders hunched, walking through the snowy New York streets with Suze Rotolo. It took only one spin of that album and a glance at the cover for me to acquire a new hero, one whose lyrics encouraged me to start reading poetry. There was a time when I could recite every word of songs such as 'Gates of Eden' and 'Mr Tambourine Man'.

Mike's sophisticated tastes were encapsulated in another album he possessed, *Green Onions* by Booker T. and the MGs, and his subscription to *Playboy* magazine, copies of which he passed on to me. Please note he didn't just buy it, he *subscribed* to it. In the early 1960s this denoted a young man of taste and discernment. His interest was in the text, particularly the short stories by writers such as Ray Bradbury, rather than the glamour shots (at least, that's what he told me). Mike smoked Senior Service untipped, the fags I would have chosen had I been able to afford them, and wore aftershave that lingered in our front room long after he'd left.

Thus Mike Whitaker came into our lives on that winter's evening in 1963. If the memories of his first date with Linda ever faded, he'd certainly never forget the second.

It was two weeks later, a Saturday evening in mid-November – the very day our gas and electricity supply was cut off because Lily had failed to pay the bills. When I returned from the milk round at about 5.30pm, our rooms were in darkness, apart from some flickering candles and a small fire burning in the back room where Linda was applying her make-up as best she could. Lily was unwell and had gone to bed to keep warm. There was nothing to eat.

Linda had agreed to meet Mike at a cinema in Edgware Road. Saturday was his busiest day and he wouldn't be finished until early evening so this arrangement made more sense. It was just as well he wasn't picking her up. She had been too ashamed to tell him we'd been cut off. When he drove her home, she told me, she had no intention of inviting him in, so our secret would be safe. She would get on to the Rowe Housing Trust on Monday to work out a plan to pay off the bills and have our power supply reconnected. It wasn't the first time we'd been in this situation but she was determined it would be the last.

Concerned about Lily, she instructed me not to go out again that night. Not only had Lily looked awful as she coughed her way upstairs to bed, she seemed somehow crushed and defeated. Linda had made sure she'd taken the assorted medications she depended on daily and offered to go to the phone box to ring for Dr Tanner but Lily had told her she just needed a good rest and that she had an appointment with the doctor on Monday anyway.

I was tired, cold and hungry. With no electricity, I couldn't watch TV or listen to records. I brought some coats down from my bed so that I could keep myself warm while I read my book by candlelight for an hour or two. We had a torch, but it was supposed to be saved for emergencies in order to preserve the battery. I used it to find my way to the outside toilet before settling down with my book in the little back room, pulling the armchair close to the fire. I remember what I was reading: *Huckleberry Finn*.

The house was silent. Every so often, I heard Lily's rasping cough above me in the front bedroom. I picked up the torch and went to see how she was, turning off the beam as I pushed open her door. 'Are you OK, Mum?' I directed my question at the mass of old coats piled on the bed. The coughing had given way to slow, rhythmic breathing. It sounded as if she was asleep. She didn't answer, didn't ask me for anything. There was nothing I could have brought her anyway. With no gas for the stove I couldn't even make her a cup of tea.

It was a cold night but the coal supply had to last through the following day so, after a couple of chapters of *Huckleberry Finn*, I decided I had better go to bed. I left the torch downstairs for Linda and felt my way upstairs in the dark. Lily's door was slightly ajar. I paused outside to listen. Silence. 'Goodnight, Mum,' I whispered. There was no response, only the wheezing lilt of her struggling breath.

I was too frightened to sleep. I lay awake anxiously wondering what to do, my ears straining to distinguish the sounds in the next room from the regular Saturday night noises of North Kensington: dogs barking, neighbours arguing, revellers passing on their way to and from the Latimer Arms. I'd seen Lily ill many times, but she'd never been so unresponsive. Eventually I fell into a fitful doze.

Linda came home at about 10pm. She'd been too worried to go straight on anywhere with Mike after the film and had asked him to wait outside in the car while she checked on Lily. She found the torch just inside the door of the back room and crept upstairs to their bedroom. Lily was still buried beneath the coats, in a state of delirium. When Linda spoke, her eyes flashed open and she screamed: 'Steve! Steve! What are you doing here? Get out, Steve, get out!' Her cry was so loud that Mike heard it from the car. He leaped out and knocked on the front door. I woke up with a start and ran downstairs to let him in.

Sheila Thompson and her husband, who lived on the top floor, called down to us. Linda told them that everything was under control. She told me to stay with Lily while she went to the phone box with Mike to summon a doctor. I sat on the bed alone with Lily, not knowing what to do or say. She seemed oblivious of my presence, of everything. Her breathing had become more laboured and she was sweating profusely. I was terrified. Finding her hand in the dark, I took it in mine and waited.

Linda and Mike were back within fifteen minutes. She found

more candles and lit them in the bedroom. I went back to bed to huddle under my coats until the doctor came. Mike waited downstairs. By the time the duty doctor arrived Lily seemed to have lost consciousness. It was a male doctor, one of the partners at Dr Tanner's practice. An ambulance had already been summoned and as we waited for it to arrive the doctor railed against the appalling condition of our accommodation, declaring that Lily must never return to living like this. The ambulance crew struggled to get her downstairs by the light of our small torch.

I wanted to go to the hospital with Linda and Mike but Linda sent me back to bed. There was nothing I could do, she said. As usual I obeyed her. Although I had no wish to stay in that freezing house on my own not knowing what was happening to Lily, I hadn't the energy to protest or the courage to insist.

And so it was that I slept while Lily was admitted to the emergency ward at St Charles' Hospital and attached to an array of medical equipment. An oxygen mask was fitted while Linda answered a plethora of questions about Lily's medication and her heart condition. She gave them the name of the heart specialist at Hammersmith and explained the opportunity he'd offered Lily to have a plastic mitral valve fitted. She asked if she could go on to the ward to sit with Lily. The matron would allow her in only briefly to say goodnight before they settled her down. She said Linda could return the following morning. Mike brought Linda home and promised to drive back from Watford the next morning to take her back to the hospital.

Linda got to bed at 2.30am only to find that it was soaked in Lily's urine. She grabbed the coats and a pillow from the bed and trooped downstairs to sleep on the settee in the front room. As she finally dozed off there was a loud rap on the front door and a torchlight beamed through the front-room window. It was the police, complete with flashing blue lights, and they were outside our house.

Linda feared the worst – that they'd been sent by the hospital with terrible news about Lily. She opened the door with trepidation. 'Is Michael Whitaker here?' asked the officer standing there.

Bewildered, Linda pieced together what had happened from what the policeman told her. Mike's mother had been waiting up for him in Watford. Alarmed when he failed to come home, she had got hold of Cheryl Roberts' parents to find out our address and then contacted the police. Linda explained that by now Mike should be arriving home. They checked. He was.

Linda, who had barely slept, woke me the next morning with the welcome news that Sheila Thompson on the top landing, realizing that we had no power, had invited us up for breakfast. I'd had nothing to eat since my milkman's lunch of half a Swiss roll and a pint of silver-top the previous morning. I fell upon those eggs and bacon like a lion on its prey.

Linda stripped Lily's bed and wheeled the sheets, blankets and pillow cases in the coal-fetching pram to a newly opened launderette in Latimer Road. There were no tumble-dryers in those early launderettes so Linda stuffed the wet bedclothes inside the pillow cases, brought them home and hung them on a line stretched across the kitchen. By this time Mike had returned. Leaving the damp clothes hanging in the damp room, the three of us drove to the hospital.

Lily was on a small ward with about three other people. It disturbed me greatly to see her attached to so many tubes and wires. Heavily sedated, she just about managed to open her eyes, smile weakly and greet us. That afternoon she was to be transferred to Hammersmith Hospital, where her specialist would talk to her again about the operation he was keen for her to have. This time, Linda wouldn't be privy to the conversation.

~

It was a week after the dreadful night of Linda's second date with Mike that we went to Hammersmith Hospital to hear the outcome of Lily's discussions with the specialist. By then, Linda had already embarked on the Herculean task of transforming our financial situation. The way she planned and executed this ambitious one-woman recovery plan is awe-inspiring – especially considering that she had only just turned sixteen.

First Linda had talked to her matron at Brook Green Nursery, who agreed to give her a week off, with pay, to sort things out. With Dr Tanner's help she secured an appointment with the senior managers of the Rowe Housing Trust. She persuaded them to restore the gas and electricity meters and to have the power supplies reconnected. The trust would settle all the outstanding bills and Linda would reimburse them through an agreed weekly payment plan.

Linda then went to see Mr Berriman in the corner shop, where she'd given up her part-time job when she began training to be a nursery nurse. Mr Berriman had heard about Lily going into hospital and was keen to help. He said Linda could work there from 9am until 3pm every Sunday, as she had done previously and, during the week she was taking off, she could open the shop at 8.30 every morning and work until midday.

As Linda was leaving, Mr Berriman went into the room at the back of the shop and returned with a box of groceries – a gift to her and to me. We were overcome with gratitude. For me, it made up in one stroke for all the humiliation I'd endured on the countless occasions I'd had to ask for shopping I couldn't pay for. There were sausages, pies, tinned beans, cakes and a fresh supply of candles. We fervently hoped we wouldn't need those again.

Linda's final job before visiting Lily was to buy her a couple of nighties, a dressing gown and a pair of slippers, none of which Lily possessed. Linda met most of the cost of these items from her wages but I was happy to make a contribution from my milk-round money. After we'd presented our gifts and pulled our seats close to her bedside, Lily told us that she'd decided to have the operation. The illness she'd suffered on that Saturday evening was the worst she'd ever experienced. If she did not have this procedure it was bound to happen again.

The surgery was planned for February or March the following year – three or four months away. She would have to stay in hospital until then, and for a few more months afterwards to recuperate. She told us how upset she was that we'd be alone at Christmas. She still had no idea that we'd already had that experience seven years earlier. We tried to put her mind at rest without revealing the precedent.

When I went to Colin's house later that week to practise with the Vampires, his lovely mother asked me all about Lily. I understood little of the medical detail of Lily's condition: if she'd spoken to Linda she'd have got a much clearer picture of the circumstances. I merely told anyone who asked that my mother was in hospital recovering from an illness. Ignorance, however, was not the only reason for the vagueness of my responses. Linda had warned me not to say too much to any-one about the length of time Lily would be in hospital. Her great fear was that somebody would interfere and we would be taken into care – or worse still, forced to go and live with Steve. She herself had told her employers at the nursery only part of the story and nothing at all was said to my school.

But that evening, 22 November 1963, the focus was not on my family's problems. The band – Colin, Jimmy and I – were in the cellar with Yvonne and Pauline. We were playing a Beatles record on the gramophone while I tried to work out the chords. It was 'Thank You Girl', which required Colin to join me in a simple two-part harmony he was finding impossible to master. As our caterwauling reached its crescendo, the door at the top of the stairs opened. It was Colin's mum. There had been a television newsflash. Something terrible had happened in America. President Kennedy had been shot and killed.

Our efforts to emulate the Beatles were immediately abandoned. Even at our age we realized what an impact this dreadful news would have on the world. And I would certainly never forget where I was when I heard that John F. Kennedy had been assassinated.

Chapter 15

LINDA WORKED RELENTLESSLY to try to ensure that when Lily came out of hospital she wouldn't have to worry about a single debt. The Provident, the loan clubs, the gas and electricity, our local shops, the rent – all arrears were cleared, all debts either settled or forgiven, all payments up to date by the New Year of 1964. It was another bad winter. Nowhere near as bad as the Big Freeze the previous year, but it was such a long one: there was snow and ice from mid-February right up to the start of spring.

Steve hadn't made any maintenance payments for months. Linda wrote to him explaining our situation. She told him about Lily's prolonged stay in hospital and that we'd had our gas and electricity cut off. He wrote back saying that with a baby to support, he couldn't afford to make these payments. His circumstances had changed since the divorce settlement. He enclosed a pound note and asked to be remembered to me. It was clear that we were on our own.

Linda wanted to write to our aunties and uncles in Liverpool. Not to ask for money – we understood they didn't have any to spare – but just to tell them that Lily was in hospital preparing for major heart surgery. Lily was adamant. We were not to worry them. When the operation was over and she had her new lease of life, we would go to Liverpool, the three of us, and show them how much better she was.

Local people were very good to us. As well as the box of groceries from Mr Berriman, we were given a stack of second-hand clothes by a woman in Walmer Road with a large family, together with a bunch of flowers to take in to Lily. Before she had gone into hospital, Lily had ordered two annuals from Maynard's to give us for Christmas. She hadn't paid for them but the newsagent passed them on anyway and wouldn't take a penny for them. Linda's was a pop-music annual; mine was *The BBC Grandstand Book of Sport*. In a fit of nostalgia for Christmases past, I actually wrapped my book and put it by my bed on Christmas Eve so that I'd have a present to open when I woke up on Christmas morning.

Lily tried to get herself discharged to be with us at Christmas but her consultant wouldn't hear of it and neither would Linda. She was determined that when Lily was discharged from hospital, she would go straight to a new home. The clinicians said that returning to the damp conditions at Walmer Road, even for a few days, would jeopardize the preparations for the operation.

Mike would be with his family on Christmas Day and would fetch Linda on Boxing Day and take her back to Watford. Mrs Cox, who was Lily's only other regular visitor, invited us to spend Christmas with her family but neither of us was keen. There were no spare beds for us to sleep in and in any case, we wanted to be at the hospital with Lily on Christmas afternoon. Instead it was agreed that I would go to the Coxes for my dinner on Boxing Day while Linda was in Watford.

So we spent Christmas morning alone again, this time six years older and wiser – Linda now knew she had to unwrap the chicken before placing it in the oven. This time she even managed to stuff it with sage and onion as well, serving it with roast potatoes that were almost as good as Lily's and vegetables that, unlike our mother's, had not been boiled to within an inch of their lives.

This feast took longer to cook than Linda had bargained for and by the time it was ready we were running late. We were determined to be at the hospital from the very start of visiting time so that Lily wouldn't be the only one without her family there when the doors opened, and we had a long walk ahead of us. I ate my Christmas dinner standing at the pull-down work surface that was a common feature of the kitchen cabinets popular in working-class homes of the 1950s and 1960s. Linda finished ironing our best clothes before gobbling down the special meal she'd cooked so painstakingly.

It was a particularly cold Christmas Day and we were pleased to reach the sterile warmth of the hospital. Of the eight beds on Lily's ward, only three were occupied. The other five patients had been allowed to go home for Christmas. The ward was decorated and had a proper tree. Linda had managed to put some decorations up at Walmer Road, but they couldn't match the quality of those in the hospital. Ours had been stored in an ancient biscuit tin for as long as we could remember, making their brief annual appearance about a week before Christmas Day: some paper chains, sprigs of imitation holly and a couple of paper bells that opened out like concertinas, which had to be Sellotaped into shape before being pushed into the ceiling with the rusty drawing pins returned to the biscuit tin with them every year. We'd never had a Christmas tree, real or fake, and we pointed out to Lily how fortunate she was to have one on the ward. She promised we'd have a tree next Christmas, when she was home, her health transformed, and we'd be living in a house with our very own front door – a house that was worthy of a Christmas tree.

Lily was as cheerful as we'd seen her since that terrible November night. She'd applied her lipstick and dabbed on some perfume. We were her only visitors but she made us feel that we were the only ones she wanted. We stayed until 8pm, when the nurse told us we had to leave. As we were about to go, Lily pulled Linda close and whispered to her that she had yet to sign the consent forms for the operation. She still wasn't sure that she should go ahead with it. For once, Linda told me what Lily had said and asked me what I thought. As we walked home through the silent streets, I confided to Linda how scared I'd been on the night Lily had been taken to hospital. I felt that if the operation was her only hope, she should agree to it for our sake as well as her own.

It was 9.30 by the time we got back to our cold, damp house, feeling distinctly unChristmassy. Sheila Thompson must have been listening out for us. She invited us up for something to eat. It was in the Thompsons' tidy kitchen-cum-living room on the top landing of 6 Walmer Road, in front of a roaring fire, that we tasted turkey for the first time in our lives. For as long as I live I will remember those sandwiches: thickly sliced bread, real butter (rather than the margarine we were used to) and deliciously moist cold turkey. There were mince pies to follow, and the feast was accompanied by Shirley Bassey on the

Thompsons' record-player. We wouldn't have to walk downstairs to our grim rooms for ages yet. This was how Christmas should be. Linda and me in the best place for us and Lily in the best place for her.

~

Lily's incarceration in Hammersmith Hospital didn't make a great deal of difference to our lives. She'd been in hospital so many times that we'd grown used to fending for ourselves. I was a pretty low-maintenance kid, requiring little attention and minimal supervision. Linda would make sure I was up and off to school each morning. She didn't need to be much of a sergeant-major to get me out of bed as I knew dawdling would spell trouble. A sixth-form prefect would be stationed every day at each of the entrances to Sloane school, and any boy arriving late would be reported to Doc Henry, who had already caned me once for persistent late attendance. Nobody at school knew my circumstances. Why should they have known? It was none of their business. Schools then seemed to have little interest in life outside their gates, and by the same token any parental curiosity about what went on within them was firmly discouraged.

Linda would toast some bread under the grill of the gas stove and put a box of cornflakes and a bottle of milk on the table for me. She had a more regimented approach to household cleanliness than Lily and was very strict about making me empty my urine bucket in the outside toilet each morning. As I took it back upstairs to my room, she'd squirt some disinfectant in it.

It didn't take me long to get ready. It wasn't as if we had a shower (nobody did then) and the bath in the basement was for special occasions. The trick in winter was to get yourself from under the coat stack to setting off on the brisk walk to Latimer Road Underground station in as short a time as possible. I had it down to a fine art. A cursory wipe of my face with the flannel and the occasional dab at my teeth with an elderly toothbrush was the extent of my toilette.

That winter of 1964 my bids to beat my record speed were hampered by the time I had to spend combing my hair. I badly wanted to look like Paul McCartney but my hair became wavier the longer it grew and it took me ages to slap it down and straighten it with cold water from our one tap over the butler sink in the kitchen. These were the days before hairstylists for the male population, when men and boys had no choice but to go to a traditional barber whose approach to styling hair was similar to an army chef's approach to cooking: basic. And it was my way or the highway. Barbers would actually tell off their younger customers for coming in with long hair. 'Don't let it grow so much next time, son,' they'd say sternly, having turned the Paul McCartney you asked for into the George Formby they preferred.

At school, I flitted between two groups of friends: the Fulham set of Colin James and the Vampires and the Shepherd's Bush set consisting of Andrew Wiltshire and John Williams (who lived on the Wormholt estate in Acton and could do a perfect imitation of Bluebottle, the Peter Sellers character from *The Goon Show*).

Unlike Colin, Andrew lived within walking distance of Walmer Road. Straight down Latimer Road, left into North Pole Road, left again at the Pavilion pub and into a small estate of attractive houses with long front gardens and gabled doorways. Andrew's parents rented 2 Nascot Street. His father Wally worked at Ravenscroft Park Hospital, where he was in charge of ordering and distributing the supplies. He was a very funny man and Andrew and his brother John shared his dark looks and sharp sense of humour.

Kath, Andrew's mother, was Wally's opposite. Well-spoken and rather prim and proper, she'd smile benignly at her husband's banter. At least once a day, on the pretext of some manufactured complaint against his wife, Wally would say to his sons, and anyone else who happened to be in the house: 'If I had the choice of spending half an hour with Marilyn Monroe or the rest of my life with your mother, who do you think I'd choose?'

Kath would smile sweetly. 'She'd never have you for half a minute, let alone half an hour, you silly old fool.'

Nothing could disguise their deep affection for one another. The Wiltshires' was a happy household, and streetwise, funny Andrew (never Andy) was to become my closest, dearest friend. Despite his short stature he also seemed irresistible to women.

One evening Cheryl Roberts knocked for Linda, who was out somewhere with Mike but due to return soon. I was there with Andrew. We'd been sitting in front of the coal fire, toasting bread on the flames with a toasting fork. Cheryl said she'd wait and so we moved to the front room, where I switched on the electric heater in her honour and we watched TV. At least, I was watching TV. As I was sitting in front of it in the armchair with Andrew and Cheryl on the settee behind me, I assumed they were, too.

There was the same age difference between Cheryl and Andrew as there was between Linda and me: three years. I was therefore shocked – yes, that's the word, shocked – when I happened to glance round to make some witticism about the programme we were supposed to be enjoying and caught them snogging. Quickly turning my gaze back to the TV screen, I sat there beetroot red and frozen with embarrassment as the sound of lips being swapped continued to emanate from the sofa. I suppose I have to admit to a tinge of jealousy. I'd been lusting after Cheryl for as long as Linda had known her, but felt she was way out of my league. As indeed she was.

When Linda didn't appear Cheryl said she had to go home. Andrew volunteered to walk with her. I can't explain how I ended up going, too – like a huge great lemon rolling along in front, while Andrew, who was an inch shorter than Cheryl for each of the three years' difference in their ages – reached up to embrace her at regular intervals.

There was no repeat of that evening and Cheryl eventually became engaged to Andrew's brother, John. I'd take you on the route between these two events if I could remember the way. Suffice it to say that if nobody else knew about that evening, Andrew knew that I knew. It gave him a certain edge as we travelled together through our rites of passage.

The Fulham set and the Shepherd's Bush set mixed only in the toilet of the Sloane school playground. It was actually more of a *pissoir* than a toilet. There were no cubicles and it consisted merely of a concrete shed with an entrance at each end and a duct along both main walls in which to urinate. Urination, however, was discouraged as this was the smoking room for third- and fourth-year boys (the fifth and sixth forms had their own facilities elsewhere). There weren't that many smokers so the place was rarely crowded. Terry Lawrence and Stephen Hackett would be there; Colin, Jimmy Robb, Andrew and John Williams were all regulars and I was a fixture during every morning break with my packet of ten Rothmans (when Lily could supply me with them) or Player's Weights (when she couldn't).

Doc Henry's office overlooked the toilet and he could be seen at the window looking down malevolently as clouds of smoke drifted through the open portals and doorways of our social club. There was little he could do because of the perfect strategic position of the shed. Since no teacher could reach us without walking across fifty yards of open playground, where he would quickly be spotted by our look-outs, catching us red-handed was impossible. It was a rare victory over our cane-happy headmaster.

I became a regular visitor to Yvonne Stacey's big house on Waltham Green. Although her German mother disapproved of Yvonne's mini-skirts and much else about the emerging 1960s culture, she encouraged her daughter to bring all her friends home. She genuinely liked the company of young people and was interested in their views. A seamstress who had longed to become a doctor, she had been forced to quit medical school at the outbreak of war.

She'd met Yvonne's father, a master baker, when he was a British soldier arriving in Germany fresh from the D-Day landings. That experience and the sights he saw in the concentration camps he'd helped liberate had deeply affected him. He spent most of his time at home sitting in silence, trying to control a temper that had been mild until the after-effects of his wartime traumas kicked in, perennially over-shadowed by his German wife's vivacious personality.

Yvonne introduced me to her parents as if I was some raving intellectual because my nose was constantly in a book. Yvonne's mother loved poetry and had read all the classics. She felt I was a young man with whom she could share this passion. On my second or third visit, she gave me a battered paperback copy of Dante's *Inferno*, which she insisted I take away with me to read. While I loved reading, fourteenth-century epic poetry was somewhat beyond me; still, I did my best. On each subsequent visit, I was asked to discuss Dante's opus – its infer-ences and undercurrents, its use of metaphor. I couldn't bring myself to tell her that I found it turgid and unfathomable. It served me right. I had become a victim of my own preten-tiousness.

∿

The date was set for Lily's operation: 26 February 1964. I didn't appreciate at the time how petrified Lily must have been. She was hundreds of miles away from her family in Liverpool, worried sick about us and facing major heart surgery at the very age her mother and grandmother had died. She never dis-cussed her feelings or fears with me. Linda was her confidante. Already carrying a huge weight of responsibility on her young shoulders, she was well aware of Lily's anguish.

When Linda, Mike and I trooped into the hospital ward the night before the operation, we found Lily in tears. Mike went for a walk at Linda's suggestion. I stayed where I was, rooted to the spot by the unprecedented spectacle of Lily crying in public. I had heard her weeping in her room during the night many times, but never like this, and never in front of other people. I was as embarrassed as I was concerned. Lily pulled me to her and hugged me. She never did that, either. She'd always insisted that I kiss her cheek when saying goodnight and she was forever tidying my hair and smoothing my clothes, but that's as tactile as it got. We never hugged. It just wasn't our way. The only time I could remember her cuddling me was on that disastrous Christmas afternoon at Ron's, and on that occasion I'd been well aware that she was making a point.

'I haven't signed the papers yet,' she sobbed to Linda. 'What if I die? What will happen to you?' Her words cut me like the surgeon's scalpel. In the space of a few minutes I'd had three new and thoroughly unwelcome experiences. I'd seen Lily cry openly, she'd hugged me for practically the first time and now she was talking about dying. This was getting dark and dangerous.

Lily still insisted that nobody in Liverpool was to be informed, not that it was possible now to notify any of her relatives in advance, with the operation only hours away, assuming she finally signed the consent form. Linda tried to soothe her by repeating what the consultant had said about the operation adding years to her life. She reminded Lily that she was in the care of some of the finest heart specialists in the world and of what the alternative would be. She pointed out how ill she'd been and would be again. 'You're not well and this operation will save your life,' she summarized succinctly.

Lily seemed to have calmed down by the time we were asked to leave. She hugged me again and gave me a radiant smile as I looked back at her from the door of the hospital ward.

She must have signed those papers because the operation went ahead as planned the next day. I went to school and Linda went to work as usual. At the hospital in the evening we were told that Lily was in intensive care following the surgery. The nurse asked if there was an adult with us. Linda explained that she was Lily's next of kin and was eventually allowed to see her. I wasn't. I whispered to Linda that I thought this was unfair, but she wasn't about to press my case, fearing that making a fuss would only lead to her being excluded as well.

A tracheotomy had been performed because Lily was having difficulty breathing and, as she was so poorly, a coma had been induced. Linda was warned about the condition in which she would find her mother. 'She will know you're there, so talk to her and tell her that she looks well,' said the intensive care sister as she shepherded Linda to Lily's bedside. 'You have to give her encouragement.' Linda described the ward to me later. Dimly lit, it was filled with the gentle hum of medical machinery and a strong smell of Jeyes Fluid. Lily lay with her eyes tightly shut, wires and tubes poking out from every part of her tiny frame.

Linda suppressed her tears and her deep disquiet. She told Lily that the operation had been a success, that she'd soon be home. She waited for a response, scrutinizing Lily's face intensely in search of the slightest twitch or flicker. There was nothing. No sign that she'd heard. No indication that she knew Linda was there. The sister asked Linda to leave and we caught the bus home.

Linda went back every day, sometimes with Mike, more often alone. If her sheer willpower could have improved the situation, Lily would have leaped out of bed and turned cartwheels. As it was, her condition deteriorated day by day. A week after the surgery, on Wednesday 4 March, Mike drove Linda to the hospital for her usual early-evening visit. She was told that Lily's kidneys were failing and that she would need another operation that evening. Linda wasn't permitted to see her, even to go through her daily routine of chatting away without receiving any response.

When Linda and Mike returned to Walmer Road, the three of us sat in the back room around the fire, saying very little but thinking a lot. At nine o'clock that night there was a knock on the door. It was the police with a message from Hammersmith Hospital. Linda was to ring them immediately. She decided to head straight to the hospital rather than waste time in the phone box. I'd given up appealing to be allowed to go with them. Linda had enough to cope with already and in truth I was frightened about what I'd have to face if I did go. Instead I was dispatched to stay with the Coxes so that I wouldn't be alone in the house. Mrs Cox was, as always, accommodating. I could sleep on the floor in her large front room. Space could be found for Linda in a bedroom upstairs. Whatever happened that night, neither of us wanted to return to the cold despair of Walmer Road.

As I disappeared into the paraffin-scented warmth of 318 Lancaster Road, and Mike's Ford Zephyr bore Linda to Hammersmith Hospital, the snow began to fall.

⁓

Linda and Mike were left sitting outside the intensive care ward for a long time before a doctor came to speak to them. He was brusque and to the point. During her second operation Lily's kidneys had failed. There was nothing more that could have been done to save her. She had died in theatre.

Linda was poleaxed. She had been utterly convinced that Lily would survive; that the surgery would be the turning point for her. That she'd return to a more tranquil life, free of debt, live in a decent house with its own front door, some reward for all those years of toil and squalor. For the operation that was to have transformed Lily's life instead to end it so prematurely was the final cruelty inflicted on a woman who had borne so much misery so courageously for so long. Linda was in such distress that she didn't think to ask to see Lily, and nobody invited her to do so.

At Lancaster Road, under some blankets on the living-room floor, I was wide awake when Linda arrived in the early hours. She took me into the kitchen on my own to break the news to me. I knew I was expected to cry, but somehow I couldn't, and didn't. I went back to my blankets, pulled them over me and lay there, trying to comprehend the enormity of what had happened. It was unthinkable that I would never see Lily again. Eventually, I drifted off to sleep. I knew that Lily deserved tears but my eyes remained resolutely dry.

～

Somebody had to deal with the aftermath, and inevitably that somebody was Linda. It is scarcely believable that my sister, at just sixteen years old, could have dealt with it all so completely, but she did.

First thing in the morning she wrote to convey the sad news

to our Auntie Jean in Liverpool, asking if she'd pass it on to Lily's siblings. Then she went to a phone box and rang the nursery where she worked to ask for time off, and Sloane school to tell them I wouldn't be attending for a while. Mike had to go to work, so next Linda and I trudged through the snow to Hammersmith Hospital.

A woman from Administration told us that Lily's body was in the mortuary. Linda must arrange for it to be collected by an undertaker as soon as possible. The woman echoed a common refrain: 'Why haven't you got an adult with you?' I felt like telling her we were fresh out of them. Linda was handed a death certificate. 'You'll need this,' she was told, 'and your mother's birth certificate. She can't be buried or cremated without both.'

Linda said she'd search for it at home. If she couldn't find the original, the administrator advised, she would be able to obtain a copy from Somerset House, where the records of the births, marriages and deaths of every person in the United Kingdom were kept. The administrator gave Linda the address printed on a card, along with a brown paper bag containing Lily's belongings. 'We had to cut her wedding ring off her finger before the operation,' the woman explained. 'It's in the bag. Oh, and we took her false teeth out as well – you might want to give them to the undertaker.' These offhand remarks stunned Linda almost as much as the news of Lily's death.

Lily had never removed her wedding ring. Perhaps it was simply because it wouldn't come off, but I suspect there was more to it; that it was just too big a step for her to take. That ring symbolized a commitment she had never broken, even if Steve had. It gave her dignity and it was a badge of the conformity that was so important to her. For her to lose it at the end, in such a brutal way, was shocking. Even I could sense that.

And as for the teeth, we'd had no idea that Lily wore dentures. We subsequently discovered that she'd had all her natural teeth removed when the National Health Service was created. Like many people then, she'd chosen that drastic course of action rather than endure a life of painful dental surgery on teeth already damaged by a poor diet and malnutrition. In the early days of the NHS dentistry was entirely free, so having every tooth taken out was an option that seemed sensible to many working-class people, including Lily and Steve. Lily must have gone to extraordinary lengths to hide the fact she wore dentures. We'd known about Steve's – they'd grinned at us from his bedside every morning – but Lily, with her lovely smile, her pearl-white teeth? False? Surely not. Yet here they were in a brown paper bag. Another vestige of her dignity stripped away at the end.

Next on Linda's to-do list was informing Steve – or at least, getting a message to him. On our way back from the hospital we went to the flat in Peabody Buildings where Steve had taken us as small children to see his mother. She was dead by this time and the flat had been passed on to Steve's youngest sibling, our Uncle Jim, a good fifteen years his brother's junior, who now lived there with his own family and an impressive collection of Frank Sinatra albums. Although Jim didn't have Steve's musical talent he was passionate about Sinatra. Jim was the only relative of Steve's we had any time for – or who had any time for us. He was now married to a lovely woman, our Auntie Betty, with one small daughter and another baby on the way. They alone had stayed in touch with Lily and she had always appreciated their empathy.

Uncle Jim and Auntie Betty were shocked and concerned for us, but Linda politely declined their offers of help. We had learned to be self-sufficient and we hadn't come looking for anything from them. All Linda asked was that they tell Steve. She promised to pass on details of the funeral when it had been arranged.

The next day the sun came out and the snow began to melt. Linda searched through the drawers, the wardrobe, the shoe boxes and the various Christmas hamper receptacles. Although she did discover an insurance policy, which she was able to cash in to pay for the funeral, she couldn't find Lily's birth certificate anywhere. That meant an expedition to Somerset House when it reopened after the weekend.

In the meantime Linda went to a funeral parlour she had noticed in the Portobello Road. A frail old man who looked more like an imminent customer than the proprietor emerged from the back of the shop. He made the usual inquiry about the absence of an accompanying adult. Linda explained the situation and told him that we would be hearing from our aunties and uncles in Liverpool soon. However, the hospital had emphasized the need for Lily's body to be collected from the mortuary quickly. She handed him Lily's dentures in their brown paper bag and asked for them to be fitted before the funeral.

The old man asked if we wanted a burial or a cremation. Linda had no idea what Lily would have wanted. It was not a question she had ever expected to be asked. Linda had only one other experience of a death in the family. Remembering that Nanny Johnson had been cremated, she chose the same for Lily. The undertaker said she should come back on Monday with

Lily's birth and death certificates, along with details of how the funeral would be paid for.

One of Lily's little homilies was that you could never be lost while you had a tongue in your head. On the Monday morning Linda duly found her way to Somerset House, rising majestically between the Thames and the Strand. She was directed to Birth Registrations, an enormous room as big as an entire school, full of banks of drawers set out in endless rows. A middle-aged woman in twin-set and pearls, a pleated skirt and sensible shoes asked why she didn't have an adult with her.

There followed an interrogation as Twin-Set and Pearls completed the required form in triplicate. Lily's full name, date of birth, place of birth, parents' names and so on. When enough information had been entered, a search was made and the certificate found amid a towering mass of paper overseen by the lady in sensible shoes who handed Linda a copy of the certificate and asked for a payment of 2s 6d. Linda had just about enough money for the certificate and her fare back to Notting Hill, where she immediately took the proof of Lily's birth and death to the funeral director in Portobello Road.

He confirmed that he'd collected Lily's body from Hammersmith Hospital. It was in a back room, still lying in a temporary coffin. The dentures had been re-affixed but he advised Linda against seeing the body because it was 'in a bit of a state'. Linda took his advice but asked if she could go into the room to spend a few minutes in private with Lily. For the best part of five years, she and Lily had shared confidences every night in the big bed vacated by Steve. Now she was talking to her alone in the back room of a funeral parlour in the

Portobello Road. Linda told Lily how much she loved her and vowed to look after me and keep me safe.

Verifying that it was actually Lily's body in there was the one grim task that was beyond my sister. I'm not certain if anyone had formally identified the body but Linda couldn't. She wanted to remember Lily as she was, the pretty face, the 'titty nose', the lovely smile. However, she had no grounds to suspect the coffin did not contain that tiny frame. She just had to trust that the undertaker had made sure Lily would go to her funeral with her teeth in.

When she got home Linda found a letter from Auntie Jean on the doormat. She and Uncle George would be driving down to London the following weekend with Auntie Peggy. Lily's favourite brother, John, and his wife would follow. Auntie Rita, though desperate to come, was due to give birth any day and it had been decided that travelling down to London would not be sensible for her. After the funeral, Jean wrote, she and George would take Linda and me back to Liverpool with them.

The idea of a holiday in Liverpool lifted our spirits. However, the implication in Auntie Jean's letter was that she intended us to stay there permanently. On that we were clear. It was kind of Lily's family to offer us a home but we would not leave the city where we'd spent our entire lives. We couldn't be certain what would happen to us in London but Linda was determined to keep us there, and, most importantly, together and well away from any kind of institution.

Chapter 16

I WAS BEWILDERED. My inability to cry nagged at me. The full force of Lily's death probably hadn't hit me yet but it felt to me as if I were letting her down.

With our Liverpudlian relatives arriving at Walmer Road, it was decided that I should stay on with the Coxes until after the funeral and a mattress was found for the living-room floor. Every night leading up to Lily's cremation, I lay there thinking of her and trying to summon the tears I felt obliged to shed. I was at a loss to understand why I was unable to grieve properly.

In my defence, tears simply weren't part of my repertoire of emotional responses. Crying wasn't something that came easily to us North Kensington boys; indeed, we were positively discouraged from showing such weakness. Steve's efforts to toughen me up in our little boxing tournaments were designed as much to familiarize me with pain as to teach me how to defend myself. The unwritten rule that boys weren't supposed to cry was just as deeply ingrained in the working-class culture of West London as it was in the rarefied, stiff-upper-lip milieu of the boarding schools I read about in Frank Richards' Billy Bunter stories.

Those around me, with the exception of Linda, also seemed to be deliberately taking care not to display their emotions. The women conveyed a kind of mute pity that among the Liverpool contingent expressed itself in tactile gestures. They'd rub my arm and smile or ruffle my hair, telling me how brave I was. Theirs was a generation familiar with death. They'd come through the war, lost brothers and sisters to disease and seen their mother and grandmother die young.

Losing Lily had come as a profound shock because they had known nothing of her worsening condition or the heart surgery. They had been shocked, too, by the conditions they found at Walmer Road. None of them lived in luxury but they were mortified to see what their sister had been reduced to. But the fact that they were undemonstrative in their grief helped me to cope.

As for the men, they treated me as though nothing whatsoever had happened. But, aside from my uncles, the three I knew the best made extraordinary gestures of kindness. On the Saturday before Lily's funeral, when we'd finished the milk round, Johnny Carter took me to his house, saying he wanted to show me something. Tough Teddy Boy Johnny hadn't uttered a word about Lily as we worked together that day. He was well aware of our sudden bereavement because Linda had dropped a note through his father's door to make sure that the family, and Jimmy in particular, knew of Lily's death. Jimmy had always got on well with Lily when he and Linda were courting and both Johnny and their father had met her on the odd occasion, too.

When we reached Johnny's house he took me straight down to the basement. There I entered an Aladdin's cave of brand-new musical instruments. Stacked against every wall were dozens of trumpets, violins, drums and electric guitars.

I didn't ask where he'd got them. Let's give Johnny Carter the benefit of the doubt: perhaps he had a sideline as a legitimate distributor of musical equipment, an essential part of the supply chain. There again, perhaps he didn't. He stood in the middle of the room, rolling a fag, his pencil behind his right ear, his hair combed into its customary elaborate sculpture. 'What are you waiting for?' he asked. 'Choose which guitar you want.' Swallowing my astonishment, I selected a solid Vox electric, mahogany with two pick-ups, a tremolo and a gingham case, which would soon bear the legend 'The Vampires', written in Linda's lipstick.

I shook Johnny's hand, thanked him and left his house with my first electric guitar. He took a long drag on his cigarette, saying only that he'd pick me up as usual the next day for our Sunday round. When Mike saw my acquisition his act of kindness was to promise to make me an amplifier for my fourteenth birthday.

The steadfast Albert Cox had said nothing at all as the drama had unfolded in his house: Linda leaving me there to go to the hospital; me sleeping on his floor; Linda arriving in the middle of the night with the dreadful news. He just pottered on, cooking breakfast for everyone, going to work, tending his allotment, watching QPR.

One day, in the period of limbo between Lily's death and her funeral, he called me into his living room. Solemnly unlocking his precious bookcase, he invited me to take any book I wanted to read. I knew exactly which one to choose. I'd studied those books, incarcerated behind the clear glass doors, often enough.

I asked for *David Copperfield* from his beautifully bound set of Dickens novels.

Thus Ham, Peggotty, Uriah Heep, Mr Micawber and Steerforth became my friends, enrapturing and distracting me with their adventures and bringing me a great deal of pleasure and comfort in the difficult months to come. I couldn't wait to look at the book. I immediately sat down in the armchair and opened it. 'Don't forget to bring it back when you've finished reading it,' said Mr Cox over his shoulder as he locked the bookcase up again. Not a gift, then, but a loan. It was a very generous one, too. And that's how *David Copperfield* became the first, and perhaps the last, book to escape from that sturdy bookcase.

∿

While I was exiled at the Coxes', our house began to fill up with Scousers. Andrew dubbed it Little Liverpool. Not all of Lily's family could make the journey to London. Our rooms were full anyway. Auntie Jean and Uncle George were sleeping in the big double bed Lily and Linda had shared. Auntie Peggy, the baby of the family, had my room and Linda slept on the settee in the front room. Lily's eldest brother, Sonny, came down from Coventry and her two other brothers, John and Norman, from Liverpool on the day of the funeral.

For Linda and me, it was a strange and novel experience. We had never in our lives had so many adults concerned for our welfare. They bickered in whispered conversations about how we could have been allowed to get into this state and what they could have done to prevent it. There was also much consternation at the absence of the chance to view their sister's body. These particular conversations were suppressed in front of me but I loved listening to the stories about growing up in Liverpool, how smart Lily had been at school, the memories of the war, the ridiculous and reprehensible behaviour of our grandfather. Although he had refused to come to his daughter's funeral, pleading infirmity, he had not wasted the opportunity to suggest that Lily was to blame for her own death. She should never have gone to London, he'd said, and he'd counselled her against marrying a 'cockney'. By ignoring his advice she'd brought all this on herself.

Lily's brothers and sisters brought to that shabby house the warmth and humour of a family Lily had missed so much and seen so rarely. She was the first of the eight siblings who had survived childhood to die – the second eldest, but still only forty-two. Peggy, the youngest, was not yet out of her twenties.

On the morning of the funeral I had to find a non-school tie to wear. I searched through the collection Steve had left behind, which Lily had kept in the gloomy old wardrobe even after the move to Walmer Road, still hanging over the piece of wire stretched across the inside door, where they'd always been. I chose a black knitted tie that was perfect for the occasion, teaming it with grey school trousers and a black jacket with six-inch vents I'd acquired second-hand from the Lane.

At 2pm, the funeral entourage arrived at 6 Walmer Road. A few neighbours had gathered in the street to watch, along with some urchins too young for school.

Linda and I stepped into our designated vehicle, the one following the hearse containing Lily in her small coffin. I knew I still owed her some tears. Linda wept quietly beside me. As well as grief I felt a sense of foreboding. Deep sorrow for Lily, yes, but also unease about what lay in store for Linda and me when things returned to normal, if they ever did.

As we crept along Ladbroke Grove, a man stopped at the side of the road and with great solemnity made the sign of the cross. I'd never seen this done before and it comforted me in a way I remember trying to rationalize at the time. This stranger was paying tribute to Lily. I was deeply moved by his gesture and for a good while afterwards, whenever a funeral procession came past me in the street, I would stop and make the sign of the cross in the hope that it would bring similar comfort to someone within the dark interiors of the passing cars.

Our last journey with Lily, from Walmer Road to Kensal Green cemetery, was short and straightforward. Left on to the Harrow Road at the north end of Ladbroke Grove, and we'd arrived at her final destination. All Souls, Kensal Green, which was inspired by the famous Père Lachaise cemetery in Paris, is among the most historic and most beautiful public burial grounds in the country. Given the miseries of Lily's brief life, it is perhaps ironic that in death she would reside at such a prestigious address, alongside the likes of William Makepeace Thackeray, Anthony Trollope and Wilkie Collins. Not forgetting, of course, Kelso Cochrane, who had been so brutally murdered on the corner of our street.

It was the first funeral I had ever attended and I was bemused by its rituals. None of the adults who now surrounded Linda and me, people from the undertakers and the crematorium, had known Lily, been with her through her travails or offered her help when she needed it, yet here they were now, respectful and solicitous, when it was too late.

It wasn't a grand affair. Women like Lily are dispatched quietly with little fuss and no obituaries. Her brothers and sisters swelled a thin congregation at the crematorium. Pat and Albert Cox were there, Mike's parents' came with him from Watford and Uncle Jim and Auntie Betty appeared, making around fifteen mourners in total.

I can remember nothing of the service but I do recall, when it was over, going into the grounds of the cemetery to see where Lily's ashes would be placed. Mike had paid for a rose bush to be planted for her and Linda had arranged for a plaque with Lily's name and dates to be displayed beside it.

As we paid our respects at Lily's resting place, I caught sight of a man standing about fifty yards away, looking over at us. He was beckoning me. It was Steve.

Linda quickly spotted him. She grabbed my arm and led me towards him. 'What are you doing here?' she said, tears pouring down her cheeks. He mumbled something about not having meant this to happen and asked if he could have a few minutes alone with me.

To my consternation, Linda left me with him. The politeness that Lily had instilled in me prevented me from being rude or turning my back on him. It's true that I was scared of him, too, but it was not fear that was crippling me now. Nor was it grief, or resentment, or anger, though I felt a measure of all three. The emotion that overwhelmed me was excruciating embarrassment. I simply didn't know this man who was talking to me as if I ought to know him. But I knew enough to be painfully aware that he bore much of the responsibility for Lily's difficult life and early death, and all I wanted was for him to go away.

The ordeal lasted for no more than a few minutes. He asked me how I was and said he had a gift for me. It was a key ring with a miniature football attached to it. I took it, thanked him and we walked away from each other. For ever.

~

Uncle George had paid a penny for a platform ticket at Liverpool Lime Street and now leaned his tall frame through the lowered sash window into our carriage, issuing firm instructions about staying in touch. If we moved we were to remember to take out a Post Office redirection. It cost nothing and would ensure that any mail sent to 6 Walmer Road would be forwarded to us.

Auntie Jean and Uncle George had made it clear that they wanted to make a home for us in Liverpool. We were adamant that we wanted to stay in London. We saw no reason whatsoever why we shouldn't just continue our life as before. We had coped on our own through Lily's countless hospital stays, the last time for over four months, and Linda was used to managing our finances as well as taking responsibility for our welfare. We intended to keep our heads down, say nothing to anybody and simply carry on living at Walmer Road.

Lily's family had taken us back to Liverpool with them for a week following the funeral. Our holiday had its sobering moments, notably our visit to the house in Warham Road in which Lily had grown up, where we experienced for ourselves the icy disregard of her irascible father. But these were easily outweighed by the warmth shown to us by the rest of the Gibson clan, including many cousins we were meeting for the first time. My favourite uncle was Auntie Rita's husband Harry, a diehard Evertonian marooned in Anfield.

Harry had himself been a promising footballer in his youth and had been signed by Blackpool before the war intervened. He took me along to Goodison Park to see Everton play Nottingham Forest. The home side had won the League championship the previous season with Albert Dunlop, Brian Labone, Jimmy Gabriel, Roy Vernon and, at centre forward, the player known as the Golden Vision, Alex Young.

On the terraces, Harry asked me if I smoked. As I'd been puffing away for years and was eager to demonstrate my masculinity, I eagerly accepted the offered cigarette. However, I didn't smoke more than about fifteen a week and Harry was a chain-smoker. Matching him fag for fag, I'd had my weekly quota by half-time. Moreover, Harry smoked Woodbine untipped – small, dark cigarettes made with black tobacco that probably belonged in a pipe, or fuelling an industrial boiler. It was like inhaling burning compost.

As half-time approached, Harry, engrossed in Alex Young's humiliation of the hapless Forest centre half, rather absent-mindedly handed me another stick of black poison. When nobody took it he looked round to find me collapsed on the terraces – completely Woodbined.

The St John's Ambulance first-aiders brought me round. Since neither Harry nor I was keen to leave, they insisted that I sat rather than stood through the second half and shepherded us to a couple of seats in the stand, close to the directors' box. It was the first time Harry had watched his beloved Everton in such comfort. As he puffed his way happily through their 6–1 victory, he told me he'd have to bring me to every game now.

To get an upgrade like this for ten Woodies was a bargain, although he'd be grateful if I could faint a little earlier in the game in future.

Back in London, we mechanically picked up the threads of our daily routine. But our plan to carry on regardless was swiftly scuppered. A letter arrived, addressed to Mrs L.M. Johnson, from London County Council. It informed us that the Walmer Road building was no longer fit for habitation and had been earmarked for demolition. As she was a medical priority, Lily's would be the first family to be rehoused. She was offered a new three-bedroomed house in Welwyn Garden City, Hertfordshire – the house she'd always dreamed of, with her own front door – two weeks after her funeral.

Linda was particularly distraught. The prospect of a house away from the slums, a fresh start in a new place, might have helped to pull Lily through if the offer had been made a year or so earlier. It might have made a world of difference to her condition. I diplomatically kept quiet about our declared aversion to moving out of London. To be fair, I think once Lily's health had taken its dramatic turn for the worse we'd have done anything to please our mother.

Linda went to the Rowe Housing Trust who, since we hadn't notified them, were unaware that Lily had died, as, evidently, was the LCC. She was asked to wait and eventually to step into the office of the man in charge. He wore a three-piece suit with a watch chain dangling from his waistcoat pocket. As Linda gave a full account of the circumstances of Lily's death, he made notes on a large ruled notepad that rested on the desk in front of him. Linda finished by passing him a copy of the letter offering Lily a council house.

He read it carefully. 'How old are you and your brother?'

'I'm sixteen and he's thirteen', she replied.

'I'm afraid that by law you have to be aged twenty-one or over to hold a rent book with us or with the council. I'm afraid you won't be able to take up this offer.'

'But my mum was on the waiting list for seventeen years,' Linda pleaded.

'Your mother may well have been on the council waiting list for seventeen years but your mother is dead. You can't simply inherit her place on the list. In any case, you're too young to have a council property in any circumstances.'

The official said he'd ask somebody from the council to visit us and a couple of days later another man duly turned up on our doorstep. He was waiting there when Linda came home from work. She invited him in, made a pot of tea and there ensued a long conversation. This man wasn't unsympathetic but he was equally unequivocal: there was no prospect what-soever of us being rehoused by the council. At sixteen she was a child and we should go to live with relatives. When Linda told him that the only relatives who could or would take us in were in Liverpool, and that she was training to be a nursery nurse in London, he had a brainwave.

'It's beyond question,' he said, 'that your brother will have to be taken into care. He's likely to be placed with foster parents. As for you, I'm sure Dr Barnardo's could facilitate your child-care studies as part of a programme of care at one of their homes.'

This did not go down well with Linda. She went through everything again: the long periods of time we'd spent alone, the bills paid, the debts cleared. At the end of her peroration she announced that if she and I weren't given a place where we could live together, we'd refuse to leave Walmer Road and they'd have to pull the house down around us.

It was a bravura performance which obviously earned her the respect of the already kindly disposed council official. He left still insisting that allocating us a council house would be impossible but promising to speak to his superiors to see what could be done. A few days later he sent a letter informing us that we'd been assigned a social worker who would be in touch with us shortly.

Needless to say, Linda dealt with all of this on her own, and I'm sure my pessimism wasn't helpful. When she told me of her plan for the Siege of Walmer Road, I pointed out that we'd be considerably easier to remove than the old piano that still occupied the front room.

I held out very little hope for our prospects of staying together, even less when Linda told me about the appointment of a social worker. He made his first appearance on a rare occasion when we both happened to be at home. His name was Mr Pepper. A tall man in his early thirties, with sandy hair, florid cheeks and a kind face, he always wore a white mac, irrespective of the weather.

Mr Pepper had evidently worked hard to follow up the council official's 'brainwave' because he had a little presentation prepared. He'd found a 'nice' foster family who lived close to my school and were prepared to take me in straight away. After Easter, Linda could have a place on an NNEB course at Dr Barnardo's at Barkingside with accommodation provided.

Coincidentally, we had visited that very institution a few years earlier after a fund-raising effort Linda had made in aid of Dr Barnardo's. This had consisted of attempting to sell bits of old tat at a penny apiece from a trestle table set up outside 6 Walmer Road. Linda had got the idea of this 'table sale' from seeing similar initiatives on the streets of Fulham, where she went to school. She had no doubt chosen Dr Barnardo's as the beneficiary because of her desire to work with children; perhaps at the time she was thinking she might work for them. Anyway, we raised something like 10 shillings, of which Lily probably contributed a shilling or two, scraped together to buy some of her stuff back.

On receiving Linda's letter and postal order, Dr Barnardo's invited her to see their children's home at Barkingside. The charity's head office was also there, and I assume it must have been their showcase London residential home. Lily couldn't go with her so she roped me in. I recall a series of houses set in a square round a kind of village green. Accommodation was allocated according to the children's ages and each building had a 'house mother' or 'house father' in charge. It all seemed jolly enough but something about the regimented existence chilled our souls. Our perception was probably unfair and undeserved but we came away feeling glad we were visitors rather than inmates.

When Mr Pepper had outlined his solution he sat back on the old brown settee, looking very pleased with himself. Linda exploded. She leaped off her chair, stood in front of him, hands on hips, and gave him both barrels. 'How dare you! You've never even met us, never spoken to me, and yet you're asking us to do what I've already said is unacceptable!' Mr Pepper looked like a schoolchild being told off by his headmistress. 'But it's all been arranged,' he pleaded.

My guess is that the council official had given a somewhat misleading account of his conversation with Linda to Mr Pepper, who had gone to a lot of time and trouble to secure what he believed we wanted.

'Well, you can just un-arrange it,' Linda retorted fiercely, 'because Alan is not going to live with foster parents and I am not going to Barnardo's.'

'But you're too young to live by yourselves,' Mr Pepper reiterated.

Linda snorted. 'Too young? It's a bit late to worry about that now. We've been living by ourselves for years.'

Linda could be very eloquent and persuasive and couldn't have failed to convince Mr Pepper of her capabilities and accomplishments – or of the truth of her succinct concluding argument: if he was concerned about our welfare, he'd keep us together, not force us apart. She was even more confident that she'd be able to pay the rent on any council house we were allocated since receiving a letter from Steve the previous day. He said he'd resume his maintenance payments, if not on the same scale: the £6 10s a week he'd been ordered to pay originally would be reduced to £2 10s because Lily was dead and Linda was earning. Nevertheless, it was something. He told us that we could rely on him, and the postal order would arrive every week. We couldn't and it didn't, but at least the thought was there.

Mr Pepper's conversion from villain to hero couldn't have been easy for him professionally. On the strength of that one meeting, he must have decided that the risk of letting us stay together was worth taking. Who knows what machinations he had to go through to achieve that for us? We just waited to hear from him, blissfully unaware of whatever battles he was fighting on our behalf.

One day I returned from school to find him on our doorstep, white mac fully buttoned despite the warm weather. I let him in and left him sitting in the front room to wait for Linda. Half an hour later she arrived and asked me, in hushed tones, if Mr Pepper had said anything. He hadn't – and he looked tense. Linda feared the worst. We went together into the front room to learn our fate.

Mr Pepper began by saying how much better off we would be if we agreed to the arrangement he had already suggested. Had we thought any further about it? Linda said we hadn't and wouldn't. He then made a point of asking me if I was of the same view. I announced, somewhat more meekly than Linda, that I was. He told us that he'd argued with the council that we should have the opportunity to remain together and had eventually managed to obtain their reluctant agreement. We could be given a place to live on two conditions. The first was that we had to find an adult householder in London to stand as a guarantor. The second was that we accepted that he would be visiting us on a regular basis as our social worker.

Linda was so overcome she almost cried. She took Mr Pepper's phone number and said she'd ring him as soon as she'd been round to Peabody Buildings to ask Uncle Jim to stand as guarantor. Mr Pepper was clearly impressed by my sister's maturity and no doubt felt they were now allies. But if he thought there'd be no further confrontations he was underestimating her.

Once Uncle Jim had agreed and Mr Pepper had been to see him with all the necessary paperwork, the council offered us a flat in Hammersmith. Linda went to take a look at it. The flat was on the top floor of a ten-storey block served by a lift that was covered in graffiti and reeked of urine. The previous tenant, an old lady, hadn't wanted electricity installed, preferring to retain gas lighting. It was in almost as bad a state as the condemned houses in Walmer Road and Southam Street. The walls were damp and cracked and there was mildew everywhere. Nowadays an enterprising estate agent might try to talk it up by describing it as 'open-plan': not a single room had a door – they had apparently all been pulled off and chopped up for firewood. We were used to unpleasant smells but the rank stench emanating from that flat, Linda declared, almost made her vomit. Wisely deciding against investigating the source of the appalling stink, she closed the door, marched to the nearest telephone box and rang Mr Pepper.

'The flat is disgusting, I'm not accepting it,' she told our hero.

'You can't refuse,' he said. 'They won't make you another offer. You're in no position to reject it. You have to go where they send you.'

'Well, we're not going there. Go and look at it yourself and if you honestly think you could live there, come round and tell me.'

Mr Pepper went to see the flat the following day. It was the last we heard of it and within a week we'd been offered another one.

PART III

AFTER LILY

Chapter 17

THE SOUTH SIDE of the Thames was uncharted territory for Linda and me. But that's where the council sent us – to Pitt House on the Wilberforce estate in York Road, on the border between Battersea and Wandsworth. Number 11 was on the first floor of a squat four-storey block built in the 1930s.

It was, it must be said, only just south of the river – about 500 yards from Wandsworth Bridge. Opposite the estate, on the riverbank, was the huge Booth's gin distillery, whose aroma covered the entire neighbourhood like a thick, pungent juniper blanket. My memory automatically generates that smell whenever I cross Wandsworth Bridge, even though the distillery gave way years ago to plush riverside apartments.

Our flat was a maisonette. Our own front door opened into a sizeable living room and there was a separate kitchen. Upstairs were two bedrooms, our first indoor toilet and a proper bathroom. To us it was pure luxury.

We left North Kensington on 4 May 1964. It was farewell to Berriman's, Maynard's and the little old lady in the 'milk shop' opposite us. Farewell to the people who'd managed to establish a community amid the squalor and poverty of Southam Street and Walmer Road. Linda would never return but for me, the umbilical cord had not quite yet been severed.

Too far away now to help Johnny Carter deliver milk or paraffin, I said goodbye to him and thanked him again for my guitar. Mike loaded our few belongings (including the Salvation Army three-piece suite) into a small hired van. We left Steve's piano behind for the demolition men, part of a Notting Hill that was disappearing for ever.

Linda paid the rent, fed the meters, bought the food, washed and swept, all with minimal help from me. Mr Pepper would call on us once a week in the early evening. On the nights he was due Linda would cook a proper meal to underline the success of our domesticity. She spent the weekends in Watford with Mike and then I would have the flat pretty much to myself.

Linda was as good as her word, never once defaulting on the rent. How she managed is still a mystery to me. Steve's contribution soon dried up, leaving her to support us on her modest wage with financial help from Mike, when he could afford it. But manage she did, and I suspect she was so obviously in control that Mr Pepper quickly realized neither she nor I required the constant monitoring that had been stipulated. As a result, though he was obliged to continue his weekly visits until Linda's eighteenth birthday, they gradually became briefer and more perfunctory.

What both Linda and I found most difficult was the antipathy of our neighbours, who seemed to resent seeing two teenagers occupying a council flat when they knew of many families on the waiting list. Given our own bitter experience, to a certain extent we could understand how they felt –

Lily had waited in vain for seventeen years for decent accommodation – but their naked hostility was hard to rationalize.

In two and a half years at Pitt House, I can't remember any of our neighbours ever speaking to us. It didn't matter much to me but Linda was gregarious and anxious for us to be accepted. It wasn't long before the situation worsened. The eldest boy in the flat next door, a lad of about Linda's age, hung around with a gang. One evening they pulled out the fuse box to our flat, which was easily accessible in the communal area at the end of the landing.

Mike reconnected everything, but it happened again and again – always our fuse box, never any of the others. Linda complained to the caretaker, to no avail. He seemed to bear us even more ill will than the tenants did.

With Linda in Watford most weekends and me out and about, it was probably only a matter of time before someone broke in. The flat would be in darkness and it was obvious nobody was at home. They would come on a Saturday. The first time they took our beloved Dansette. The second time they took my Vox electric guitar (which could have been divine retribution, given how Johnny probably acquired it in the first place). The third time they didn't take anything because there was nothing left to steal. We had no insurance and we didn't report the break-ins to the police, or to Mr Pepper. If we'd told Mr Pepper his Plan A could have been resurrected, and if we'd told the police they'd have told Mr Pepper.

Pitt House was a palace compared to where we'd lived before. If the price we had to pay to stay there was a bit of nastiness from the neighbours and the caretaker's indifference, it was worth it. What mattered most to Linda and me was being together, free from any institutions.

The Wilberforce estate was much closer to my school than Walmer Road. Indeed, I often walked there and back. The sixteen months I remained there after Lily died was the only period of my time at Sloane I enjoyed, thanks to the arrival of two new teachers I liked and who inspired my interest in their subjects.

Mr Pallai had left his native Hungary during the 1956 uprising. He moonlighted with the BBC World Service, broadcasting back to Hungary, while spending his days teaching us history and a new subject on the curriculum, economics. Peter Pallai was built like a rugby player – broad shoulders, slim physique – and wore his thinning hair close-cropped.

Half the teachers at Sloane seemed to me to be deeply uninterested in both their subjects and their pupils. 'Dolly' Harris, who taught us French, was so soporific that boys had been known to sleep peacefully through entire lessons. Mr Woosnam, our geography teacher, at least made an attempt to engage us in his classes. 'What would you like to do in geography?' he asked keenly. 'Play football,' came the depressing reply.

My favourite teacher was Peter Carlen, who had taken over from Mr Smith as our English teacher part way through my third year. By the time I entered my fourth and what turned out to be final year, he'd become the second most important adult in my life (Mr Pepper just clinched the top spot). In class Mr Carlen led us, line by line, through Wilfred Owen's 'Anthem for Doomed Youth', exploring the context and the background and pointing out the power of alliteration ('the rifles' rapid rattle');

he analysed *Animal Farm*, explaining the subtext and how Orwell used his characters to satirize the descent of the Russian Revolution into totalitarianism. He took us to the theatre to see Spike Milligan in *Oblomov* and musicals such as *Oliver!* and *Half a Sixpence*.

Outside his lessons, he maintained his interest in our welfare. He once saw me reading the copy of *David Copperfield* I'd borrowed from Mr Cox and asked me what else I read. I told him about the paperback crime thrillers I'd begun to pick up for a few pence at the Quality Book Shop in Shepherd's Bush Road. By then I'd swapped a whole stack of *Charles Buchan's Football Monthly* magazines for a shelf full of crime mysteries by Agatha Christie, Leslie Charteris, John Dickson Carr and Edgar Wallace. He suggested that I write a review of every book I read at the back of my English exercise book and guided my reading, giving me a list of books he thought I ought to read and would enjoy. On his recommendation I was introduced to Geoffrey Household, Ian Fleming, H.G. Wells, Arnold Bennett and C.S. Forester.

Mr Carlen was in his early thirties and wore his already greying hair fashionably long, which must have frustrated Doc Henry, who was for ever sending me home to have mine cut. The timbre of his voice commanded attention. I never heard him raise it. There was no need: nobody misbehaved in Mr Carlen's lessons.

By this time I'd decided I wanted to be a writer as well as a rock star. I told Mr Carlen of my ambition and he encouraged me to develop characters, pre-plan plots and submit my stories as school projects. I created Mr Midnight, a black-clad super-hero with a mission to avenge the wrongs done to innocent citizens, and a detective, Inspector Andrews – basically a synthesis of all the detectives created by the authors whose books I devoured. Having noticed in the novels I'd read that so many important conversations took place in restaurants, I made Inspector Andrews a regular at The Golden Egg, one of a chain of garishly decorated budget eateries. Apart from Renee's Pie and Mash Shop on the Golborne Road, it was the only restaurant I was aware of.

I was so convinced my future career as a writer was assured that I used the lessons that bored me (basically all of them except English, history and economics) to try to teach myself to write left-handed, on the basis that if I was going to make a living out of writing I would need to be ambidextrous in case I broke my right arm. I suspect the fact that my hero Paul McCartney was left-handed also had something to do with it.

After Mr Carlen told me about the *Writers' and Artists' Yearbook*, which offered advice to budding writers and a useful directory of newspapers and publishers of books and magazines, I began to send off my pathetic stories and poems to various magazines and built up an impressive collection of rejection slips. I comforted myself with the knowledge that all writers had to face the disappointment of having their work declined on their way to becoming famous.

One day Mr Carlen handed me the money to purchase four copies of a book for the school library from a bookshop on the King's Road. 'Which book?' I asked.

'Whichever one you think boys like you would like to read.'

It was noon on a summer's day and I was delighted to be released from school to browse in a bookshop entrusted with the assignment of spending the school's funds, which after some consideration I allocated to George Orwell's *Keep the Aspidistra Flying*. I felt very adult and, like Mr Carlen, a little bohemian. I remember lighting a cigarette as I strolled down the King's Road in the sunshine. I'd left my school blazer and tie in the cloakroom so that, for this expedition at least, I could imagine I was a struggling writer seeking inspiration rather than a schoolboy on an errand.

Mr Carlen knew I intended to leave school at the end of that academic year and wanted me to sit my mock O-Level in English a year early, perhaps reasoning that if I passed I'd be motivated to stay on and take the real thing. As I remember, the mock exams were used to test whether a child was good enough to take the prestigious O-Level or should instead be entered for the inferior CSE. I was keen on the idea but it needed the headmaster's approval. Doc Henry refused to allow it unless I made a commitment to stay on. I had made up my mind, however, and being deprived of sitting an exam was hardly going to change it.

Despite our precarious financial situation, Linda never pressurized me to leave school. Quite the opposite. She was scrupulous about going to see my teachers on parents' evenings. They must have been uncomfortable talking to a 'parent' who could have been in the sixth form of the girls' school next door. Linda always gave me the same advice following these consultations, which was basically work harder, stay on, fulfil your potential. She'd tell me how much Lily would have wanted me to take O-Levels and how I'd be throwing away the advantages of my grammar-school education if I left prematurely. When I pointed out that she herself had left school at fifteen, she made the reasonable point that she'd continued her education at college and, in any case, she had known what she wanted to do, whereas I didn't.

Oh, but I did. I would be a songwriter and pop star. The rejection slips had convinced me that I needed to concentrate on music first and take up writing later, perhaps after the fourth bestselling album.

By now I was playing in a duo with Andrew Wiltshire – me on guitar and vocals, Andrew on his gradually expanding drum kit – but only in the bedroom Andrew shared with his brother, John. Our market research was conducted at the Marquee in Soho, where we saw a Mod band called the Action and, later, a great 'blue-eyed' soul singer called Rod Stewart. After paying the entrance fee, we usually didn't have enough money left for the bus fare home and would walk from the West End to Pitt House, often stopping to sit on steps leading down to the Thames by Putney Bridge to contemplate our futures in the hush of the small hours.

We'd both decided to leave school and were determined to forge a career in music but we didn't know how. As the end of the school year approached, I was sent to a careers advice office on the Fulham Road and, at Mr Carlen's suggestion, asked about a job that involved writing. The very helpful man asked if I'd be interested in producing the blurbs for books and LP records, encapsulating the plot or describing the tracks. This sounded very exciting but nothing ever came of it. Andrew and I told everyone at Sloane that we were going to play in a group that would be touring the country. To us it was more of a prediction than a fib.

In July 1965, two months after my fifteenth birthday, I duly left Sloane, with no regrets. I'm sure that as far as the headmaster was concerned, the feeling was mutual.

Dereck Tapper, whose path through the education system had mirrored mine since we were five years old, had blazed a trail at Sloane as he had at Bevington – my Sloane school photograph from 1964 shows only three black pupils apart from him. He stayed on and continued to do well after we parted company.

Five years after leaving school, I opened a national newspaper to see a photograph of Dereck playing Romeo in an Exeter University production of *Romeo and Juliet,* deemed newsworthy because the girl taking the role of Juliet was white and mixed-race casting was considered to be a startling innovation at the time. The characteristic I most associate with Dereck is courage. He knew how to stand up for himself, although when our paths diverged I still had little real comprehension of exactly what it was he'd had to stand up to.

Despite the unhappiness of most of my time at Sloane, Mr Smith, Mr Pallai and in particular Mr Carlen had begun to prise open a window on the world for me. The school had also happened to place me at the centre of an area that was coming to epitomize 'Swinging London' for trend-setters and teenagers across the country and beyond.

Carnaby Street, a favourite stamping ground for Colin James and me (though I only remember once buying any clothes there) was already at the beating heart of pop culture. Chelsea had for many years been a district towards which artists, musicians and theatrical types had gravitated and its inhabitants tended to be in the vanguard of new fashions and social changes. When I started at Sloane, King's Road was still a street of butchers and bakers, newsagents and grocers, like any other London high street. As I left school the cutting-edge, psychedelic boutiques for which the road would become renowned were beginning to appear. Yet I don't remember it occurring to me that I was living my life at the hub of Swinging London. History exists only in retrospect and besides, as someone once said, if you can remember the 1960s, you weren't there.

The Establishment was changing, too. In the 1964 general election the country had elected its first Labour government since I was a baby. Under the new prime minister, Harold Wilson – a former grammar-school boy – we would see the introduction of a whole series of social reforms. By the end of the decade, comprehensive education had been expanded nationwide, polytechnics and the Open University had been created, abortion was legal, capital punishment abolished and homosexuality decriminalized.

While I didn't listen to the radio as often as I had when we'd had a set wired into that Bakelite switch, I kept abreast of current affairs. When I got my first full-time job I decided to buy *The Times* to read on my way to work. It seemed an adult thing to do – and I now considered myself an adult.

~

I began work the Monday after I left school, as a postal clerk with Remington Electric Razors at their headquarters on Kensington High Street. I was paid £10 every fortnight, from which I gave Linda a few pounds towards the rent, and received five luncheon vouchers a week, worth 3 shillings (15p) each. Losing free school meals at Sloane (where the dinner ladies gave me seconds and sometimes thirds) was a blow, but I found a café that served steak pie, chips and baked beans for exactly 3 shillings and that's what I ate, every single lunchtime.

My job was to log in all the shavers being returned for repair by registered post and dispatch them back to their owners once they were mended; to frank letters on the Pitney Bowes machine and to take the mail to the Post Office in Kensington High Street every day at 5pm. It was far from absorbing and left me plenty of time to dream of the future. Those daydreams never featured working for Tesco, yet that's where I ended up six months after leaving school.

I got the job through Ronnie Handley, a neighbour of Andrew's, who lived with his dad a few doors away from the Wiltshires in Nascot Street. We showed Ronnie great respect as he had his own scooter and an M-51 fishtail parka, the pukka parka, so to speak. He was about twenty and worked as a warehouse manager at Tesco in King Street, Hammersmith.

Supermarkets were just becoming a familiar sight on London's streets and this was one of the bigger stores in West London. Ronnie told me he needed an assistant. The pay was much better than at Remington's – £8 a week, plus luncheon vouchers, too – so in January 1966 I moved on to Tesco, where my principal function was to support Ronnie, ordering stock for the warehouse and helping to unload the deliveries. The Tesco managers (including Ronnie) wore tunic-style cream linen jackets. The non-managers (including me) wore awful black nylon overalls that flapped around our knees.

Andrew was training to be a butcher. He liked the sound of the customer-free environment of the Tesco butchers' department. It was based at the warehouse, from where cuts of meat were transferred to the shop already shrink-wrapped, which meant Tesco butchers never had to deal with the public. A few months later, he joined me there.

By day we were unassuming supermarket workers, but every moment of our spare time was devoted to the pursuit of our dream to become pop stars. We longed to form a proper band. Luckily so did Danny Curtis, elder brother of my childhood friend Walter, who was engaged to Tony Cox's sister, Carole. Danny had a passable voice, bags of energy and few inhibitions. At nineteen years of age, Andrew and I felt he was getting on a bit, but on the other hand that brought certain advantages. He drove a van, he could talk his way in and out of anything and he knew how to mend fuses and cable wire.

Danny came over to Pitt House to talk me through his ideas. He would be our singer/manager and would make bookings, provide the transport, set up the gear and distribute our earnings. He volunteered to advertise in *Melody Maker* for two guitarists. We christened the band the Area and painted the name on the side of Danny's ancient Bedford van. Our base was to be the Fourth Feathers Club in Edgware Road, one of a series of Feathers youth clubs across London.

Our advert brought us bass guitarist Ian Clark, a red-haired Scot studying music at university in London, and, on lead guitar, Tony Kearns, who'd left his native Chester to seek fame and fortune in the capital and owned an exotic Futurama instrument.

When it became obvious that my small amplifier – the one Mike had made for me as promised for my fourteenth birthday – wasn't powerful enough, Danny blagged me an old Marshall from the Small Faces, who also practised at the Fourth Feathers, as did a band called the Wild Angels. The famous impresario Don Arden, who was managing the Small Faces at the time and whose son Dave played with the Wild Angels, was a frequent visitor.

It was just as we were putting the group together that my Vox was stolen in one of the Pitt House break-ins. My saviour, to my surprise and gratitude, was Lily. She had left £40 for me – whether in a savings account, or from an insurance policy, I no longer remember – which Linda hadn't mentioned, having intended to set it aside for me until I was older. When I lost my guitar my sister decided to give me the money. I used it to buy a gorgeous red Höfner Verythin from a shop in Wardour Street for £35.

Once my guitar had been replaced, we were up and away, playing in pubs and clubs that Andrew and I were too young to drink in. We had a regular spot every Wednesday night at the Pavilion opposite Wormwood Scrubs, a big music venue where we occasionally supported the Symbols – a band that made the lower reaches of the charts with an early cover of the Four Seasons' 'Bye Bye Baby'. On one exhilarating evening we played in front of 1,000 people at Aylesbury College – not quite Shea Stadium but a lively enough venue. When the crowd made it clear that they wanted to hear us rather than the headline band, Fifth Dynasty, we really felt we were going places. And we hadn't the slightest doubt that the principal place we were going was the top of the charts.

Chapter 18

As my musical career was launched in 1966 our two-and-a-half-year occupancy of the Pitt House maisonette was drawing to an end. Linda and Mike were going to be married on 24 September and Mike had found a house for them in Watford, close to his parents. Linda had by now qualified as a nursery nurse and would be transferring from Brook Green to a nursery closer to her new home. The house Mike was buying had three bedrooms and they wanted me to move there with them. The idea was the topic of several heated discussions between Linda and me but she knew in her heart that I wouldn't leave London. I was a Londoner, born and bred, my whole world was in the town and I had no intention of relocating to what I saw as the countryside. The problem was, where would I live once she was married?

Linda came up with an elaborate plan to enable me to stay on in the flat after she moved to Watford, which involved Mike's sister, Barbara, a single mother living in a caravan in Surrey. Linda asked the council if Barbara could move into the flat in her place. The woman from the LCC was in no mood to discuss this option. No, she replied curtly, that would not be possible. When would Linda be returning the keys? At least the threat of foster parents had diminished. Children in care were generally turfed out at the age of sixteen.

The solution came from 318 Lancaster Road. Linda contacted Mrs Cox, who said I could stay there, sharing a room with my erstwhile best friend, Tony. I would pay a few pounds in rent from my wages as I'd done at Pitt House. After two and a half years away from Notting Hill, I was going back to my manor.

I had no romantic notions of returning to my roots, nor had I missed Notting Hill. I'd been particularly glad to escape our miserable accommodation. But there were practical reasons why it was good to be back. Living with Mr and Mrs Cox was perfect for me, and for the Area, with Danny living opposite and Andrew within walking distance. Although Tony and I never resumed our close friendship, we always got on fine. While he wasn't actually a Mod, he had a Lambretta and a parka with 'The Who' emblazoned on the back. I'd ride pillion as we buzzed around town with his mates from Kilburn in a scooter cavalcade.

Picturing the Coxes' large living room brings so many memories of that time into sharp focus. It was there that one evening, after returning from a gig at the Fourth Feathers, I watched the horror of Aberfan – the collapse of a mountainside colliery waste tip sited above a Welsh village, which engulfed a terrace of homes and a primary school – unfolding on the TV screen. The disaster claimed the lives of 116 children and twenty-eight adults.

Most of the memories, though, are happy ones. It was in that room that we gathered to watch the midnight movie every

Saturday night on BBC2. Though this new channel had been launched in 1964, initially it could only be picked up by a particular kind of receiver, which limited its audience, and I had never had access to it before. Pat and Albert would nestle together on the long settee as they had always done in the evenings. Their youngest son would perch at the end, with Danny, Carole, Tony and me sprawled across the armchairs and the floor, gripped by black-and-white classics such as *On the Waterfront* and *Dial M for Murder*.

And it was here that Andrew, a frequent visitor, met his future wife, Ann Cheetham. Ann, who was Pat's niece, had been at Wornington Road Infants' School with me until her family were moved out of Notting Hill to Aylesbury in Buckinghamshire. Ann and her sister Irene would come to visit their cousins in Lancaster Road, both looking like Twiggy, gamine in their tiny mini-skirts, with lots of eye make-up and false eyelashes. Andrew was instantly smitten by Ann and the relationship began in earnest after the Area concert at Aylesbury College, which Ann had helped Danny to arrange.

If reminiscing about the Coxes' living room brings back feelings of warm contentment, it is the kitchen that dominates my memory of their home and carries the most comforting associations. It's difficult to describe my obsession with food without sounding melancholic and sentimental. It was simple, really. I'd never been able to eat as much as I wanted to. I was a skinny kid who had relied on those free school meals to an unhealthy degree. At work, the luncheon vouchers ensured I had one meal a day, which was basically all I was used to. One meal a day. It was never enough for an active teenager who was fast developing into a man, and hunger gnawed away at me perpetually like a dull toothache.

Now I was included in Mr Cox's big, hot breakfasts. Every morning, once we were allowed into the kitchen after Carole's strip wash at the sink (there was no bathroom at Lancaster Road), Mr Cox would preside over the meal while his wife scampered around polishing her youngest son's shoes, which always struck me as over-indulgence. Albert wore an immaculate white vest tucked into a thickly belted pair of trousers. He always had a tea towel tossed casually over one shoulder. Porridge bubbled on the stove for starters, to be followed by egg, bacon and tomatoes and a constant pot of freshly brewed tea. Albert cooked, cleared the table, washed up and went to work – planting a firm kiss on Pat's lips before he left.

~

The month Linda and Mike got married, Ronnie Handley handed in his notice at Tesco. He was leaving to become a rep for Smith's Crisps. Reps were an integral part of supermarket life then. They were always men, wore suits and drove company cars. Their job was to try to persuade managers to buy more of their products and to give them a more prominent position in their shops.

The manager of Tesco in King Street was a large ex-copper of capricious nature called Mr Dawson. When Ronnie announced his departure, Mr Dawson asked if I'd take over temporarily as warehouse manager. I asked if I could temporarily receive Ronnie's wages, too, but he said it would only be for a couple of weeks and not worth the disruption to the payroll. There was nobody to temporarily assist me, but the biggest disappointment was that I would not be allowed to wear the manager's natty jacket. Even temporarily.

None the less I carried on doing my job and Ronnie's, loading and unloading produce, taking it up in the lift to the warehouse floor, collecting and compressing acres of cardboard and dealing with the paperwork from orders and deliveries. September passed, then October, with no sign of a replacement for Ronnie or anyone to help me. I'd always felt a pay rise was a vain hope but I did think Mr Dawson would at least release me from the nylon smock.

The situation hadn't changed by the time 'Christmas pressure' began in early December. That was always a time of chaos in the warehouse, with the surge in demand on the shop floor matched by frantic activity behind the scenes.

Ten days before Christmas the regional manager paid a surprise visit and obviously had words with Mr Dawson about the performance of the store. At the start of my lunch break at 12.30, I was walking down the stairs from the warehouse, putting on my coat, when I met Mr Dawson coming up the other way. 'Where do you think you're going?' asked my foul-tempered manager, in full sergeant-major mode.

'I'm going to lunch.'

'No you're not. You'll go to lunch when you've tidied the warehouse.'

'I'll tidy the warehouse when I've had my lunch,' I replied.

By now, Mr Dawson had reached the top of the stairs and I was at the bottom. His voice boomed down at me. 'If you don't come back now,' he fumed, provoked by my defiance, 'you won't have a job to come back to.'

I'm not proud of my rejoinder. I wanted it to be succinct and wittily scathing, to encapsulate in a pithy sentence my months of frustration at doing a manager's job without the pay, without an assistant and, most importantly for my morale, without that cream linen jacket. A Wildean one-liner so wounding that Mr Dawson would fall sobbing to the floor, pleading for my forgiveness through his tears. But all I managed was: 'Stick the job up your fucking arse.'

In high dudgeon, I marched off to have my lunch at the pub Andrew and I had begun to frequent along with the more senior Tesco butchers and greengrocers. Andrew came over later with a message from Mr Dawson. 'He says if you apologize you can come back.' He added that he thought I should stand my ground against an unpopular manager and that everyone was on my side.

I stood my ground. I had another job within a fortnight, though admittedly the pay was 10 shillings a week less than I had been earning, and there were no luncheon vouchers. Andrew had told Ronnie Handley what had happened, and he alerted me to the availability of a job at a small Anthony Jackson's supermarket in the Upper Richmond Road, East Sheen. By New Year's Day 1967, I had started work there. Thankfully, I wasn't asked for a reference from Tesco. They would no doubt have insisted that they'd sacked me, whereas as far as I was concerned, I'd resigned on a point of principle. Either way, my sense of outrage remained with me, as did the conviction that not only should the voices of workers be heard but they needed some protection against exploitation.

Mr Dawson went on to become the manager of the biggest Tesco store in the country, but there is an interesting codicil to this story. A few years after our showdown I read in a Sunday tabloid about a Tesco manager who had claimed his family had been held to ransom by masked bandits demanding that he hand over the store's takings. The masked bandits did not exist. It was a hoax he had devised himself in a bid to rob Tesco of thousands of pounds. The miscreant was none other than Mr Dawson. I rest my case.

I was happy stacking shelves at Anthony Jackson's, which wasn't much more than a large corner store. Ironically, it's now a shoe shop called Johnson's. There was one girl, Kath, on the till, two shelf-stackers (myself and Sandra, a cheery redhead with a permanent cold) and a workaholic manager, a Maltese guy called Johnny Farugia. Johnny was about thirty-five years old, short with a significant paunch that defied all sartorial attempts to contain it. He was for ever either hitching up his trousers – a task he insisted on performing with his elbows while at the same time checking his flies with his fingers. It was an awkward manoeuvre and one he repeated every thirty seconds or so.

I've never known anyone work as hard as Johnny Farugia. He helped on the tills, squabbled with the reps, flattened cardboard boxes, stacked shelves, often doing all four jobs simultaneously while smoking a cigarette, conducting staccato conversations with several people at once and executing the ritual that stopped his trousers falling down.

Johnny loved his wife, England, Anthony Jackson's and his car, in that order. He'd worked his way up to a nice semi-detached in Sutton and had acquired a cream-coloured Rover upon which he lavished the love and attention he'd have devoted to a child, if he'd had one. It was washed and polished every few days. Odour-repellents, a miniature George Cross and a Union Jack adorned the inside. On the outside it boasted every modern gadget known to man: wing-mirror extensions, AA badges, a gleaming roof-rack and windscreen-wiper enhancements.

His favourite pastime at work was standing on a table at the rear of the store so that he could monitor the shop floor for light-fingered customers through the two-way mirror. He happened to be doing this on the day we were the victims of a robbery. Kath had opened the till to give some change when the man she was serving leaned across her and snatched up all the banknotes. She screamed and the guy rushed out and jumped into a car waiting for him outside, its engine running.

Johnny came charging out from the back of the shop like a bull on to the streets of Pamplona. As the getaway car pulled away from the kerb, he flung himself across the windscreen, clutching on to the wipers. He managed to cling on for about five minutes as the driver accelerated, swinging the steering wheel from side to side and reversing to try to shake him off. When he succeeded and the pair sped away through the quiet avenues of East Sheen, Kath, Sandra and I ran outside to help Johnny out of the gutter into which he'd been thrown. Up he bounced, shouting, swearing and hauling up his trousers. The local paper carried the story of the robbery on its front page (not a great deal happened in East Sheen) and Johnny sent a copy home to his parents in Malta, proud of his contribution to law and order in his beloved England.

∼

Pat Cox had been a true friend to Lily. Her generosity in taking me into her already over-populated home is something for which I will be eternally grateful. However, I was well aware that it couldn't last.

Notting Hill was beginning its biggest phase of demolition since it suffered the unwanted attentions of the Luftwaffe during the war. Most of Southam Street was already no more. All that remained of our end was the Earl of Warwick on the corner and, further along on the other side of the road, Southam House, a small block of flats built in the 1930s. The eastern end, on the other side of Golborne Road, had disappeared completely. On the corner where the bagwash had once been, the Brutalist-style Trellick Tower, thirty-one storeys high, was slowly rising in its place. By 1972 – when the social problems of high-rise tower blocks were already emerging – it would be casting its gaze across the capital like the Eye of Mordor. Walmer Road was now being laid to waste and soon the bulldozers would be descending on our end of Lancaster Road, the next area to be flattened to make room for the Westway.

When Albert Cox removed the Old Holborn roll-up from the side of his mouth (where it usually managed to cling on even when he was speaking) and cleared his throat, I knew he had something difficult to tell me. We were alone in the big front room at Lancaster Road, early in the winter of 1967. Mr Cox explained that he'd received a letter offering the family the council house for which they'd been waiting for so long. It was on the Roehampton estate, near my old school's playing fields.

The hard part for kindly Mr Cox was breaking the news that I couldn't go with them. I had never expected this arrangement to last, so it wasn't as devastating as the Coxes evidently thought it would be. I could picture Mrs Cox urging Albert, in whispered conversations, to have a talk with me while there was nobody else around, which wasn't easy. The house was seldom quiet, and I'd never known it quieter than it was that afternoon. Perhaps the rest of the family had been instructed to keep out of the way. I imagine the uncomplaining Tony would have wanted his bedroom to himself in their new house. Transplanting our cramped sleeping conditions to Roehampton wouldn't have suited either of us.

I found somewhere else to live very quickly. Mrs Kenny, an elderly Irish widow, advertised for a tenant to rent a furnished room in her spacious flat in Hamlet Gardens at the Chiswick end of King Street in Hammersmith, close to where I had worked for Tesco. This was not the kind of flat I was familiar with. That is to say it was nothing like Pitt House. The front door opened on to an apparently endless hallway. The accommodation was L-shaped, and my room was on the left as you turned into the lower part of the 'L'. It was thirty paces – I counted them once – from my door to the kitchen, at the very top of the 'L'.

Mrs Kenny was a warm and maternal woman. She didn't ask for a guarantor, even though I was still only sixteen, telling me merely that I could move in whenever I liked. The room, equipped with a wash basin, bed, wardrobe, standard lamp and a plush armchair, would cost me £2 a week and there was a separate meter I would have to feed with shilling coins for my electricity supply. I was invited to join her and her grown-up son, who also lived there, in the living room to watch TV whenever I liked.

I rarely laid eyes on Mrs Kenny after that first meeting. I left my rent on the kitchen table for her every Friday, and beyond that there was no necessity for our paths to cross. I was shy and uncomfortable in the company of strangers. As for her son, he might have been a phantom for all I knew, because I never saw him once. When I came back from work I'd stay in my comfortably fusty room, leaving it only to make the occasional foray to the kitchen, or to use the bathroom next door. I would hear the television as I sneaked past the living room on my way up and down the hall, but I never crossed its threshold. Johnny Farugia let me take the portable radio home from the back of the shop every evening and I'd listen to that for entertainment, or read one of my collection of books, which I kept in a large coffin-shaped cardboard box – the most substantial item I'd brought with me from Lancaster Road.

Thus Mrs Kenny, her unseen grown-up son and I lived our lives completely independently of one another while occupying the same address. My friends envied me such freedom but, used as I was to being on my own, Hamlet Gardens could feel lonely after the clamour and bustle of the Coxes' home. Andrew was going steady with Ann so I didn't spend much time with him when we weren't practising or performing with our band. I'd had a few girlfriends myself, from Susan Kelly, who'd bought me 'You're My World' by Cilla Black for my fourteenth birthday, to Stephanie Bates, who lived in the prefabs on the notorious White City estate. Even though I chivalrously risked being beaten up by the local gangs when I walked her home every night, she dumped me unceremoniously for her cousin. All of these romances had, however, been short-lived.

None of that mattered when I stood on stage with the Area. The band was still doing well and we truly believed that stardom was just a recording contract away.

Chapter 19

O<small>N ONE GLORIOUS</small> evening, 4 March 1967, to be precise, we played at a dance in Shepherd's Bush. That afternoon, I'd been at Wembley to see QPR beat West Bromwich Albion 3–2 in the League Cup final. It was the first such final to be played at Wembley and the first time a Third Division side had triumphed in the competition. That cup remains the only major trophy QPR have ever won. That season, they went on to complete a double by winning the Third Division title as well.

Although I never made the association, it was the third anniversary of Lily's death. Had Linda, living quietly in Watford, registered what a momentous day it was for all Rangers fans, she would have told me, as she so often did, that Lily's spirit was guiding our lives.

That night of celebration found the Area in the heart of Rangers territory, playing at a wedding reception attended by about a hundred jubilant fans. The atmosphere was amazing, with the band at one with the audience. Their constant chant of 'Rodney, Rodney' was turned into a nifty little drumbeat by Andrew, and this collective tribute to the most skilful player I've ever seen on a football pitch, the incomparable Rodney

Marsh, who'd scored a fabulous second goal that afternoon, punctuated the evening.

A month earlier, Danny had managed to hire Regent Sound Studios in Denmark Street in Soho for an hour. Studio time was expensive, particularly at a place like Regent, where many top artists recorded. Danny met the cost with the aim of getting a return on his investment when the demo disc we were there to produce was picked up by one of the major labels. We recorded two numbers, 'Hard Life' written by Ian and Tony, and one of my songs – 'I Have Seen'. Having taken so long getting 'Hard Life' right, we had only ten minutes left for my song. No time for retakes or to overlay the harmonies, but thanks to Andrew's exceptional drumming and the chance to hear the song played back over the state-of-the-art equipment at Regent Sound, we were happy. It sounded brilliant to us and we left the studios convinced that a record deal was achievable.

By this time, Andrew and I had grown so confident of our abilities that, unbeknown to our fellow band members, we were both keeping our options open by responding to ads placed in the music press by established groups with vacancies to fill.

Danny couldn't have tried harder with the Area's demo disc. He hawked it round all the established labels and took it to a new one, Deram, that was enjoying a lot of publicity at the time. He managed to interest Don Arden, who was considering hiring us as a support act for a Small Faces tour and releasing 'Hard Life' as a single at the same time. But London was brimming with talented musicians and up-and-coming bands. Making the breakthrough was a matter of luck and timing as well as public appeal and musical prowess, and we couldn't all succeed. Neither the Area nor the record was bad, just not good enough.

The end came for the band when somebody broke into the Fourth Feathers, where we stored our instruments between gigs, and stole the lot – Andrew's drums, the mikes, Ian's and Tony's guitars and amps. Luckily, I had taken my Höfner Verythin home that night to practise, but I lost the new amplifier I'd bought on hire purchase with Johnny Farugia as my guarantor. It wasn't insured. None of the equipment was. There was no way we could afford to replace all the instruments and so the Area was no more: killed off by the crime wave that seemed to be following me around.

∼

A few months later, Danny Curtis told me that a band he knew were interested in recruiting me. I wouldn't need to worry about buying another amp, he assured me: one would be provided for me. The In-Betweens were a proper semi-professional group, with a manager and even a small fan club. What was really interesting and unusual about them was that their manager, Arif Ali, was Asian and the band was multi-racial. The bass guitarist, Sham Hassan, was from the Caribbean; the drummer, Mike Bakridon, was Indian; Ivan, the lead guitarist, was Indo-Italian and others flitting in and out had Indo-Guyanese and West Indian backgrounds. Their greatest asset was a stunningly beautiful lead vocalist named Carmen. It was rare then for bands to have any female members, let alone for a woman to be fronting a group as Carmen did. The daughter of an Indian mother and a German father, she had big brown eyes, long black hair and a fabulous figure.

And so I joined the In-Betweens as the white guy on rhythm

guitar and backing vocals. We played soul – Stax, Tamla, Atlantic – but with a fair smattering of pop, songs like 'The First Cut is the Deepest', the Bee Gees' 'To Love Somebody' and our classic rendition of the Troggs' 'Wild Thing'. I took lead vocals on this while Carmen danced seductively around me, draping herself across my shoulders in a way I wouldn't have appreciated Danny Curtis doing.

Our base was a pub called the Pied Horse at the Angel, Islington, opposite the Post Office's Northern District head-quarters, where bass guitarist Sham worked as a postman. North London was a foreign land to me and getting there involved a circuitous tube journey at least once a week for our regular Friday-night gig at the pub and on the odd Saturday when we weren't booked elsewhere.

Afterwards I'd make my way back to my solitary billet in Hamlet Gardens.

Andrew and Ann urged me to find myself a girlfriend so that we could go out in the evenings as a foursome. I had been nursing a serious crush on Carmen, our exotic vocalist, but, much to my amazement, she preferred Mike, the drummer. So when Linda invited me to a party, I was unattached.

It was a New Year's Eve party at Mike and Linda's house in Watford. Or, to be more accurate, a New Year's Eve Eve party. There was no Bank Holiday on New Year's Day back then, and with 31 December 1967 falling on a Sunday and everyone due to greet 1968 at work, the event was held on the Saturday night to ensure that the occasion could be properly celebrated.

Somehow I managed to perform with the In-Betweens and get to Watford for the party, arriving on the last train well after midnight. Everyone was bopping away in Linda's house when I arrived. Among her friends and neighbours was an attractive black-haired girl with a lovely smile who had come alone. I asked Linda who she was, sotto voce, as she fussed around getting me a drink in the crowded kitchen. The only part of the reply I caught was the girl's name, Judy Cox, and Linda's insistence that I'd met her before. Given her surname, I assumed this would have been at Lancaster Road and that she must be a relative of Pat and Albert's.

In fact, as I discovered, Judy was nothing to do with the Lancaster Road Coxes. She'd trained as a nursery nurse with Linda, they had become close and I'd met her one afternoon when Linda had brought three of her friends to Pitt House. I remembered, then, trying to impress them in my pretentious way by offering them a cigarette from my flat box of Du Maurier's, which I considered the height of sophistication. I recalled thinking how pretty she was as she took one.

Judy was a few months older than my sister. She had been engaged to an Italian who had been in England training to be a teacher. They had been together for three years when Judy fell pregnant and her fiancé fled back to Italy, breaking off all communication. Her daughter Natalie was now fifteen months old and sleeping upstairs with Mike and Linda's baby daughter Renay while the celebrations proceeded noisily below. When the party was over, the other revellers had all gone home and our hosts had retired to bed, Judy and I were not ready for the night to end. We stayed up into the small hours, talking and getting to know one another, with the radio playing softly in the background – hearing 'Nights in White Satin' always reminds me of that New Year's Eve. As the old year ebbed away, my increasing loneliness went with it.

Judy's upbringing hadn't been conventional. She had been just sixteen months old when her mother died of peritonitis in pregnancy at the age of twenty-four. The baby had been still-born. Her father was a drunken bully who had immediately married the woman with whom he was already having an affair. They put Judy's two brothers in a children's home and sent her to live with one of his relatives. Her maternal grandparents tracked her down and took her back to live with them at Camelford Road, a turning between Ladbroke Grove and St Marks Road in Notting Hill. It was a leased war-damaged house that Judy's grandparents were eventually forced to sell to a slum landlord because they didn't have the money to repair it.

Judy's father cut off all contact and it was some time before her grandparents were able to trace her brothers, who were living in separate Barnardo's homes. There they remained until they were sixteen. All this time Judy's dad was still living in Notting Hill. It took her some while to realize that the man who crossed the street to avoid her whenever he saw her approaching with her grandparents was her father.

Now Judy was an unmarried mother, which still carried a stigma in the late 1960s, albeit not to the extent it had ten years previously. The 'sexual revolution' was by no means as sweeping as is sometimes supposed: the concept might have been *de rigueur* among pop stars and metropolitan radicals but it certainly didn't filter through to ordinary families, where having babies outside marriage was still frowned upon. Judy and Natalie – the loveliest child I'd ever encountered, with huge, melting brown eyes and a mass of curly hair – still lived with her grandmother, her grandfather having died when Judy was six.

We went out on our first date on Judy's twenty-first birthday a couple of weeks after Linda's party. I bought her a box of Cadbury's Milk Tray, which was all I could afford and which must have signalled to Judy that there would be nothing extravagant about our courtship.

~

For a while in 1968, the In-Betweens were doing so well that the prospect of music as a sustainable career didn't seem entirely fanciful. The band was in demand and we had at least two bookings every week. We were becoming more daring in our repertoire, adding our take on Vanilla Fudge's hard-rock version of 'You Keep Me Hanging On', which became a bit of a showstopper with its power chords and piercing crescendo. There was interest from a well-known A & R man at the time, Iain Samuel, and Pat Meehan from EMI sent a talent-spotter to one of our gigs in South London.

The EMI scouting mission resulted in an audition at a recording studio in Shepherd's Bush, which in turn led to the prospect of a recording contract and a short film centred on the racial diversity of the band. Johnny Farugia gave permission for me to be filmed at work in the store in East Sheen. However, before shooting could begin it was all brought to a shuddering halt by what was by now becoming a familiar disaster: the room above the bar at the Pied Horse was broken into and all our equipment was stolen – this time including my precious Höfner Verythin. Perhaps the Victims would have been the most appropriate name for any band I played in.

After the theft Sham, my closest friend in the In-Betweens,

asked me to form another band with him but I knew the time had come for me to take a sabbatical from my life as a musician to concentrate on domesticity with Judy and Natalie and, most pressingly, to find an occupation that would bring us some financial stability.

Judy and I had decided to get married that July, two months after my eighteenth birthday. With a wife and daughter to support (I later adopted Natalie to make my paternity official), I needed to forget my pipedreams of making a career out of music or becoming a writer and knuckle down to a steady job.

Sham suggested that I should apply to work alongside him at the Post Office. There were hundreds of vacancies for postmen because the basic wage was so poor, but the low staffing levels meant the opportunities for overtime were virtually limitless. I liked the idea of being a postman, but not in North London.

The bus I took to East Sheen from Hammersmith every morning passed through leafy, well-heeled Barnes. On summer days, I'd watch a postman on his round along the main drag, bleached white sack tied across his back, crisp brown summer jacket with the sleeves rolled up, dark blue serge trousers with a neat red stripe down each leg. It seemed to me to be an idyllic job, being out delivering mail in those pleasant streets close to the Thames.

It was that rather romantic image that led me to the GPO recruitment office in Lavender Hill, Battersea, shortly after my eighteenth birthday. I completed what I was satisfied was a successful interview, in which I correctly placed Southend in the county of Essex and Brighton in Sussex, and spotted in the initiative test that, on a picture of a bicycle, the chain was wrongly attached to the front instead of the back wheel.

The very nice manager explained to me that, as civil servants, postmen effectively worked for themselves. The General Post Office was still a government department (the following year, under the Post Office Act 1969, it would become a statutory corporation known simply as the Post Office), headed by the postmaster general. This was a Cabinet position and therefore occupied by an elected politician answerable to the government and ultimately to the public. As members of the public, the manager argued, this meant we were his boss. It never seemed plausible to me.

As it happened the postmaster general at the time, and indeed the last incumbent of that office, was John Stonehouse who, six years later, famously faked his own death, leaving a pile of his clothes on a Miami beach and decamping in secret to Australia in a bid to set up a new life with his mistress. He was found after only a month, and later deported back to Britain to face an array of charges including fraud, theft, forgery and wasting police time.

It's a wonder I got the job at all. I was obliged to supply my full name on my application form, which meant I couldn't leave out my hated middle name, Arthur. In a small act of protest, I tried to distance myself from it by spelling it differently.

'Is this how you spell "Arther"?' asked the friendly post office manager. 'With an "e"?'

I thought I handled this skilfully by taking him through a peculiar family history, invented on the spot, in which 'Arther' had been handed down through generations of my branch of the Johnson clan. Unfortunately, his own name was Arthur, which made him a bit of an expert on the subject. My application was successful, but 'Alan Arthur Johnson' was what appeared stubbornly on my job offer, Arthur at the Post Office clearly having been unimpressed by my tortuous explanation.

So I signed the Official Secrets Act, as we civil servants were required to do, and spent two weeks at the London training school in King's Cross, where I learned to tie a slip-knot, memorized the London postal districts and mastered the technique of hand-sorting letters into a forty-eight-box fitting with reasonable accuracy.

At eighteen years of age I was about to move house for the seventh time. I'd left school, had four jobs, been in two bands and fallen for the woman I was about to marry, in the process becoming a father as well as a husband.

My male friends in particular had been envious of my independence, but for Judy and me, the imperative was different. Domesticity appealed to us. We wanted to be a part of family life, not to get away from it. We were bound not only by our desire to be together but, I suppose, by a shared aspiration to create the kind of loving, two-parent family neither of us had known as children.

For me, family life was to be found with Judy, her grandmother and Natalie at the house in Notting Hill where Judy had been raised. Judy's grandmother was very disapproving of the shelf-stacker-turned-postman who was to marry her precious charge. She hardly spoke to me at first although she mellowed over time. The four of us were to occupy the two top floors of 2 Camelford Road and I would cycle to Barnes every morning to pursue the occupation that I fully expected to take me into retirement.

My destiny was not, after all, to become a professional

musician. Nor was it to be a writer. Ultimately the Area and the In-Betweens had failed, but we had our moments, and we had so much fun failing that it didn't matter. The joy of making music with like-minded friends at the Fourth Feathers or the Pied Horse, rather than alone in my bedroom, and the thrill of being able to play in front of an audience, never left me, even if the ambition to succeed in that world finally had.

~

The one big chance I was given to fulfil my ambition to be a rock star was, as it happened, nothing to do with the Area or the In-Betweens.

Before the demise of the Area, when Andrew and I were answering ads for musicians in the music press, we were both called for auditions. Andrew very nearly became the drummer for the Mindbenders, whose single 'A Groovy Kind of Love' reached Number 2 in the charts in the UK and the US in 1966. He narrowly lost out after making the final shortlist.

If the band for which I auditioned didn't have the cachet of a Top Ten hit on both sides of the Atlantic, they were just as famous in Britain for covering other artists' top ten hits and are often described as having been the best warm-up act of the 1960s. This rather backhanded compliment didn't do them any harm; indeed, they had a reputation for stealing the limelight from some of the bigger bands they supported.

Peter Jay and the Jaywalkers were ubiquitous on the BBC pop programmes broadcast every weekday lunchtime in the pre-Radio 1 days when restrictions on 'needle time' – which had led to the rise of offshore pirate radio stations capable of circumventing them – were in force. These regulations meant that the BBC had to use live bands to cover pop songs and the Jaywalkers were in demand for their ability to provide rather more authentic renderings of hits by beat groups than the old boys in the Joe Loss Orchestra, who were considerably more at home with Glenn Miller than the likes of the Kinks or the Troggs.

I'd answered an advertisement placed by the band in *Melody Maker* for a rhythm guitarist/backing vocalist and was invited to audition. I was a few months short of my seventeenth birthday and felt I looked a lot like Peter Frampton, who was just a few weeks older than me and soon to become the boy wonder of the pop world as front man of a band called the Herd. I should say that nobody else thought I remotely resembled Frampton, but I was deemed to have the pretty-boy look fashionable at the time. The audition was in Soho. The summer of love was on the horizon, and even we Mods were putting foulards round our neck, if not flowers in our hair. I went dressed in my favourite outfit, a light, tight-fitting double-breasted cotton jacket, white with a thin black stripe, tight black trousers and Chelsea boots. Not only was I convinced I looked the part, I was certain I was the prodigal talent the world of popular music was waiting for.

Peter Jay was the band's drummer but someone else was on drums for the auditions, freeing him up to sit with his management team and closely observe each applicant's performance. The song I was asked to sing and play with the band was a Beatles number called 'This Boy'. I knew it well enough but had never played it before. They gave me the sheet music and asked me to take lead vocal in a three-part harmony.

The key they were using had a tricky D major 7th chord, but I mastered that and we did the whole song straight through twice and the middle eight once more on its own, from which I deduced that I was in serious contention for the job. I'd been word- and note-perfect and Peter Jay chatted to me afterwards, advising me that if I joined the band I'd need to turn professional and sign up with the Musicians' Union. He said they had a few more applicants to audition and they'd contact me.

They never did but for a few glorious days I was convinced that 'This Boy' had landed me the career I craved.

I was ecstatic as I left the audition and caught the tube back to Notting Hill. For some reason I'd jumped into one of the few carriages reserved for non-smokers, which were rarely full. This early in the afternoon, the carriage was practically empty. Looking at my reflection in the dark window, something made me think of Lily. Was it the guitar I was carrying in its red case, bought with Lily's small legacy? More likely it was the 'No Smoking' directive displayed across the famous London Underground symbol on the glass. Lily was for ever telling us about an entertainer of the 1930s who had taken his stage name, Nosmo King, from a no-smoking sign. Every time we travelled on the tube together she'd repeat the story, insisting it was true.

Something strange happened. I saw Lily's face, heard her voice and, as the train carried me towards what I was convinced would be a brilliant future, hot tears began to flow. I thought of my mother and cried.

EPILOGUE

THE SUMMER OF 1968: my wedding day, twenty-three years after Lily's. We were married at Hammersmith Register Office. Judy travelled there with Natalie and her grandmother on the Metropolitan line from Ladbroke Grove. Andrew was my best man and the Coxes were in attendance. There had been no official photographer at Lily's wedding and there wasn't at mine, either, just some black and white snaps taken on Linda's camera to mark the event. We'd come through so much in the four years since Lily had died and had managed to evade what my sister always referred to as 'the authorities', who we feared would ensnare us. Linda, heavily influenced by Lily's belief in spiritualism, was convinced that Lily was our spirit guide; that she'd protected us in some mystical way. I was never in any doubt about who'd protected me: it was Linda.

On Christmas Eve 1968, Judy gave birth to our daughter Emma in St Charles' Hospital. Linda's second child, Tara, was born shortly afterwards and by early 1969 we had two daughters apiece: the grandchildren Linda had so badly wanted Lily to live to see.

Only Linda and I knew the true extent of Lily's heroic

attempts to overcome adversity. Only I could testify to the extraordinary courage and determination of my sister. Lily would always be the light inside us, and our inspiration as we set out on an adult life that was only just beginning; one that would, for both of us, be infinitely better than her own.

Acknowledgements

My grateful thanks to:

My sister, Linda Edwards, for relating so many of the experiences recorded here.

My agent, Andrew Kidd, and my friends Charlotte Greig and Becky Milligan for all their enthusiasm, encouragement and help with this book.

Sue Utting, a former Number 10 'Garden Room Girl', whose typing was impeccable.

Doug Young and his colleagues at Transworld.

Caroline North, who my publishers rightly described as the best editor in the business.

My Auntie Peggy and recently departed Auntie Rita for reliving their childhoods for me.

Yvonne Tozer (née Stacey), Colin James, Danny Curtis, Tony Kearns, Arif Ali, Jimmy Robb and the late Carmen Samad for sharing their memories.

Catherine Bramwell and Caroline Reynolds for their out-of-hours help.

Mrs Eve Stonelake for reminding me of some of the vast array of shops in Golborne Road.

Mark Olden, for sending me his splendid book *Murder in*

Notting Hill (Zero Books, 2011) and acquainting me with *London's Newcomers: The West Indian Migrants* by Ruth Glass (Harvard University Press, 1960), which provided me with a useful context for my childhood experiences.

Picture Acknowledgements

Unless otherwise credited, all photos are from the author's collection. Every effort has been made to trace the copyright holders of photos reproduced in the book. Copyright holders not credited are invited to get in touch with the publishers.

Photos on pages 2–3, 5 (bottom) and 7 (top right) of the picture section courtesy of Mary Evans Picture Library/Roger Mayne.

Index

Index